COLORFUL
Crochet Cables

COLORFUL
Crochet Cables

STACKPOLE
BOOKS
Essex, Connecticut
Blue Ridge Summit, Pennsylvania

Noelle R. B. Stiles

STACKPOLE BOOKS

An imprint of Globe Pequot, the trade division of The Rowman & Littlefield Publishing Group, Inc.
4501 Forbes Blvd., Ste. 200
Lanham, MD 20706
www.rowman.com

Distributed by NATIONAL BOOK NETWORK
800-462-6420

British Library Cataloguing in Publication Information available

Library of Congress Cataloging-in-Publication Data

Names: Stiles, Noelle R. B., author.
Title: Colorful crochet cables : how to crochet celtic cabled designs in
  vibrant multicolored hues / Noelle R. B. Stiles.
Description: First edition. | Essex, Connecticut : Stackpole Books, [2024]
  | Summary: "With a bit of planning, you can crochet beautiful Celtic
  cables and actually enhance the design with your choice of a
  multicolored yarn. With practical examples and 20 patterns, Noelle
  Stiles shows how crochet designs can feature both a multicolored yarn
  and an intricate cable to gorgeous effect"— Provided by publisher.
Identifiers: LCCN 2023050149 (print) | LCCN 2023050150 (ebook) | ISBN
  9780811772907 (paperback) | ISBN 9780811772914 (epub)
Subjects: LCSH: Crocheting—Patterns. | Decoration and ornament, Celtic.
Classification: LCC TT825 .S7424 2024 (print) | LCC TT825 (ebook) | DDC
  746.43/4041—dc23/eng/20240124
LC record available at https://lccn.loc.gov/2023050149
LC ebook record available at https://lccn.loc.gov/2023050150

♾™ The paper used in this publication meets the minimum requirements of American National Standard for Information Sciences—Permanence of Paper for Printed Library Materials, ANSI/NISO Z39.48-1992.

First Edition

CONTENTS

This book is dedicated to:

My grandmother and parents.
Thank you for introducing me to impressionist art.
This book is inspired by its enchanting textures and effervescent colors.

And my beloved and ingenious husband.
Thank you for your constant support and encouragement of my fiber art.

PREFACE: COLORFUL CABLES

A few years ago, I was reading a thread on Facebook in which crocheters and knitters were discussing their worst projects. For most people, the projects they showcased were their first few fiber creations, such as misshapen hats and mittens with uneven tension and crumpled stitches. Each person gloried in how far they had come in their craft since their earlier perhaps not-so-successful projects. However, one project in particular caught my eye. It was a perfectly fashioned pair of socks with delicate cable stitching. What was wrong with this project? The maker lamented that the multicolored self-striping yarn she used was too busy and obscured the intricate cable motif she had labored so hard to create. For this single error in yarn selection, the entire project was downgraded (in her view) to one of her worst. From my perspective, this is the most tragic of outcomes, not just because of the wasted skill and effort but also because the error is so simple and easy to fix.

In this book, we will address the challenge of merging cable stitches (or texture) and colorful variegated yarn. We will discuss the types of multicolored yarns that enhance crochet texture and then design and make twenty crochet projects based on these skills. But before we start, let's discuss why a crocheter would want to make a multi-colored cabled project in the first place.

Crocheted fabric is known for its beautiful texture. Basketweave patterns, bobbles, popcorns, ridges, and cables are just a few examples of the panoply of crochet stitches. The most traditional knit and crocheted highly textured garments, accessories, and blankets have been made from a single color, often off-white, to highlight the visibility of the complex stitches. These traditional fisherman's sweaters, Gansey (or Guernsey) sweaters, and Celtic Aran motifs are continually re-emerging as "new" popular trends.

At the same time, modern crocheters love color. Hand-painted yarns made in small artisanal batches have enlivened the fiber world with a new level of creativity. These hand-painted yarns showcase small, short bursts of vibrant hues, which seem to swirl and flow through each other. In addition, gradients of color have excited yarn enthusiasts and have made beautiful canvasses for shawls and sweaters.

Crocheters should not have to choose between multicolored yarns and highly textured patterns. And the good news is that they don't have to!

In this book, we will cover the steps of selecting a yarn that both showcases texture and is beautifully multicolored. In particular, we will discuss the role of brightness, shadow, and color in yarns, and we will provide an easy technique for matching multicolored or gradient yarn to textured patterns. We will also consider stranded colorwork with multicolored yarns and cables and give examples of how to organize a colorful stranded project. Finally, we will review tips for photographing textured patterns, including the impact of backgrounds, light sources, and cameras. After building this toolset, we will then apply it to twenty crochet projects that range from accessories through garments to blankets and pillows.

As a vision scientist, I am excited to share with you the basics of color and texture perception as applied to fiber projects. After reading the tutorial chapters and making the projects provided, you will be able to choose yarns for future projects that have vibrant, diverse hues but also don't obscure stitch definition.

Let's get started!

PART 1

Color, Shadow, and Texture in Crochet

Crochet Color

THE FASCINATION OF COLOR

Our perception of the myriad colors in our environment is one of the most aesthetically pleasing aspects of vision. The bright blues, dashing purples, and searing reds and yellows can blend to make a painting entirely captivating and transport us to another realm of imagination and enchantment. In this chapter, we will discuss the basic properties of color perception and share tips for the selection of solid colors that harmonize in your fiber projects.

HOW DO OUR EYES AND BRAIN PROCESS COLOR?

We sense color with three different types of photosensors called cones in the retina of the eye. These cones primarily respond to different wavelengths of light in the electromagnetic spectrum (as shown in Figure 1.1). The *visible* electromagnetic spectrum includes the range of wavelengths of light that we can see, but the spectrum extends far beyond just light waves, reaching from cosmic rays and x-rays that are very high energy (short wavelength) and damaging to the human body, down to microwaves that are very low energy (long wavelength) and the basis of our mobile communication networks. The range of light within the visible electromagnetic spectrum is perceived by us as a variety of colors and extends from red (lower energy, longer wavelength) to blue (higher energy, shorter wavelength). The different types of cones in our eyes sense different parts of the spectrum and include cones that are sensitive to red colors, cones sensitive to green colors, and cones sensitive to blue colors. The brain then uses the varying strengths of activation of these three types of cones to distinguish among the various colors. For example, strong activation of the red cones, and weak activation of the green and blue cones, makes us perceive the color red. However, strong activation of the blue cones at the shortest visible wavelengths (which also slightly activates the red

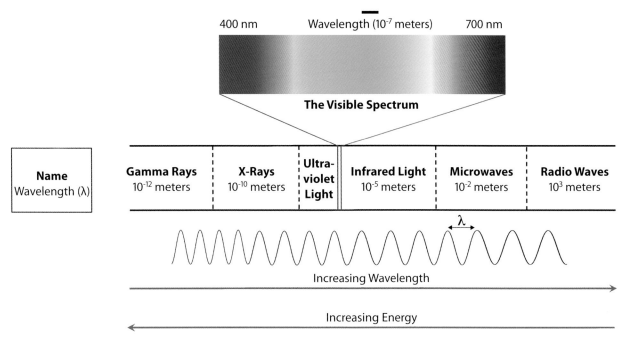

| | Wavelength (10^{-7} meters) | |
| 400 nm | | 700 nm |

The Visible Spectrum

| **Name** Wavelength (λ) | **Gamma Rays** 10^{-12} meters | **X-Rays** 10^{-10} meters | **Ultra-violet Light** | **Infrared Light** 10^{-5} meters | **Microwaves** 10^{-2} meters | **Radio Waves** 10^{3} meters |

λ

Increasing Wavelength

Increasing Energy

Figure 1.1: The Electromagnetic Spectrum. The visible colors within the electromagnetic spectrum.

cones) makes us perceive the color violet. This basis for human color perception is called the "trichromatic theory" (or three-color theory) and is the reason many colors on our computers are expressed as varying levels of three numbers: R, G, and B (RGB, or Red-Green-Blue). As a side note (just for fun), other animals have different types of eyes with different numbers of cones, and therefore they have quite different color perception than us. For example, dogs have only two cones and therefore less color differentiation than we have, but the mantis shrimp has up to sixteen types of cones, which could aid in inter-animal signaling (Franklin 2013).

In addition to combining the three types of cone activations to make the colors of the rainbow, our eyes and brain exhibit "color opponency" processing. The different types of cones (or sensors) in the eye send signals to other types of cells in the eye before sending the signals to the brain. One of these types

of cells, called retinal ganglion cells, pairs together inputs from two different types of cones to make a push-pull type of processing. In other words, one type of retinal ganglion cell could be excited when a substantial intensity of red light is present *and* green light is entirely absent. The colors paired together in this "opponency" or push-pull processing are red-green and blue-yellow. This type of "opponent" color pairing helps us to see subtle differences in color.

The best perceptual evidence for this opponency process is derived from the phenomenon of afterimages. To experience an afterimage, view a red apple for a few seconds, and then move your gaze to a blank sheet of white paper or an empty white countertop. On the empty countertop, you will see a green image or "afterimage" of the apple you previously viewed. The afterimage of the apple is green because that is the opponent color to the apple's red color.

INSET I: COLOR ILLUSIONS

An entertaining way to investigate how the brain perceives color is to experience and then interpret illusions. Illusions unveil a hidden level of processing performed by our eyes and brain that is used to make sense of complex and unreliable visual information. Therefore, by discovering and studying illusions, scientists can better understand the mechanisms and algorithms the brain uses to interpret the visual world.

Color illusions are particularly compelling to experience. For this reason, I have included a few vibrant visual illusions for you to enjoy.

Troxler Fading Illusion

To experience this illusion, fix your gaze on the central black cross in Figure 1.2 for several seconds (it may take some people longer than others to stabilize and focus your gaze; be patient). After several seconds, most people perceive that all the colors in the background fade to gray. The reason for this startling effect is that visual stimuli need to constantly change to prevent our brain from adapting to the images and then ignoring them. When you stabilize your eyes, you reduce the alteration of the visual stimulus and increase the likelihood that the stimulus will fade.

References

Bonneh, Yoram S., et al. 2014. "Motion-Induced Blindness and Troxler Fading: Common and Different Mechanisms." *PLoS One* 9, no. 3: e92894.

Martinez-Conde, Susana, and Stephen L. Macknik. 2017. "Unchanging Visions: The Effects and Limitations of Ocular Stillness." *Philosophical Transactions of the Royal Society B: Biological Sciences* 372, no. 1718: 20160204.

Color Spreading Illusion

For this illusion, fix your gaze on the white cross at the center of Figure 1.3 for several seconds. Then observe whether the colors in the boxes change.

If you perceive the illusion, the colors in the boxes on the left and the right edges of the image will morph from green to red. It will appear as if the color from the central boxes is spreading into the peripheral boxes.

This color spreading occurs because of differences in how your central vision (where you fix your vision) processes color and how your peripheral vision (the left and right edges of what you can see) processes color. Your central vision is more sensitive to differences in color and therefore will dominate over the color perceived in the periphery—thus the outward spreading of colors from the image center to the outer edge.

Reference

Kanai, Ryota, et al. 2006. "Discrete Color Filling beyond Luminance Gaps along Perceptual Surfaces." *Journal of Vision* 6, no. 12: 4–4.

Lilac Chaser Illusion

The lilac chaser illusion is a dynamic illusion (a movie); therefore, to view it, you need to visit this website:
https://michaelbach.de/ot/col-lilacChaser/

Figure 1.2: Troxler Fading Illusion

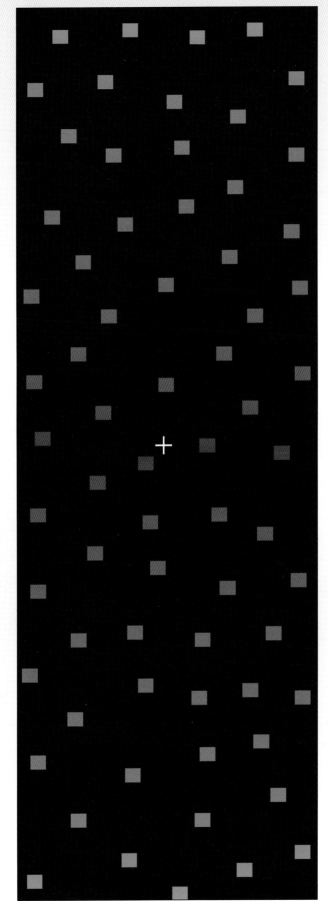

Figure 1.3: Color Spreading Illusion

When you view the illusion, you should initially see a ring of small lilac disks with one disk missing. The missing disk moves around the ring clockwise. After fixating on the cross in the center of the ring for several seconds, you may start to see other visual effects. For example, you may see a green circle appear in the absence of the lilac circle. When you fix your gaze for several more seconds, you will see the purple disks disappear altogether and only the moving green dot remain.

During the course of this illusion, there are several effects occurring at once. The green dot is perceived because of color afterimages (we discussed afterimages earlier in this chapter). After viewing a lilac circle for several seconds in any one location, the perception of the complementary green afterimage begins to appear. Therefore, when the lilac circle is taken away in one location, the green afterimage circle remains.

In addition, the static purple dots fade because of the Troxler Fading Effect discussed at the beginning of this section. In other words, the lilac dots are stable on your eyes (i.e., not moving or jittering around), and therefore over time the brain begins to neglect them. All of this leaves the green afterimage dot, which is still moving from location to location around the circle.

For more information about this fascinating illusion, read the comments on the website listed above.

WHEN DEFINING COLOR, WHAT ARE HUE, SATURATION, AND LIGHTNESS?

When artists and psychologists define color, they typically use three different properties: hue, saturation, and lightness (Palmer 1999). A color's hue determines whether the color is perceived as blue, red, or yellow, among others; in other words, it defines the perceived variation of colors within the rainbow (i.e., which cones are activated in the eye, the red, green, and/or blue cones). Figure 1.4 shows the range of hues that can be used with an example crochet swatch. Saturation represents the *pureness* of the color and ranges from the pure color to gray for a given level of hue and lightness. In neuroscience terms, this property is defined by how strongly certain types of cones are activated with respect to the other types of cones in the eye. Finally, the lightness of the color is a measure of how "white" the color appears and ranges from black through gray to white. Lightness is also frequently called brightness, colloquially, and relates to a different balance among the types of cone activation in the eye. Figure 1.5 showcases the effects of varying the saturation and lightness instead of the hue for the same example crochet swatch shown in Figure 1.4.

The properties of hue, saturation, and lightness can be used to define a space with all the possible colors that we perceive, in which each of the three dimensions (or axes) has a different color property. A simplified version of this three-dimensional space is a two-dimensional color wheel, which includes the properties of hue (varying along the edge of the wheel) and a range of lightness (varying from the center of the wheel outward) (as shown in Figure 1.6). We can now use this color wheel to discuss color pairings for crochet projects.

Figure 1.4: Variation in Hue within One Crochet Swatch. This figure shows the range of colors that can be perceived in crochet by altering only the property of hue. Each column has a range in hue from the original swatch in green at the top to magenta at the bottom. In the column on the left, the colors progress *counterclockwise* around the color wheel, while the colors in the column on the right progress *clockwise*. These color changes are equivalent to one complete circumnavigation of the perimeter of the color wheel. The color variations were generated by changing the property of hue in Adobe Photoshop. The original swatch was made with Knit Picks Stroll Yarn in Peapod with a US size F-5 (3.75 mm) hook.

Figure 1.6: The Color Wheel. This image shows the variation of hue around the perimeter of the circle, as well as a range of lightness values from the center of the circle to the edge.

Figure 1.5: Variation in Saturation and Lightness within One Crochet Swatch. This figure shows the range of green colors that can be perceived by altering either the property of saturation or the property of lightness in a crochet pattern. The color variations were generated by changing the properties of saturation and lightness in Adobe Photoshop. The original swatch was made with Knit Picks Stroll Yarn in Peapod with a US size F-5 (3.75 mm) hook.

HOW DO I MATCH DIFFERENT COLORS?

One of the goals of this chapter is to understand how to choose colors that go well together. To do this, we start by matching colors of the same saturation and lightness but of varying hue (for example, the colors around the edge of the color wheel shown in Figure 1.6).

The most basic attractive color combination is called the Analogous Color Plan, and it utilizes a handful of colors that neighbor each other on the color wheel (Wolfrom 2014) (see Figure 1.7). This type of color scheme could be described as warm when reds and oranges are used (Figure 1.7, Left Side, Middle Row) or cool when blues and greens are used (Figure 1.7, Left Side, Bottom Row). This color plan is also a typical style for color gradient yarns, which can have a gradual, continuous color shift from, for example, orange to red to pink. Figure 1.8 presents three crochet projects that used the Analogous Color Plan, with the key colors in each design highlighted on the right side of the figure.

Another common color plan is called the Complementary Color Plan (Wolfrom 2014) (Figure 1.7, Center). For this combination of colors, one would choose two or more colors that are on the opposite sides of the color wheel. For example, pinks would be paired with greens (Figure 1.7, Center, Top Row), or oranges would be paired with blues (Figure 1.7, Center, Middle Row). Figure 1.9 shows three fiber work projects that follow the Complementary Color Plan (one crochet pillow and two knit sweaters), with the key color pairs indicated on the right side of the figure.

Complementary colors are likely related to the opponent color processing (discussed above), although they are a bit different (opponent colors: red-green and blue-yellow; complementary color examples: red-cyan and blue-orange). A recent study by Christopher Tyler of the Smith-Kettlewell Eye Research Institute found that afterimages (once believed to be a direct effect of color opponency), when tested precisely, are not in fact typically perceived as the opponent colors predicted from the retinal cells of the eye (e.g., red-green and blue-yellow) but are rather perceived as the corresponding complementary colors (such as red-cyan and blue-orange). This means that perhaps color opponency and complementary colors are more closely related than artists and scientists previously thought, linked through the phenomenon of afterimages.

Finally, the Triadic Color Plan (Wolfrom 2014) is a three-toned color combination that is rooted in the trichromatic (three color cones) basis of human vision (see once again Figure 1.7). The most basic version of this type of plan uses red, green, and blue colors that are equally spaced around the color wheel (Figure 1.7, Right, Top Row). However, this plan can also include shifts in the basic red-green-blue triad to other color combinations, as long as the three key colors used are equally distanced around the color wheel (Figure 1.7, Right, Middle, and Bottom Rows). Figure 1.10 includes three crochet blanket examples that employ the Triadic Color Plan, with the three key colors used in each presented on the right side of the figure.

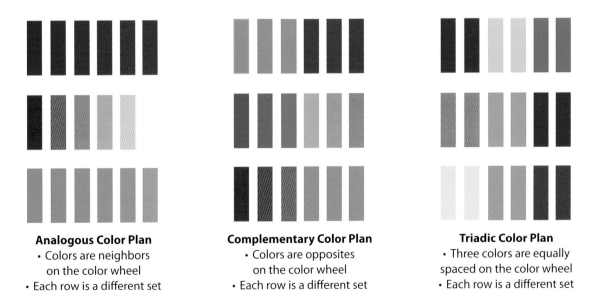

Analogous Color Plan
- Colors are neighbors on the color wheel
- Each row is a different set

Complementary Color Plan
- Colors are opposites on the color wheel
- Each row is a different set

Triadic Color Plan
- Three colors are equally spaced on the color wheel
- Each row is a different set

Figure 1.7: Examples of Color Plans. Three examples for each of the three key color plans are presented. Each row shows a different set of colors that follow the guidelines for the particular color plan in each column.

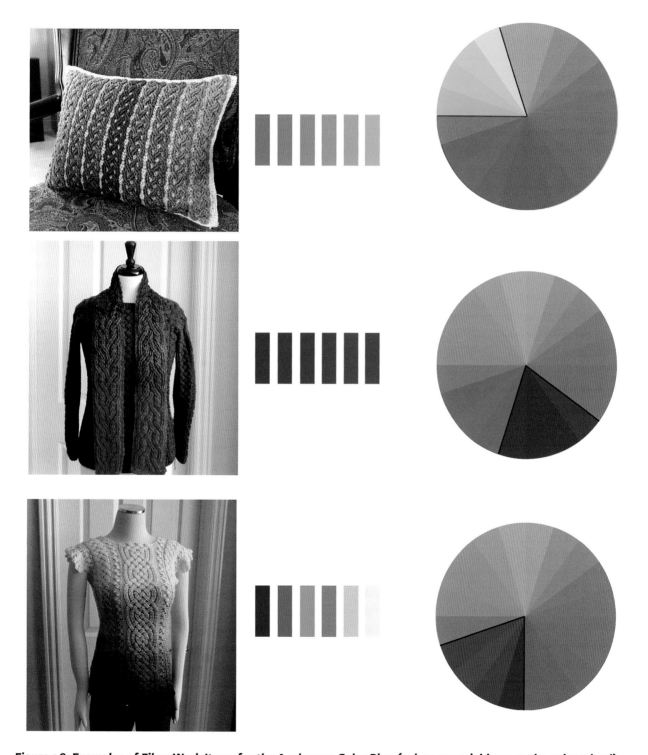

Figure 1.8: Examples of Fiber Work Items for the Analogous Color Plan (colors are neighbors on the color wheel).
Images are from Rebecca's Stylings Crochet (designed by Noelle Stiles).

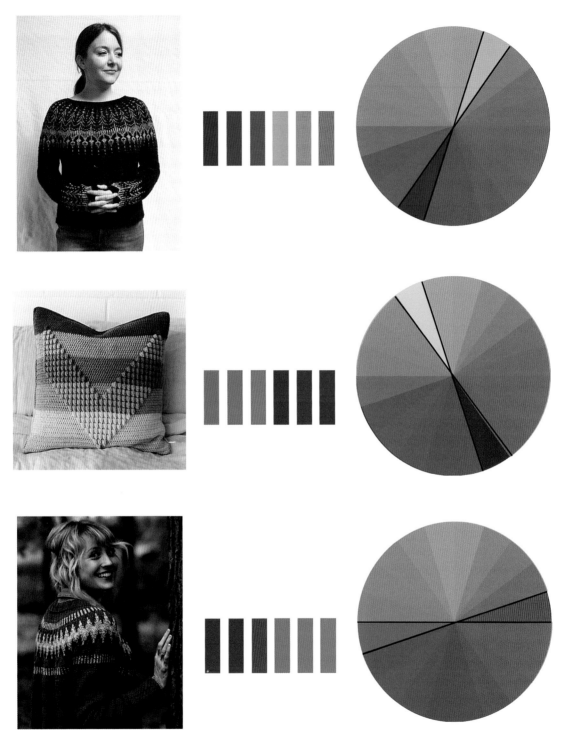

Figure 1.9: Examples of Fiber Work Items for the Complementary Color Plan (colors are opposites on the color wheel). Images are in descending order from Knit.Love.Wool (designed by Jennifer Steingass), from Haak Maar Raak Crochet (designed by Kirsten Ballering), and from Drea Renee Knits (designed by Andrea Mowry).

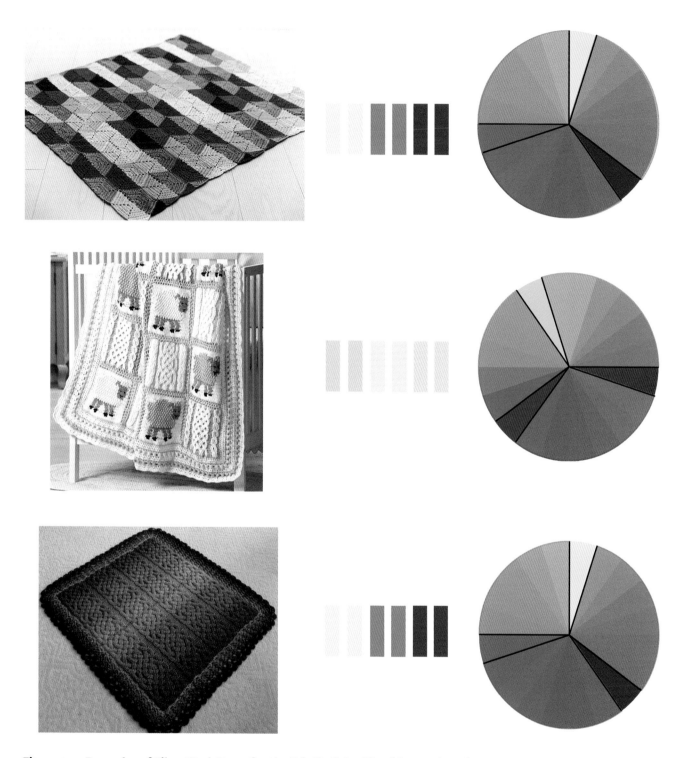

Figure 1.10: Examples of Fiber Work Items for the Triadic Color Plan (three colors that are equally spaced on the color wheel). Images are in descending order from Haak Maar Raak Crochet (designed by Kirsten Ballering), Herrschners (designed by Noelle Stiles), and Rebecca's Stylings Crochet (designed by Noelle Stiles).

When you are choosing yarns for a crochet project, I recommend using one of these color plans to guide your color selection before you head out to the store or browse online. In addition, if you have several colors that you would like to include in a crochet project and would like to be able to carefully match the color that you have already chosen to the yarn that you will purchase, try using a yarn line with a large variety of colors available, such as WeCrochet's Palette yarn line.

Saturation and lightness also change a color's appearance and can be used to advantage in a color plan. The color plan that uses saturation and lightness the most is the Monochromatic Color Plan, which uses one key hue with varied saturation and lightness. This type of color plan requires skill to add complexity and nuance to a set of relatively similar colors. Saturation and lightness can also be used to add depth to the color plans outlined above. For example, for the Complementary Color Plan you can choose two complementary colors and then vary the saturation and lightness of those colors to add complexity to the design.

HOW DO COLORS AFFECT EACH OTHER?

Colors have the amazing ability of changing their appearance, depending on their surroundings and lighting. This is why a pillow color can look like a lovely mauve hue in the store, but then, when you bring it home and put it on the couch, it transforms into a garish pink! Therefore it is always wise to take a photograph of your yarn color combinations or, even better, swatch them before starting a project. A photograph of the yarn colors always gives another perspective on the texture and hues used, whereas a swatch provides an idea of the yarn combination appeal and color synergy in the fabric itself. If you do make a swatch, make sure to look at it in its intended environment, whether that is with the other clothing you will wear with a sweater or the couch the pillow will call home.

How do colors influence each other? A basic understanding of the push-pull dynamics of color interaction will help you predict and plan good color combinations. In the scientific field, the influence of neighboring colors on each other is called Lateral Brightness Adaptation (for the influence of brightness) and Lateral Chromatic Adaptation (for the influence of saturation and hue). In general, the surrounding colors of a central color patch will push the perceived color of the patch to be more opposite to the surround than it "really" is. This effect is a way for the brain to heighten the contrast between the central patch and its surround. For brightness, a dark surround will make a central color patch appear lighter, and a lighter surround will make a central color patch appear darker. For an example, look at the top row (Effect 1) of Figure 1.11, in which the same color patch or swatch is surrounded by two different colors—a lighter color on the left and a darker color on the right. You will notice that although supposedly the two swatches are identical (you can cover up the surrounding color with your fingers to check this for yourself), the two central swatches look quite different. The left central swatch looks darker than the right central swatch because the brain is taking each of the surrounding colors into account and enhancing the perceived differences between the center and the surround of each color grouping. This is the power of color context!

Color saturation and hue also have similar effects. A high color saturation surround will make the central swatch look more dull, and a low color saturation surround will make the central swatch look more vibrant. The second row (Effect 2) of Figure 1.11 shows this example of saturation context. The central swatch in Effect 2 of Figure 1.11 is the same color on the left and the right, but despite this, the

Effect 1: Lightness (Brightness)
The brightness of adjacent colors affects color perception. The central swatch on the left and right are the same color, but the left center swatch appears darker than the right center swatch because the left center swatch is surrounded by lighter colors.

Patchwork 1: Light Surround

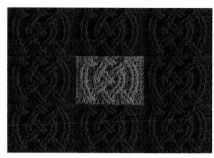
Patchwork 2: Dark Surround

Effect 2: Saturation
The saturation of adjacent colors affects color perception. The central swatch on the left and right are the same color, but the left center swatch appears more dull than the right center swatch because the left center swatch is surrounded by brighter colors.

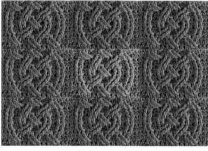
Patchwork 1: Bright Surround

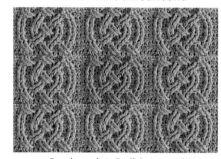
Patchwork 2: Dull Surround

Effect 3: Hue
The hue of adjacent colors affects color perception. The central swatch on the left and right are the same color, but the left center swatch appears more yellow-orange than the right center swatch because the left center swatch is surrounded by a pink color and the right center swatch is surrounded by a yellow/green color.

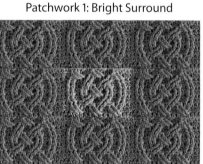
Patchwork 1: Pink Surround

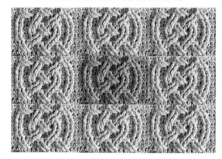
Patchwork 2: Yellow/Lime Green Surround

Figure 1.11: Colors Affecting Colors. Images of swatches surrounded by swatches of different colors to show the effects of adjacent colors on our perception of different lightnesses, saturations, and hues. The best way to view the differences between the left and right center swatches is to fix your gaze between the two columns (for example, between patchwork 1 and 2), and make note of the center patch color.

left central swatch looks more dull than the right central swatch because of their differing surrounds.

The hue of a color can also influence its neighbor by pushing the neighboring color farther away on the color wheel. For example, Figure 1.11, third row (Effect 3), has two central swatches that are the same color, but the vibrant pink surround on the left makes the orange central swatch appear more yellow, and the yellow surround on the right makes the orange central swatch appear more reddish.

Now that we understand how surrounding colors influence central color swatches, how can we choose colors so that they go together? Of course, swatching and photographing help, but it also is good to note which color you are using the most of and how that background or most frequent color will affect its neighbors. For example, imagine that you are making a crocheted sweater with a navy background and light green accents. The light green color will look brighter and more yellow in the sweater relative to when it is in the skein on the shelf (assuming it is surrounded by a white or off-white background). Alternatively, if you fall in love with a green yarn because of the accents it makes in a navy-blue sweater your friend made, be aware that when you go to purchase the green yarn by itself, it will appear darker and less yellow than it looked in the sweater. The moral of this story is that swatching and color planning are your friends and can help with sorting out any variation in color due to their surrounds.

ATTENTION-GRABBING COLORS: WHEN AND WHERE TO USE THEM

The eyes and brain are attracted to some colors more than others (a feature called saliency in vision science). Highly saturated and light colors, neon colors, and bright reds and oranges steal our attention more strongly than duller, darker colors (lower brightness and saturation) and the blues and greens. This is why stop signs are a bright red color; they are purposely designed to arrest our attention from our busy surroundings.

Colors that are excessively bright such as reds and neons will compete with the textures in your item for your attention, so use bright colors judiciously

Figure 1.12: Image of the Shocking Pink Pillow. The pattern for this pillow can be found on page 82 in Chapter 8.

and expect to use extra lighting from a side angle in your photography to highlight texture (see Inset IV on photographing crochet). For an example of attention-grabbing yarn and how to work with these types of colors, the Shocking Pink Pillow (page 81) in this book uses a yarn with bright neon colors (Figure 1.12).

HOW DO I CHOOSE DIFFERENT COLORED YARNS FOR A PROJECT?

Whenever you start a new crochet project, the key questions are always what colors you want to use to make the item and which type of yarn you want to use. You are often limited in the yarn lines you can choose from by the yarn weight and the yarn fiber required to make the project. In turn, the yarn line you choose restricts the color choices you have for your item. Given these restrictions, you can first select the color plan followed by the yarn colors that best fit your plan. However, given the restrictions of yarn selection, you may have to adapt your ideal color plan to fit the color palette available.

There are also other color considerations, depending on how color is used in the pattern in question. One possible use of color is in a patchwork blanket, in which squares are made with a specific pattern or texture and then multiple squares are joined to form a blanket (see Figure 1.13). In this case, it is ideal to choose the colors for your blanket with similar levels of lightness (i.e., brightness) because then your eye will focus on the texture in each square rather than on the brightness edges between the squares (more detail is included on brightness edges in Chapter 3). As an example, refer to Figure 1.13 and compare the harmonious perception of Patchwork 1, with similar levels of lightness across the patchwork squares, with the disjointed perception of Patchwork 2, with highly variable levels of lightness across the patchwork squares. The differences in texture perception

Patchwork Styles

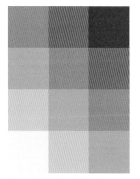

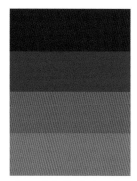

Patchwork 1: Similar Saturation and Brightness
- Allows the texture in each square to be visible
- Makes the colors more apparent

Patchwork 2: Different Saturation and Brightness
- Makes the edges between the darker squares and lighter squares more apparent
- Reduces the visibility of the texture in each square

Patchwork 3: Fade Patchwork
- Each row of squares changes significantly in lightness or saturation
- Makes the edges between the squares more apparent

Colorwork Styles

Colorwork 1: Similar Saturation and Brightness
- The colorwork is less visible

Colorwork 2: Different Saturation and Brightness
- The colorwork is more visible

Figure 1.13: Schematics of Patchwork and Colorwork Styles. Three examples of patchwork color combinations and three examples of colorwork color combination are shown.

between Patchwork 1 and Patchwork 2 are illustrated in Figure 1.14, which uses crochet swatches to showcase the different visibilities of cable stitches implemented in the two types of patchworks. Choosing patchwork colors that have similar lightness and saturation will also emphasize the colors (i.e., hues) in your patchwork design because your eye will not be distracted by multiple brightness edges between the squares. Finally, if you want a patchwork quilt of crocheted squares that starts with a darker color and then fades to a lighter color or even white, then you should select highly saturated colors with low lightness at one end of the blanket and increase the color lightness toward the faded end (an example is shown in Figures 1.13 and 1.14, Patchwork 3).

Patchwork 1: Similar Saturation and Brightness

Patchwork 2: Different Saturation and Brightness

Patchwork 3: Fade Patchwork

Figure 1.14: Patchwork Styles with Crochet Swatches. Three examples of patchwork color combinations are shown with crochet swatches to highlight the texture perception differences among the different patchwork types. The color variations were generated by changing the properties of saturation and lightness in Adobe Photoshop. The original swatch was made with Knit Picks Stroll Yarn in Peapod with a US size F-5 (3.75 mm) hook.

Another type of crochet pattern uses colorwork, in which you interleave stitches of different yarns to make a motif or image, such as the letter N (Figure 1.13, Bottom). In this case, you should select yarns with very different lightness (or brightness), which will emphasize the edges between the motif and the background, and therefore enhance the visibility of your design. For example, in Figure 1.13 compare the difficulty of reading the letter N in Colorwork 1 that incorporates colors of similar lightness with the ease of reading the letter N in Colorwork 2 that instead incorporates colors of different lightness. An easy way to compare yarn lightness is to take a gray-scale photo of the two or more yarns that you want to use. If the yarns have different brightness levels in the grayscale photo, they are a suitable choice for this type of colorwork.

INSET II: YARN DYE LOTS— A CAUTIONARY TALE

Yarn color can vary dramatically between different dye lots of the same yarn. For example, the pillow in Figures 1.15 and 1.16 was made with the same yarn but was taken from two different dye lots. The left image shows the pillow's appearance when a single dye lot was used, and the right image shows the result when two different dye lots were used. Therefore, it is essential to use yarn from the exact same dye lots in order to achieve consistency of color in your crochet projects. Unfortunately, some hand-painted yarns do not have dye lots, so in this case I recommend matching the hue and brightness of the skeins you buy in the store by eye. If you can't find matching skeins, don't be shy about asking to see additional skeins of the yarn from the back. Small yarn stores that carry hand-painted yarns are aware of this challenge and are often eager to help.

Figure 1.15

Figure 1.16

SUMMARY

Colors have three key features—hue, saturation, and lightness—that, taken together, define the range of colors that humans can see or perceive. There are many types of color plans that can be used to design beautiful and colorful crochet projects, including the Analogous, Complementary, Triadic, and Monochromatic color plans. When starting a crochet project, you should consider the type of project that you are making (such as a patchwork project versus a colorwork project), in addition to your project's color plan and available yarn color selection, before purchasing your yarn of choice.

REFERENCES

Franklin, Amanda M. 2013. "Mantis Shrimp Have the World's Best Eyes—But Why?" The Conversation. https://theconversation.com/mantis-shrimp-have-the-worlds-best-eyes-but-why-17577.

Palmer, Stephen E. 1999. *Vision Science: Photons to Phenomenology*. Cambridge: MA: MIT Press.

Tyler, Christopher. 2020. "Human Color Perception Complementary or Opponent?" *Investigative Ophthalmology and Visual Science* 61, no. 7.

Wolfrom, Joen. 2014. *Color Play: Transparency, Luminosity, Depth & More*, second edition. Concord, CA: C&T Publishing.

ADDITIONAL READING ON COLOR IN ART AND CRAFTING

Albers, Josef, and Nicholas Fox Weber. 2013. *Interaction of Color: 50th Anniversary Edition*. New Haven, CT: Yale University Press.

Bruecher, Tacha, Brioni Greenberg, Lynne Goldsworthy, and John Adams. 2014. *Quilt Colour Workshop: Creative Colour Combinations for Quilters. Fat Quarterly*. Exeter, England: David and Charles.

Edwards, Betty. 2004. *Color by Betty Edwards: A Course in Mastering the Art of Mixing Colors*. New York: TarcherPerigee.

Fassett, Kaffe. 2021. *Kaffe Fassett in the Studio: Behind the Scenes with a Master Colorist*. New York: Abrams.

Hauser, Rachel. 2019. *The Quilter's Field Guide to Color: A Hands-On Workbook for Mastering Fabric Selection*. Austin, TX: Lucky Spool.

Ostermiller, Jesie. 2020. *The Colorwork Bible: Techniques and Projects for Colorful Knitting*. Loveland, CO: Interweave.

Sutton, Tina. 2020. *The Pocket Complete Color Harmony: 1,500 Plus Color Palettes for Designers, Artists, Architects, Makers, and Educators*. Beverly, MA: Rockport Publishers.

Thomas, Heather. 2014. *A Fiber Artist's Guide to Color & Design: The Basics & Beyond*. Mount Joy, PA: Design Originals.

Wolfrom, Joen. 2014. *Color Play: Transparency, Luminosity, Depth & More*, second edition. Concord, CA: C&T Publishing.

ADDITIONAL READING ON COLOR TRENDS AND THE HISTORY OF COLOR AND FIBER

Adams, Sean. 2017. *The Designers Dictionary of Color*. New York: Abrams.

Eiseman, Leatrice, and Keith Recker. 2011. *Pantone: The Twentieth Century in Color*. San Francisco, CA: Chronicle Books.

Finlay, Victoria. 2014. *The Brilliant History of Color in Art*. Los Angeles, CA: J. Paul Getty Museum.

Finlay, Victoria. 2004. *Color: A Natural History of the Palette*. New York: Random House.

Finlay, Victoria. 2003. *Color: Travels through the Paintbox*. London, England: Hodder & Stoughton.

St. Clair, Kassia. 2017. *The Secret Lives of Color*. New York: Penguin Books.

Crochet Texture

2

THE BEAUTY OF ARAN-STYLE CROCHET TEXTURE

In this chapter, we will discuss the steps to make crochet texture with a focus on the foundational stitches for cable and Aran motifs. These stitches grace the surfaces of the classic fisherman's and gansey sweaters. Aran motifs add depth and complexity to shawls, mittens, and hats designed to be extra thick in order to resist the bite of the bitter winter wind in the northern reaches of the Irish Isles.

The complex cables from the Aran islands are beautiful. They remind me of the interweaving ripples of a flowing brook, bouncing and crossing as they negotiate some rocky riverbed hidden beneath the water's surface. The lyrical and rippling strands from cables are a symphony of visual delights mirroring the river's blend of nature and art.

The cable stitches highlighted in this chapter will be used in Chapters 8–12 when we discuss making the highly textured items with multicolored yarns. Crocheted Aran or Celtic motifs are emphasized in the patterns for this book because they are both especially beautiful and a personal favorite of mine among highly textured crochet motifs. Although it is often advised to use only off-white yarn while making Celtic motifs to highlight the cable texture, we will show that proper design principles make the use of multicolored yarn not only possible but also intriguing as an expansion of the design space. We will now explore how to use multicolored yarn with these cable motifs.

TYPES OF STITCHES GENERATING CROCHET TEXTURE

Aran and Celtic crochet stitches and motifs are not the only kinds of crochet texture; different textured crocheted fabrics can be generated with variations on nearly every crochet stitch. I think it is important

Figure 2.1: Skara Brae Cable Blanket from Rebecca's Stylings Crochet

21

to emphasize that one of the primary reasons patterns exist and hundreds of crochet stitches have been studiously generated and documented is to create distinctive textures on the surface of crocheted fabric. Texture is a fundamental property and feature of fiber arts and has delighted crafters for hundreds of years.

Texture appears everywhere in crochet, and the lessons for combining color and texture potentially apply to all types of patterns, not just cable crochet. In other words, one mustn't conclude from the choice of cables in this chapter and the Aran and Celtic styles of my patterns that the lessons on merging color and texture are useful only for these types of crochet. The lessons in Chapters 3–6 are universal and apply to the many varieties of textured fabric made through crocheting or knitting.

For other types of crochet stitches and texture beyond those highlighted in this chapter, I recommend that you look at crochet stitch dictionaries, which often list and provide instructions for hundreds of crochet stitch types as used in hundreds of crochet texture styles.

POPCORN, BOBBLE, AND PUFF STITCHES

Popcorn, bobble, and puff stitches make small nubs or bumps on the fabric surface (Figure 2.2). Typically, these types of stitches are worked into a larger motif that outlines a particular shape, such as a diamond, heart, or footprint. To make one of these stitches, you typically make several full stitches or partial stitches in the same stitch in the previous row and then connect them to form a nub. Popcorn stitches are generated by making several double crochets in the same stitch and then slip stitching the first and final double crochet. A bobble stitch also makes multiple double crochets in the same stitch, but for the bobble stitch you don't perform the final

yarn over and pull through two loops of the double crochets. Therefore, you leave a loop on your hook for each partial double crochet. Then, after you finish the partial double crochets, you yarn over and pull through all the loops on hook. The final type is the puff stitch. For the puff stitch, you pull multiple loops through the fabric. To make a loop, you do the following: yarn over, insert your hook in the fabric, and then pull through. Next, you leave the previous loop on the hook, and you repeat the previous instruction (yarn over, insert your hook in the fabric, and then pull through) multiple times. Finally, you yarn over and pull through all the loops on your hook to complete the stitch. Therefore, the popcorn stitch is composed of complete stitches, the bobble stitch is made of half-completed stitches, and the puff stitch is made of yarn loops. After you complete any of these stitches, you usually need to adjust the stitch so that it is bulging out on the front side of the fabric (simply pull the center of the stitch up away from the fabric) and is flat on the back side of the fabric. In my experience, the puff stitches are the smoothest and smaller than popcorn and bobble stitches, and this is the reason I have used puff stitches in the patterns in this book.

Figure 2.2: Popcorn, Bobble, and Puff Stitch Swatch. This swatch shows columns of popcorn stitches, bobble stitches, and puff stitches (left to right order). The swatch was made from Knit Picks Swish Worsted Weight Yarn in the Haze Heather colorway with a US size I-9 (5.5 mm) hook.

RIDGES AND RIBBING

Ridges or ribbing are typically used for the borders of blankets or the cuffs, collar, and waistband of sweaters. This fabric has a zigzag shape (with a front ridge, then back ridge in repeating order) in depth, which gives the fabric a stretchiness that is perfect for gripping around the wrists, necklines, and waists in sweaters. Ribbing is generated in crochet by one of two methods: the first by working rows in the front or back loops of previous rows, and the second by the use of alternating front and back post stitches.

Back-Loop Ribbing

This technique makes an edging for sweaters in short rows; the edging can be either slip-stitched to the edge of the sweater as the rows are worked or sewn on after it's completed (see Figure 2.3 for an example of a sweater waistband using this technique).

After you complete a row of stitches, the tops of single or double crochet stitches look like small V's or dual loops. When the fabric is facing you, one of the top loops (or sides of the V) is close to you—this is the front loop—and one of the top loops (or sides of the V) is far away from you, which is the

back loop. To make the ridges with this technique, make all your stitches in the back loop, rather than through both loops of the crochet stitches. This method generates a small edge or ridge on the front side of the fabric between the first and second row. Then turn your work over and continue to work in the back loop.

This type of ribbing is the best technique to use if you would like to make a collar, waistband, or cuffs on a sweater that is variable in width. For example, if you would like to make a shawl collar, the flexibility in the width of each row can allow the collar width to expand from the narrow button band to the wide collar at the neck, thereby creating a "shawl," which is easier than using long rows that are parallel to the neckline or extend the whole length of the neckline. Collars, cuffs, and blanket edgings with a wavy edge are also in style and can be made with this ribbing technique.

Post-Stitch Ribbing

Post stitches are made by inserting your hook around the stitch in the row below, yarning over, and pulling through, rather than inserting your hook through the crochet fabric and then yarning over and pulling through. If you make the stitch by inserting your hook around the stitch on the front side, then you pull the stitch below forward, and the stitch you make is also pulled forward, making a bump on the front of the fabric. This is called a front post stitch. If you make the stitch by inserting your hook around the stitch in the previous row

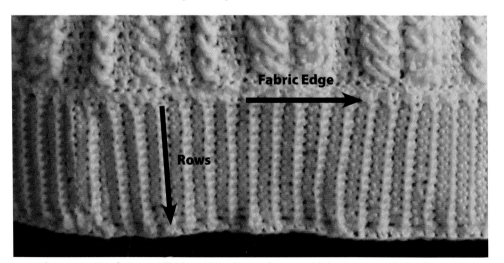

Figure 2.3: Back-Loop Ribbing. This photo of an unpublished sweater design from Rebecca's Styling Crochet shows the texture of back-loop ribbing at the bottom edge of the sweater. The sweater was made from Knit Picks Stroll Fingering Weight Yarn in the Bare colorway with a US size F-5 (3.75 mm) hook.

on the back side, then you pull that stitch backward, and the stitch you make is also pulled backward, making a bump on the back side of the fabric. That type of stitch is called a back post stitch. To make a ribbed fabric, you just need to start with a chain, followed by a row of single crochets or double crochets; for the next row, make a front post stitch and then a back post stitch, repeating these two stitches across the row. This method consequently makes a front bump and then a back bump and then repeats the zigzag in depth across the row. An image of this type of ribbing at the edge of a blanket is included below (Figure 2.4). Note that the rows of this edging are parallel to your fabric edge (the ridges are perpendicular to the fabric edge), so you can attach your yarn to the edge of your sweater or blanket and then work several rows of front and back post stitches to make the border or cuff.

Most ribbing in my patterns uses this technique, in part because it generates more pronounced ridges than the back-loop stitch technique. In addition, as you work rows of the ribbing in this technique, the ribbed fabric will narrow slightly, which adds to the shaping of the sleeve or sweater you are making. Finally, with this technique you can complete multiple long rows of post stitches until the ribbing appears to be the right width, which I find more straightforward than the back-loop method, which uses short rows for a pre-estimated width of the ribbing that then needs to be sewn onto the project.

We should note that post stitches are not just used for ribbing; they are the key stitch used to make most crochet cable stitches and twist stitches. We will discuss the post stitch's role in crocheted cables in the following section.

Figure 2.4: Post-Stitch Ribbing. This image of the Large Irish Lullaby Blanket from Rebecca's Styling Crochet shows a post-stitch ribbing on the edge of the blanket (bottom of photo). The blanket was made from Knit Picks Biggo Yarn in the Dove Heather colorway with a US size M/N-13 (9.0 mm) hook.

Basketweave Stitch (Two-Dimensional Ribbing)

Post stitches can also be used to make the basketweave stitch (see image below), which looks like the in-and-out woven structure of a basket. The basketweave stitch is often used to make panels of texture in crochet cable blankets, sweaters, and other large projects. In many ways, the basketweave stitch is a texturized and more complex form of ribbing with a vertical ribbed variation (generated by switching between back and front post stitches from row to row) to match the horizontal variation of traditional ribbing (generated by switching between back and front post stitches from stitch to stitch). In this way, the basketweave stitch can be thought of as a two-dimensional (horizontal and vertical) ribbing.

To make the basketweave stitch, you perform three front post stitches followed by three back post stitches and repeat this pattern across the row. After chaining and turning your work, you work front post stitches into the last three back post stitches you made in the previous row and then three back post stitches into the next three front post stitches you made in the previous row. Then chain and turn

your work. You now switch the back post stitches for front post stitches and vice versa in each of the next two rows. To make the weave or pattern bigger, just increase the number of stitches in each repeat of the front and back post stitches; for example, increase from three stitches to four, five, or six stitches. If you are interested in trying out this motif, the Imperial Yellow Washcloth (Figure 2.5) uses a basketweave pattern with a ten post-stitch pattern repeat (five front post stitches and then five back post stitches).

Twist Stitches (a Post Stitch and a SC Stitch)

Twist stitches combine a post stitch and a single crochet stitch to make a small cable. The post stitch is always in front of the single crochet stitch and forms a tilted ridge on the fabric. Frequently, two twist stitches tilting in opposite directions are combined to form a V and then repeated from row to row to make an interleaved wreath-like cable (see example in Figure 2.6). These stitches are excellent as accents to a larger cable motif in an Aran-style sweater or blanket. You can see twist stitches used in this manner in the Vermilion Shawl pattern (page 130).

Figure 2.5: Basketweave Motif. The Imperial Yellow Washcloth (pattern on page 93) is decorated with a basketweave post-stitch texture.

Figure 2.6: Twist Stitch Swatch. This swatch shows pairs of twist stitches forming a V shape. The swatch was made from Knit Picks Swish Worsted Weight Yarn in the Haze Heather colorway with a US size I-9 (5.5 mm) hook.

INSET III: CABLED MOTIFS AND EDGES: REDUCING WRINKLING IN CROCHET EDGING

Dense cabled fabric inevitably leads to puckering or wrinkling at the base of the cabled fabric. This is most apparent for Aran (typically densely cabled) sweaters and blankets that are large and have many cable stitches.

What causes this effect is that every cable stitch is narrower than the base of four or six double crochet stitches. Therefore, when you add a cable following a series of rows with double crochet stitches, the row shrinks in width and the edge or double crochet base wrinkles to fit this new smaller width.

Is there a way to prevent this annoying and unsightly edging? I have found that I can reduce this puckering effect by reducing the number of chains and by single crocheting twice in the stitches between the cables of the first cable row, and single crocheting once in the stitches between the cables of the second cable row. This method is shown in detail in the accompanying stitch diagrams. Images of the wrinkling in the crochet edging of a blanket and the puckering-reduced method as performed with a similar blanket are shown following the stitch diagrams.

To reduce puckering at the beginning of the blanket, follow these instructions. First, look at the recommended number of chains for the base of the project. Count the number of cable stitches and subtract this number from the number of chains. Then make the reduced number of chains for the base and continue with the first row of single or double crochet stitches. Follow the pattern for the first row of cables, but rather than making each prescribed single crochet (sc) in a separate stitch, sc twice in one stitch after each cable. To be clear, you are making the same number of single crochets as recommended in the pattern, but you are just bunching them together so that two of them are in one stitch of the previous row (it will be helpful to refer once again to the stitch diagrams). Now continue normally with the pattern. The base will turn out to be straighter and flatter, so that it will be easier to add the appropriate edging at the end of the project. I also find that by using this method, I don't have to block my projects as often.

Figure 2.7: Example Blanket with Edge Puckering

Figure 2.8: Example Blanket Without Edge Puckering

Diagram to Demonstrate Wrinkle-Reducing Method

Example Cable Motif 1: Normal Cable Layout

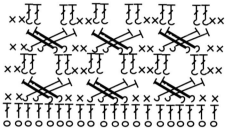

Row 3: 3 Cable stitches, and
8 Single crochet stitches

Row 2: 20 Double crochet stitches
Row 1: 20 Chain stitches

Example Cable Motif 2: Cable Layout without Puckering

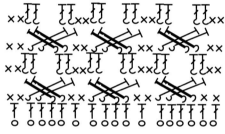

Row 3: 3 Cable stitches, and
8 Single crochet stitches

Row 2: 17 Double crochet
stitches
Row 1: 17 Chain stitches

┬ Double Crochet
✕ Single Crochet
o Chain

Front Post
Double Crochet

Back Post
Double Crochet

Cable: All stitches are
treble post stitch

Note: Bold stitches are in front
of other stitches

Figure 2.9: Stitch Diagram to Demonstrate Wrinkle-Reducing Method

CABLE STITCHES

Cables are most often the central motif or theme of Aran items. Ultimately cables are made using the same post stitches as post-stitch ribbed motifs, but cable stitches are simply made of post stitches created in different spatial orders. For example, cables can skip the first half of post stitches, perform the second half first, and then revisit the first half of post stitches. They can also skip the first stitch, then work the rest of the post stitches, and finally make the last post stitch in the skipped stitch. Figure 2.10 shows an overview of these different families of cable stitches and how they make all kinds of beautiful stitches. The first diagram for each column in Figure 2.10 (each column has a different number of post stitches—e.g., four, six, or eight post stitches, left to right) shows the stitch order for just post stitches alone (no cabling). This means the post stitches are made one at a time from the right side of the fabric to the left side of the fabric. The second diagram in each column of Figure 2.10 shows the traditional cable stitch, which performs the second half of the post stitches first and then the first half of the post stitches second. The remaining diagrams for four post stitches and eight post stitches in Figure 2.10 show other more complex variations on cables. Note: For each of these cable stitches, if you look at the tops of the post stitches, they are always in the same order as the post stitches alone (first diagram in that column). However, if you look at the bottom of the post stitches in each cable, they are crossed in different ways. This is the essential feature of a cable stitch: the order of the stitches is different at the top of the cable stitch in comparison to the bottom of the cable stitch. Now we will discuss an overview of each of these cable stitch types.

Figure 2.10: Cable Stitch Diagrams with Color-Coded Stitch Order. These sets of diagrams show how cables change the shape of the stitch by reordering the post stitches within the cable stitches. The diagram is divided into three different numbers of post stitches in cables (four, six, and eight post stitches), one for each column. The first stitch for each column is the order of the stitches without any cabling, with post stitches alone. The subsequent rows in each column are different types of cable stitches. The color coding is used to indicate the order in which the stitches are generated so that it is easy to compare the order of the stitches with no cabling (top row) and the order of the stitches with different types of cabling (subsequent rows).

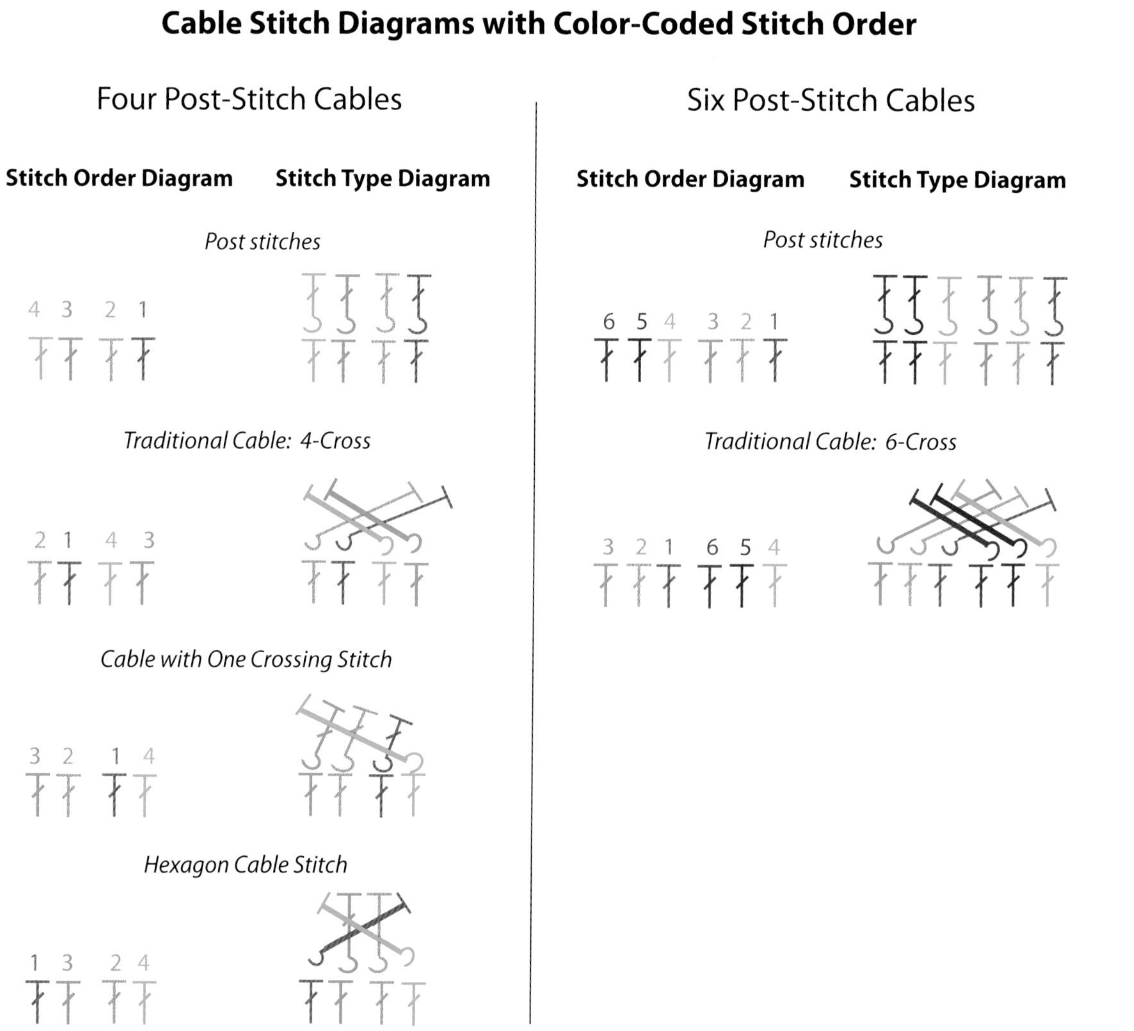

Cable Stitch Diagrams with Color-Coded Stitch Order

Four Post-Stitch Cables

Stitch Order Diagram **Stitch Type Diagram**

Post stitches

4 3   2 1

Traditional Cable: 4-Cross

2 1   4 3

Cable with One Crossing Stitch

3 2   1 4

Hexagon Cable Stitch

1 3   2 4

Six Post-Stitch Cables

Stitch Order Diagram **Stitch Type Diagram**

Post stitches

6 5 4   3 2 1

Traditional Cable: 6-Cross

3 2 1   6 5 4

Traditional cables have the first half of the post stitches crossing the other half of the post stitches (Columns 1–3, Row 2 of Figure 2.10). These cables can also have two different directions of crossing. The first two post stitches can cross in front (shown in Row 2 of Figure 2.10), and therefore point to the upper left (i.e., have a negative slope), or the first two post stitches can cross behind, making the cable appear to point to the upper right (i.e., have a positive slope). These two flavors of traditional cables can be used in combination to make larger braided motifs such as the Saxon braid, which we will discuss later in this chapter.

Eight Post-Stitch Cables

Stitch Order Diagram	Stitch Type Diagram

Post stitches

8 7 6 5 4 3 2 1

Traditional Cable: 8-Cross

4 3 2 1 8 7 6 5

Nested Cable 1

2 1 4 3 8 7 6 5

Nested Cable 2

4 3 2 1 6 5 8 7

A cable stitch can also be made by creating one post stitch that crosses over the front of other post stitches (shown in Column 1, Row 3 of Figure 2.10). In addition, a cable stitch can be generated in which two post stitches cross (shown in Column 1, Row 4 of Figure 2.10) in front of two other vertical post stitches, as we will detail in the hexagon cable stitch subsection later. Finally, a larger cable stitch can be made in which a small cable stitch (two stitches crossing two stitches) is hidden within a larger cable stitch (four stitches crossing four stitches), as we will detail in the section on the nested cable stitch (shown in Column 3, Rows 3–4 of Figure 2.10).

Traditional Cable Stitches

Traditional cable stitches (as mentioned in the previous section) are created by making post stitches that cross over each other. The post stitches that make up these cables are divided into two equal groups, half that pass behind the other group (visible on the back side of the fabric), and half that pass in front of the other group (visible on the front side of the fabric). This type of cable is made (like all other cables) by making the stitches out of order. For example, to make a 2-cross cable, you skip one stitch and then make one front post stitch in the next stitch. Then you return to the stitch you skipped and make a front post stitch either in front of or behind the post stitch you just made (a front cross cable and back cross cable, respectively). This type of traditional cable is typically made with two post stitches (one post stitch crossing one post stitch—e.g., a 2-cross cable), four post stitches (two post stitches crossing two post stitches—e.g., a 4-cross cable), six post stitches (three post stitches crossing three post stitches—e.g., a 6-cross cable), or eight post stitches (four post stitches crossing four post stitches—e.g., an 8-cross cable). Figure 2.11 shows a shawl that includes each of the traditional cable stitches described above; the 8-cross cable stitch is in the center of the shawl, and then, as you move

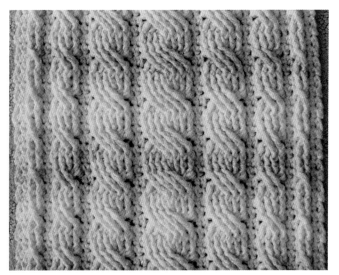

Figure 2.11: Traditional Cable Stitches. This photo of the Kelly Green Shawl (pattern on page 86) shows four different traditional cable stitches with two post stitches, four post stitches, six post stitches, and eight post stitches (moving far left to center).

toward the left or right edges of the shawl, there is a 6-cross cable stitch, a 4-cross cable stitch, and a 2-cross cable stitch.

The more post stitches within a cable stitch, the wider the stitch becomes and the more dramatic the cable twist appears. You can also vary the tightness of the twist of the cable by changing how often you make a cable stitch. For example, you could make a cable stitch in every row of the fabric, which will make the cable twist very tight, or you could make a cable stitch every two, three, or four rows, which would make the cable twist progressively less tight. The rows between the cable stitches (for less twisty cables) frequently just use post stitches to continue the cable without adding any twist. For the wider cables, a row or two of post stitches between cable stitches makes the cable less tight and easier to see on the fabric (for an example, view Figure 2.11). In contrast, a cable stitch in every row or every other row makes the 2-cross cable look more rope-like and beautiful (in contrast to the looser look of the 2-cross cable in Figure 2.11).

A Cable Stitch with One Crossing Stitch

A cable stitch can also be made with only one stitch across three post stitches (Figure 2.12). This stitch is made by skipping one stitch, then making three front post stitches in the next three stitches, and finally returning to the first stitch and working a front post stitch in front of the previous three post stitches. This type of cable stitch has the appearance of a thread or strand wrapped around a vertical column, which is different from the rope-like appearance of the traditional cables from the previous section.

Figure 2.12: Cable Stitch with One Crossing Stitch Swatch. This swatch shows a four-post-stitch cable with one crossing stitch. The swatch was made from Knit Picks Swish Worsted Weight Yarn in the Haze Heather colorway with a US size I-9 (5.5 mm) hook.

The Hexagon Cable Stitch

The hexagon cable stitch is rare compared to the previous cable stitch types and is a variation on the cable stitch with one crossing stitch described in the previous section. The hexagon stitch consists of four post stitches and is made by skipping three stitches to make a front post stitch and then returning to the second and third skipped stitches to make front post stitches behind the first post stitch, and finally returning to the first skipped stitch to make a front post stitch in front of all the stitches (Diagram in Figure 2.10). The crossing X of post stitches cinches in

Figure 2.13: Hexagon Cable Stitches. The Inverness Cable Scarf from Rebecca's Stylings Crochet has a hexagon cable stitch on the left and right sides of the scarf motif. The scarf was made from Knit Picks Simply Wool Yarn in the Winnie colorway with a US size H-8 (5.0 mm) hook.

the left and right side of the cable and generates the appearance of a series of connected hexagon shapes (Figure 2.13). This hexagon stitch followed by three rows of post stitches (back post stitches on the back side of the fabric and front post stitches on the front side of the fabric) generates the pattern repeat to make the cable shown in Figure 2.13. This unusual cable can be employed as an accent to a larger motif of cables or other textured crochet designs.

Nested Cables: A Cable Within a Cable

Nested cables, or cables within cables, are the most advanced form of cable stitches we will review in this book. This unusual cable stitch permits the use of smaller cable stitches to add texture to strands within a larger cable motif. For example, in Figure 2.14, the nested cable is used to make one strand of the larger cable appear intricate and textured, while the other

strand of the cable appears to just have the normal vertical striations (from the individual post stitches). In general, a nested cable is possible only if the traditional cable stitch you are using has two or more post stitches in each half of the stitch. Therefore, you could make a nested cable with a 2-cross cable within a 4-cross cable stitch; however, in this section we will just discuss a 4-cross cable within an 8-cross cable stitch. We will be using this example because the larger stitches make the complex texture more visible and easier to perceive relative to the overall motif structure.

The stitch order for a nested cable is easiest to understand if divided into two halves. Half of the 8-cross nested cable is four post stitches (no twist); the other half is the 4-cross cable. For example, to make the first half of the Nested Cable 1 in Figure 2.14, first skip six stitches, then make two front post stitches in the last two stitches, and finally make two front post stitches in the fifth and sixth stitches skipped. Note that the last two post stitches are made in front of the first two you made. This first half of the Nested Cable 1 is a 4-cross cable. Then, for the second half of the Nested Cable stitch, you

Figure 2.14: Nested Cable Stitches. The Rosslyn Cable Scarf from Rebecca's Stylings Crochet has a cable within a cable stitch (nested cable stitch) on the left and right side of the scarf motif. The scarf was made from Lion Brand Fisherman's Wool Yarn in the Natural colorway with a US size H-8 (5.0 mm) hook.

return to the first four stitches you skipped, and make four front post stitches behind the four post stitches you have already made. The only difference between this Nested Cable stitch and the traditional 8-cross cable is the order in which you make the stitches. You can use Figure 2.14 to carefully compare the different stitches and look at these stitch order differences.

CABLE MOTIFS

Cable motifs use the combination of multiple cable stitches as well as post stitches (outside of a cable stitch) to generate larger and more complex designs. Cable motifs can have the cable stitches directly next to each other, or they can have single crochet stitches or double crochet stitches inserted between the cable stitches. The additional single or double crochet stitches between the cable stitches can add space and elegance to the cable motifs while simultaneously making it easier for our eyes and brain to parse the cable motif into sections and lines. However, the cable motifs without the single or double crochet stitches between the cable stitches are easier to crochet. While this type of cable motif has less curve to it, it can appear similar to braids that are made in hair, knotted ropes, and macrame jewelry.

We will discuss in this section three standard cable motifs (including the three-stranded braid, the Celtic Weave, and the Saxon Cable), variations on those standard cable motifs, and then other, more unusual and adventurous types of cable designs.

A Three-Stranded Braid

The well-known three-stranded braid is often donned by girls and milkmaids (and other braid enthusiasts!) and can be made in crochet by pairing a vertical strand of post stitches next to a traditional cable stitch.

Figure 2.15: Three-Stranded Braid Swatch. This swatch shows two three-stranded braids made of a 6-cross cable stitch and three post stitches. The swatch was made from Knit Picks Swish Worsted Weight Yarn in the Haze Heather colorway with a US size I-9 (5.5 mm) hook.

Figure 2.15 shows an example of the three-stranded braid with a 6-cross traditional cable stitch and three front post stitches in each row. The first front-side row in the left cable on the swatch has back 6-cross traditional cable and then three front post stitches. A back 6-cross traditional cable is made by skipping three stitches, making three front post stitches in the next three stitches, and then working *behind* the three stitches just made to make three front post stitches in the skipped stitches. The second row of the three-stranded braid is six back post stitches worked on the back side of the fabric. The third row of the three-stranded braid is made by first working three front post stitches and then working a front 6-cross cable. A front 6-cross traditional cable is made by skipping three stitches, making three front post stitches in the next three stitches, and then working *in front of* the three stitches just made to make three front post stitches in the skipped stitches. The final row of the three-stranded braid is completed by making back post stitches in each of the stitches of the cable.

Therefore, the three-stranded braid is made by changing both the order of the cable stitch and post stitches and the direction of the cable stitch from row to row. This cable motif does not traditionally have single or double crochet stitches between the cable and post stitches, making it an easy starting place for learning cable motifs. A thin three-stranded cable can be made with a 4-cross cable and two post stitches, or even a 2-cross cable and one post stitch. If you would like to try out a three-stranded cable, this cable motif can be found on page 82 in the pattern for the Shocking Pink Pillow.

Celtic Weave

A Celtic Weave motif has two alternating cable stitch rows. One cable row has all the strands of the braid twisted into cable stitches (shown in Figure 2.16). The second row of the motif has two strands of post stitches, one on the left edge and one on the right edge, and cable stitches in the center (these cables are the opposite direction of the cables in the motif Row 1). Note: There may be rows before the cable rows to begin the fabric and additional rows between the cable rows made of post stitches in order to

Figure 2.16: Celtic Weave. This swatch shows the Celtic Weave motif made of three 6-cross cable stitches. The swatch was made from Knit Picks Swish Worsted Weight Yarn in the Haze Heather colorway with a US size I-9 (5.5 mm) hook.

spread out the cables vertically so that the motif is not twisted too tight. By changing the cable direction between cable rows, all the cable strands that are crossed in front in a given row are then crossed behind in the next row. This in-and-out weaving of the cable strands makes the braid look harmonious without any strand not properly tucked into the motif.

The Celtic Weave motif can use traditional cables that are of any size (2-cross, 4-cross, 6-cross, or 8-cross), although most commonly the 4-cross and 6-cross cables are used because they have more bulk than the lightweight 2-cross cable stitch and yet are not unwieldy like the 8-cross cable stitch. The Celtic Weave can be made with stitches (single crochet or double crochet) between the cables and stand-alone post stitches or without any stitches between the cables and stand-alone post stitches. I prefer to add stitches in between the cables because this reduces gapping (discussed in detail later in this chapter), and it spreads out the cable stitches so that it is easier to see their woven pattern. I also perform a row of post stitches without any cables for each of the back-side rows (between the cable rows), which also tends to spread out the cables vertically and (in my opinion) make the cable motif more attractive. If you would like to further spread out the cable motif vertically, you can add an additional front-side row and back-side row of post stitches between each of the cable rows. If you are new to cable motifs, it is fun to explore how small changes in the cable stitch size, number of post-stitch rows between cable rows, and number of stitches between cable stitches change how this motif appears.

Variations on the Celtic Weave

A Celtic Weave cable motif can be changed in small ways to make a plethora of cable motifs. The easiest modification is adding a repeat of one of the cable rows to the cable motif, which adds the appearance of a loop in the cable. For example, in Figure 2.17, the large cable motif in this blanket is a variation

Figure 2.17: Other Types of Cable Stitches. The Braemar Cable Blanket from Rebecca's Stylings Crochet has a large central cable made of 6-cross cable stitches that has a combination of twist, loops, and braids. The blanket was made from Manos Del Uruguay, Gloria, Superwash Merino in the Natural colorway with a US size H-8 (5.0 mm) hook.

Figure 2.18: Other Types of Cable Stitches. The Isle of Skye Cable Blanket from Rebecca's Stylings Crochet includes a large cable made of 6-cross cable stitches that generates a large V motif. The blanket was made from Knit Picks Simply Wool Worsted in the Wanda colorway with a US size I-9 (5.5 mm) hook.

of the Celtic Weave stitch, with the first cable row repeated once before moving to the second cable row. This adds the look of a nice extra loop or twist to the cable motif.

Another way to modify the Celtic Weave is to change the directions of the cable stitches. For example, in Figure 2.18 the main cable motif of the blanket is a variation of the Celtic Weave, in which the cable stitch directions (front cross or back cross) are made to be directed away from the cable center, making with multiple cable row repeats the appearance of a V-shaped design.

These are just two examples of variations of the Celtic Weave cable motif. Many more variations can be made by further changes to the number and frequency of repeats of cable stitch rows and the directions of the cable stitches in each row.

Saxon Cable

A classic cable motif is the Saxon Cable motif (Figure 2.19, center cable). The Saxon Cable motif has a repeat of four cable rows, making it twice as complex as the Celtic Weave motif. The main defining feature of the Saxon Cable is the decrease in the number of cable stitches in each row, until just one cable stitch is left, and then the increase in cable stitches in each row until all braid strands are back in cable stitches. This design means that the number of post-stitch strands (not in a cable stitch) increases toward the center of the motif and then decreases toward the end of the motif. A classic aspect of this design is the bowing of the shape of the cable to form a rounded, almost scalloped, edging. The reason the cable widens at the center is that cable stitches shrink the fabric width, so by reducing the number of cables in a motif, the motif widens.

The Saxon Cable motif, like the Celtic Weave motif, can be made with or without stitches between the cable stitches. However, this particular motif appears the most curvy when single or double crochet stitches are included between the post stitches and cable stitches. As with the Celtic Weave motif, my version of the Saxon Cable motif includes a row of post stitches (and single crochet stitches) between the cable rows, to stretch the motif vertically and make the cable motif less tight.

The Saxon Cable motif can be made with traditional cable stitches of any size, although it is most commonly made with 4-cross and 6-cross cable stitches. A Saxon Cable motif can also be made any number of cable stitches across, although the most common are three or four cable stitches in the first cable row.

Variations on the Saxon Cable

There are many ways to generate variations to the Saxon Cable motif. Simple variation may include repeating a cable row of the cable motif to add length to the cable or adding a cable stitch on the left or right edges halfway through the design.

In Figure 2.20, the left scarf image shows a Saxon Cable variation with an added cable stitch on the left and the right edges midway through the design. This variation can be used to highlight the center cable and to reduce the curve of the design.

Another, more complicated variation of the Saxon Cable is the right image in Figure 2.20, which shows the removal of cable stitches in the first cable row and the variation in stitch direction in the other cable rows to generate the appearance of woven strands through the cable motif.

Trees, Leaves, and Cables

Motifs of post stitches can be morphed into tree, vine, and leaf shapes by increasing or decreasing the number of post stitches from row to row. Since cable stitches are also made with post stitches, often these two types of motifs are intermingled to generate complex and beautiful designs. In Figure 2.21, the

Figure 2.19: Saxon Braid. The Vermilion Shawl (pattern on page 130) includes a large Saxon Cable in the center of the cable motif. The Saxon Cable is flanked by a double-twist stitch forming a V shape and a puff stitch on the far edges.

Figure 2.20: Variations on the Saxon Cable. These scarves include variations of the Saxon Cable. The scarf patterns are the Bordeaux Cable Scarf (left) and the Louvre Cable Scarf (right). The left scarf added extra cable stitches to the left and right edges of the Saxon Cable halfway through the cable repeat (on the rows that are halfway through the total number of rows to repeat the pattern). The scarf on the right changed the direction of the cable stitches and removed two cable stitches to generate the appearance of two strands weaving through the Saxon Cable. The Bordeaux Cable Scarf used Malabrigo Sock yarn in the Archangel colorway and a US size D-3 (3.25 mm) hook. The Louvre Cable Scarf used Rowan Cashmere yarn in the Cream colorway and a US size H-8 (5.0 mm) hook.

Figure 2.21: Trees, Leaves, and Cables Examples. This figure includes a photo of the Celtic Garden Cable Blanket (left) and the Limerick Tree Cable Scarf (right) from Rebecca's Stylings Crochet. The blanket on the left shows post stitches made into leaves, which appear to sprout from a Saxon Cable. The scarf on the right shows a tree made from post stitches that morphs into three cables. The Celtic Garden Cable Blanket used WeCrochet Swish Worsted Weight yarn in the Wonderland Heather colorway with a US size H-8 (5.0 mm) hook. The Limerick Tree Cable Scarf is made from Berroco Ultra Alpaca yarn in the 6273 colorway with a US size H-8 (5.0 mm) hook.

blanket shows leaves and flowers seeming to sprout out of the sides of a Saxon Cable. Also, in Figure 2.21, the scarf shows that a tree motif can be morphed so that the tree's branches transition seamlessly into cables. These types of designs are advanced, as they require the merging of post stitches (a decrease stitch but using post stitches) or the expansion of post stitches (making multiple post stitches into one post stitch in the previous row).

Lacy Cables

Cabled fabric is not just for the cold winter months. Cables can be combined with chain stitches to make a light, lacy, airy fabric. Most commonly, the single or double crochet stitches between the cable stitches in a large cable motif, such as a Saxon Cable, are replaced with chain stitches, which generates lacy gaps in the fabric. This type of lacy cable is frequently combined with other crochet lace motifs to make summer clothing or lacy baby blankets, as shown in

Figure 2.22: Lacy Cables. The Fiona Cable Lace Blanket from Rebecca's Stylings Crochet uses chain stitches and cable stitches to make lacy cables. The blanket was made from Cascade Yarns, Longwood Sport, Superwash Extrafine Merino Wool yarn in the number 46 colorway with a US size H-8 (5.0 mm) hook.

Figure 2.23: Lacy Cables. The Fiona Cable Lace Top and Cable Lace Poncho from Rebecca's Stylings Crochet use chain stitches and cable stitches to make lacy cables. The top was made from Scheepjes Whirl yarn in the Blueberry Bambam colorway with a US size D-3 (3.25 mm) hook. The poncho was made from Knit Picks Swish Fingering Weight yarn in the bare colorway with a US size G-6 (4.0 mm) hook.

Figures 2.22 and 2.23. In addition, lighter and finer yarn is used to make the items less heavy, more intricate, and more suitable for warm weather wear. It is important to note that, as with any other lacy crocheted fabric, these items require blocking before use. For those unfamiliar, blocking is performed to stretch a fabric to its final shape. To block these lacy items, typically you wet the item with water and then pin it to a blocking board in the desired stretched shape. It can take a couple of iterations of blocking (wetting, stretching, and pinning) before the lacy item is in its final form and ready for gifting or use. This book does not include any lacy crochet cable project, and none of the projects herein should require blocking.

Interconnected Cable Motifs

One of the beautiful aspects of Celtic braided designs emerges when multiple braids of the same or different type are interconnected into a maze of mesmerizing complexity. These types of designs can make a blanket with cables that interconnect every cable strand into a continuous but orderly web of Celtic beauty. These fully connected cable designs are one of my favorite types of cable motifs and feature in many of the crochet patterns posted on my crochet design website, Rebecca's Stylings Crochet.

One way to think about interconnected cables is to start with a typical cable motif, such as a Saxon Cable, and then connect neighboring Saxon Cables with one cable stitch. In this way, an interconnected cable design is like making a patchwork blanket all in one piece, but with each cable motif connected to its neighbor with a single cable stitch. This type of interconnected, repeating Saxon Cable blanket is shown in Figure 2.24, where the Saxon Cables are connected laterally with a single cable stitch in the middle of their cable motif repeat. Figure 2.25 shows another interconnected design, in which a Shamrock

Cable motif is repeated across the blanket (each cable repeat is four 6-cross cable stitches wide at the base of the blanket) and then connected to its neighbor halfway through the cable pattern repeat (or halfway through the number of rows to repeat the pattern).

You can also imagine interconnecting two different types of cable motifs that have the same number of rows in their cable pattern repeat (such as a Saxon Cable and a Shamrock Cable). This approach was used in the blanket in Figure 2.26, which shows a Saxon Cable connected to a Shamrock Cable, again where connection between the cable motifs is halfway through the motif repeat (or halfway through the number of rows to repeat the pattern).

These fully interconnected blanket designs are more advanced because the pattern is more complex and difficult to break into parts. However, the interconnected patterns shown in this section all use relatively few stitch types, including only one traditional cable stitch (with two stitch directions), extended single crochet stitches, and post stitches. Therefore, once a crocheter has mastered the basic concepts and stitches of cable crochet, they can begin exploring even these seemingly complicated designs.

Figure 2.24: Interconnected Cable Motifs: Saxon Cable. The Aberdeen Baby Cable Blanket from Rebecca's Stylings Crochet shows a Saxon Cable that has a connection between the motifs. The blanket was made from Patons Classic Wool Worsted in the Jade colorway with a US size I-9 (5.5 mm) hook.

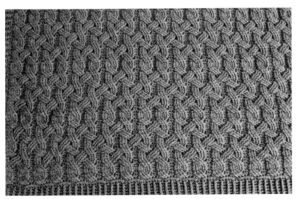

Figure 2.25: Interconnected Cable Stitches. The Large Bulky Shamrock Cable Blanket from Rebecca's Stylings Crochet shows a Shamrock Cable that has a connection between the motifs. The blanket was made from Knit Picks Biggo Bulky Weight in the Cobblestone Heather colorway with a US size M/N-13 (9 mm) hook.

Figure 2.26: Interconnected Cable Stitches. The Stonehaven Cable Blanket from Rebecca's Stylings Crochet shows a Saxon Cable that has a connection with a Shamrock Cable. The blanket was made from Patons Classic Wool Worsted in the Natural Heather colorway with a US size I-9 (5.5 mm) hook.

GAPPING BETWEEN CABLE STITCHES

One of the well-known downsides to cable stitches is that they tend to generate holes, or gaps, on their left and right sides due to the stitches pulling in to overlap each other. This type of gapping between stitches is the most noticeable when you use a heavier yarn and have multiple cable stitches next to each other. Therefore, to diminish gapping, my designs use lighter yarns for garments (such as fingering weight), and my patterns almost always have extended single crochet stitches next to the cable stitches (instead of double crochet stitches). Since the extended single crochet is shorter than a double crochet stitch, it diminishes the effect of the gapping.

Other designers have discovered and innovated many other advanced techniques to reduce the gapping between cable stitches. Jason and Shannon Mullett-Bowlsby have developed the shadow-stitch technique (details in the online article referenced at the end of this chapter), in which additional single crochet stitches are worked behind the cable stitches, which covers the cable stitch gaps. Another advanced method for making crochet cables is called Infinity Crochet by Briana K Designs (https://brianakdesigns.com/infinity-crochet), which, like the Mullett-Bowlsby technique, makes the post stitches in front of a background of consistent single crochet stitches. Nancy Smith has also innovated a similar shadow single crochet technique with cables to reduce gapping and uses it in the Starburst Afghan in the second edition of *The Complete Photo Guide to Crochet*. Finally, Susan Perez has developed the Live Loops Method (book referenced at the end of this chapter), which holds multiple loops on the hook before making a cable stitch. While the Live Loops Method is more advanced, it does reduce gapping and makes beautiful cables that look very similar to knitted cables. If you are concerned about gapping in your crochet garments and are interested in even more advanced cable crochet, you can explore these novel methods.

SUMMARY

Texture is one of the most beautiful features of crocheted fabric. All varieties of crochet stitches generate different types of fabric with a wide range of stitch architectures, tactile features, and visual hallmarks. In this chapter, we focused on crochet texture from Celtic motifs, including ribbing, popcorns, bobbles, puff stitches, and cable motifs. This chapter just scratches the surface of the wide range of crochet Celtic textures available, and for the enthusiast it can be a jumping-off point to the many resources, patterns, and tutorials available online. In addition, we will explore a variety of crochet textures even more with each of the patterns in the second half of this book.

ADDITIONAL READING ON THE HISTORY AND TYPES OF CABLE KNITTING

Gaughan, Norah. 2016. *Norah Gaughan's Knitted Cable Sourcebook: A Breakthrough Guide to Knitting with Cables and Designing Your Own.* New York: Abrams.

Starmore, Alice. 2010. *Aran Knitting*, expanded edition. New York: Dover Publications.

ADDITIONAL READING ON CABLE CROCHET

Online Articles

Anderson, Brenda K. B. 2017. "Learn This New Kind of Crochet Cable!" Interweave.com. https://www.interweave.com/article/crochet/learn-new-kind-crochet-cable.

Barker, Bonnie. 2019. "A Twist on Crocheted Cables." Interweave.com. https://www.interweave.com/article/crochet/twist-on-crocheted-cables.

Dudek, Sara. 2018. "New to Crochet Cables? This Is the Project to Get You Started!" Interweave .com. https://www.interweave.com/article/crochet/crochet-cables-get-started.

Dudek, Sara. 2018. "3 Brilliant Ideas to Perfect Your Crochet Cables!" Interweave.com. https://www .interweave.com/article/crochet/3-brilliant-ideas -to-perfect-your-crochet-cables.

Mullett-Bowlsby, Jason, and Shannon Mullett-Bowlsby. 2018. "Shadow-Stitch Cables: Your New Crochet Obsession." Interweave.com. https://www.interweave.com/article/crochet/shadow-stitch-cables.

Mullett-Bowlsby, Shannon. 2021. "Untangling Cables: Creating Crochet Cables with Post Stitches." Interweave.com. https://www.interweave.com/article/crochet/creating-crochet-cables -post-stitches.

WeAreKnitters. 2020. "How to Crochet Cables." The Blog, We Are Knitters, November 11. https://blog.weareknitters.com/crochet-stitches/how -to-crochet-cables.

WeCrochet. 2020. "How to Crochet Cables + Good Beginner Crochet Cable Patterns." WeCrochet Blog, September 22. https://blog.crochet.com/how-to-crochet-cables-good-beginner-crochet-cable-patterns.

Books

Barker, Bonnie. 2016. *Celtic Cable Crochet: 18 Crochet Patterns for Modern Cabled Garments & Accessories*. Loveland, CO: Interweave.

Hubert, Margaret. 2014. *The Complete Photo Guide to Crochet*, second edition. Minneapolis, MN: Creative Publishing International.

Laitenberger, Manuela. 2017. *50 Crochet Cable Stitches*. CreateSpace Independent Publishing Platform.

Perez, Sue. 2020. *Live Loop Cables in Crochet: A New Way to Make Cables in Crochet Fabric*. Self-published.

Texture and Shadow in One Color 3

WHAT IS TEXTURE?

Crocheted fabric can have beautiful stitching that generates an intricate pattern of texture. But what exactly *is* texture, and how do we see it? Texture refers to variations in the surface elevation of stitches; just like a topographical map with mountains and valleys, crochet fabric has bumps and fissures on its surface. These variations in surface elevation (height) are not visible by themselves (unless you have phenomenal depth perception!); rather, they become visible as the result of *shadows*. When you walk on the sidewalk in the early evening, you cast a shadow that varies in length depending on where the sun is, varies in darkness depending on how completely you block the sun, and varies in form depending on the shape of your own body. Each of the bumps on your crocheted fabric also has a shadow, and these vary in darkness, size, and shape depending on the stitch properties and where the sun is (or where the light source is after dark). Therefore, the source of the texture that you see on the fabric is generated by shadows and depends on two things: the bump (or stitch) topography and the illumination.

Highlights can also contribute to texture perception. Highlights are bright regions where the light hits the cable stitch or bump on the fabric and reflects more light. However, shadows seem to have a much stronger effect on the perception of crocheted fabric texture than highlights do. This observation is supported by the stronger perception of texture in white yarn garments (which have a limited range of highlights) in comparison to the perception of texture in black yarn garments (which have a limited range of shadows). Therefore, we will focus on discussing shadows from now on.

HOW DOES YARN BRIGHTNESS AFFECT TEXTURE VISIBILITY?

Let's now turn to the brightness of the yarn used to make the fabric. How does yarn brightness affect the texture that you see? It is often recommended that people use light-colored yarn (such as cream or white) to make highly textured garments. This advice is for a good reason. The texture (as we established above) is generated mostly by the perception of shadows. Shadows are simply darkened regions on the surface of the fabric generated by the blocking of light by bumps or ridges in the fabric. The more completely the light is blocked by a stitch, the darker the shadow. Therefore, if the fabric has a light color background, many gradations of shadows (from light to very dark) can be seen against the light background. This variability is what gives the texture intricacy and detail. However, if the fabric is a dark color (such as a charcoal gray), then when shadows darken the fabric further, only a few additional levels of gray are visible before that region of the garment appears to be completely black. In this case, the details of the shadows (and details of the texture) are drowned out by the darkness of the background color.

For example, imagine drawing the outline of a shadow on black asphalt versus attempting the same task on white cement. The white cement would be much easier! Of course, for this reason black is one of the worst types of yarn to use in making a textured garment, as the shadows cannot make regions of the garment appear to be much darker than the background color, and therefore the texture is nearly invisible. (Note: Of course, shadow effects depend to some degree on the camera settings, background, and lighting that you use to photograph an item. Detailed suggestions on the photography of crochet are provided in Inset IV.)

For a visual comparison of different yarn brightnesses in textured patterns, see Figure 3.1. The top right swatch in Figure 3.1 is a light gray and shows the pattern texture in vivid detail. By way of contrast, the bottom right swatch is made from a much darker yarn. This darkness limits the complexity of the shadows that can be seen and therefore limits the pattern visibility.

HOW DOES YARN COLOR AFFECT TEXTURE VISIBILITY?

Let's now consider cases in which the yarn is a solid color (such as green, for example). The texture is still generated by shadows of different darknesses against the color background. Therefore, the same rule of "the lighter the yarn, the better" applies here as well. Choose colors that are pale and bright and avoid colors that are dark and close to black. If it

Figure 3.1: Texture with Solid Color Yarn. The three swatches on the left are texture patterns made in a natural yarn, a light green yarn, and a dark green yarn. The texture is more apparent in the natural and light green yarn than in the dark green yarn, as the highlights and shadows generated by the variation in surface height (i.e., texture) can be easily seen. The grayscale image on the right side shows that the natural yarn is a light gray in brightness, the light green yarn is a medium gray in brightness, and the dark green yarn is a dark charcoal gray in brightness. The swatches were made from Knit Picks Stroll Yarn in Bare, Peapod, and Forest Heather colorways with a US size F-5 (3.75 mm) hook.

is difficult for you to tell the brightness of the yarn color, simply take a photo and convert the image from color to grayscale, and then decide whether you will be able to see shadows against that shade of gray. Using this photo method, I recommend colors that translate to a medium gray or lighter. I would avoid colors that translate to charcoal gray or darker (when converted to grayscale). For an example of textures crocheted in solid colors, see Figure 3.1. The light green yarn in Figure 3.1 (just like the light gray yarn) has many shadows and therefore pattern details. The darker green yarn in Figure 3.1 (photographed in the same lighting) has much less detail and complexity visible in the cable stitching.

INSET IV: TIPS FOR PHOTOGRAPHING CROCHET TEXTURE

Photographing texture on crochet fabric has its own unique challenges. Here is a brief list of tips to improve your crochet photography.

Do:

- Have a strong light source on one side of the cable pattern. Usually, a side window works the best, but extra internal lighting helps also.
- Lay out or hang your item so that it is flat. This is important so that the wrinkles in the fabric do not also cast shadows that distract from the texture or cabling.
- Use natural lighting as much as possible, as this will highlight the colors and generate beautiful shadows.
- Use a background that highlights but does not wash out your item. For example, for dark yarns I use dark wood backgrounds, as this lightens the item as perceived relative to the background and highlights the subtle shadows (see the example to the right).

Don't:

- Use a flash. A flash will wash out all of the shadows and will tend to make your item look flat.
- Photograph the item at night, as you will never get enough light to take a nice photo.

Figure 3.2: Dark Scarf on a Dark Background with Side Lighting. The cables are highlighted and not washed out.

Figure 3.3: The Same Scarf with the Same Lighting but Placed Instead on an Off-White Background

HOW DO YARN FIBER, TWIST, AND WEIGHT AFFECT TEXTURE?

Four other yarn features are valuable to consider in making highly textured garments: fiber type, fiber twist, fiber weight, and fiber fuzziness. We will briefly review these features here.

Yarn fiber can be made from animal wool, plant fibers, silk, and artificial materials (acrylic). The animal fibers such as sheep wool, goat wool, or rabbit fur have strands with ridges along their length. These ridges allow for felting of the fiber, hold textured patterns well over time, and generate an elasticity within the fiber. The plant fibers, silk, and artificial materials have smooth strands, which hold textured patterns less and, in the case of plant fibers (such as cotton), can stretch out over time.

Overall, it is preferable to use animal wool for highly textured patterns, as the texture will be more apparent. However, this is not a hard and fast rule. If cared for properly, other materials can also make beautiful items, even though they may be less durable and lose shape over time. Yarn that combines wool and nylon (often used for socks) is excellent for scarves and hats, as it combines the texture benefits of wool and the durability of nylon. For more details on fiber types, I recommend several of the books listed at the end of this chapter.

Fiber weight (or yarn weight) has an impact on textured patterns as well. Heavier yarns will make texture that is easier to see. Bulky weight yarn can be used to make Aran patterns that leap off the surface of the fabric and arrest the viewer's attention. However, bulky yarns are not always ideal for Aran patterns, as they make items with occasional gaps (not great for a sweater!) and tend to create very large motifs. Fingering and DK weight yarns will generate a lighter weight fabric with more drape, which in general is better for sweaters and tops. Lighter weight yarns also make smaller stitches that allow the pattern to be more intricate and complex.

It is important to be aware of these pros and cons when choosing a yarn weight for a textured project. If you want to make an item that is similar to the pattern that you are using, I recommend using the same yarn weight as the example in the pattern. As a rule of thumb in crochet, which tends to make a stiffer fabric than knitting does, I recommend using fingering weight yarn for garments, scarves, and hats, and worsted or bulky yarn for blankets (depending on blanket size, cost, and pattern).

The fiber twist is the ply of the yarn (how many threads make up the yarn) and the direction in which it is twisted. There is a wide variety of yarn-making techniques that generate yarn consisting of anywhere from one to four threads twisted together (among other braiding techniques). In my experience, the best yarn type for textures and cables is a multiple-ply yarn with a significant amount of twist. The multiple twisted plies make the yarn more durable (less likely to pill) and add elasticity to the fiber, which in turn makes the stitches more uniform. While highly twisted yarn is the best for textured patterns, the effect of yarn twist is relatively modest, so don't avoid your favorite yarn for this reason alone.

Finally, yarn fuzziness (or loft) has a strong impact on the visibility of textured patterns. Yarns such as Mohair that have a halo can make beautiful fabric. However, the fuzziness tends to reduce the stitch definition and the clarity of texture edges. For this reason, it is ideal to choose yarns with little to no halo for cabled and textured projects.

SUMMARY

In this chapter, we reviewed the visual perception of texture, and noted that shadows and highlights are the primary visual basis for fabric texture. In addition, we showed that lighter color yarns emphasize texture better than darker color yarns. Finally, we reviewed the basics of yarn features and discussed the best yarn fiber, weight, twist, and fuzziness for heavily textured items. In the next chapter, we will discuss the use of multiple colors and how to choose the best multicolored yarn for a highly textured project.

REFERENCES

Cavanagh, Patrick, and Yvan G. Leclerc. 1989. "Shape from Shadows." *Journal of Experimental Psychology: Human Perception and Performance* 15, no. 1: 3.

Palmer, Stephen E. 1999. *Vision Science: Photons to Phenomenology*. Cambridge, MA: MIT Press.

Robson, Deborah, and Carol Ekarius. 2011. *The Fleece and Fiber Sourcebook: More than 200 Fibers from Animal to Spun Yarn*. North Adams, MA: Storey Publishing.

Sulcoski, Carol J. 2019. *Yarn Substitution Made Easy: Matching the Right Yarn to Any Knitting Pattern*. New York: Lark Crafts.

ADDITIONAL READING ON YARN FIBER, TWIST, WEIGHT, AND FUZZINESS

Parkes, Clara. 2007. *The Knitter's Book of Yarn: The Ultimate Guide to Choosing, Using, and Enjoying Yarn*. New York: Potter Craft.

Robson, Deborah, and Carol Ekarius. 2013. *The Field Guide to Fleece: 100 Sheep Breeds and How to Use Their Fibers*. North Adams, MA: Storey Publishing.

Robson, Deborah, and Carol Ekarius. 2011. *The Fleece and Fiber Sourcebook: More than 200 Fibers from Animal to Spun Yarn*. North Adams, MA: Storey Publishing.

Sulcoski, Carol J. 2019. *Yarn Substitution Made Easy: Matching the Right Yarn to Any Knitting Pattern*. New York: Lark Crafts.

4

Multicolored Yarns with Multi-Textured Patterns

*I*n the last chapter, we discussed how fiber texture is made visible by the presence of shadows and how lighter yarns showcase texture better than darker yarns. In this chapter, we will examine multicolored yarns as well as how changes in coloration interact with the visual perception of texture.

BRIGHTNESS EDGES: IS THAT EDGE A SHADOW OR A STRIPE?

How do we interpret the visual world around us? It is not quite as simple as it first appears. For example, a table could be made of two different woods, such as oak, which is quite bright, and mahogany, which is quite dark. How does the brain know that the table is made of two different woods? In addition to their inherent difference in color, the two woods have different brightnesses, which allows the interfaces between them to be accentuated. However, changes in brightness could also be caused by shadows on the table's surface and not by a change in wood type. The brain makes assumptions about details in the environment based on both historical knowledge and context, which allows us to distinguish (in most cases) between shadows and changes in the nature of the surface materials. However, the brain is not always

perfect, and changes in intrinsic surface brightness can conflict with the perception of shadows.

Why is this important? In Chapter 3, we discussed the critical role of shadows in the perception of fabric textures. It is through the perception of shadows that the beautiful cable stitches in our crochet projects come to life. Therefore, what do you predict would happen if we change yarns back and forth between a black yarn and a white yarn while making a cable motif? You're right! The brightness edges from the yarn changes (between black and white) would make it much more difficult for the brain to locate and visualize the shadows. Consequently, the *pattern* details are more difficult to see and sometimes disappear altogether. For example, look at the bottom row of Figure 4.2. The black-and-white splotches of brightness make the cable pattern (which is identical to the pattern in the top row) extremely difficult to see.

Therefore, in *cable* projects you most often want to avoid choosing two or more yarns that change in brightness. But this does not mean that the only yarn you can use is a solid gray or a solid color. There are many yarn options that don't vary in brightness. To discuss this concept in more depth, we will first review the psychological properties of color that we introduced in Chapter 1.

COLOR EDGES AND LIGHTNESS EDGES: ISOLUMINANT COLORS AND TEXTURE

Colors have three basic properties: hue (variation across the rainbow), saturation (vividness), and lightness (brightness), as illustrated in the crochet swatches shown in Figure 4.2. In Chapter 1, we focused on understanding color perception and then on making crochet project color plans with solid color yarns based on the color wheel. In this chapter, we will apply this understanding of color perception to the luminance edges (or brightness edges) in multicolored yarns.

When you are adding colors to a white canvas, the various colors can have several different types of interfaces. One color could neighbor another color that has the same saturation and lightness but is different in hue (for example, a vivid blue next to a stop-sign red). The neighboring colors could also have the same saturation and hue, but different lightnesses (for example, a baby blue next to a navy blue). In general, our visual system is most sensitive to differences in lightness in terms of visualizing edges and lines, as well as in determining the locations of borders, and not as sensitive to differences in hue and saturation. Most important, differences in hue and saturation do not compete strongly with shadow perception, which represents a brightness edge. However, if two colors next to each other have different lightnesses (or brightnesses), then the border between the colors will appear to be nearly as apparent as a brightness edge between a gray yarn and a black yarn. This lightness difference will *compete* with the perception of shadows and make it more difficult to see the texture of the surface. Therefore, if we are choosing yarn that varies in color, we need to choose yarns that have beautiful variations in hue and saturation but as little as possible variation in lightness. In visual science, these families of colors are called "isoluminant," or of the same

luminance (*or* lightness), and are frequently used in the study of the visual system.

As an example of a nearly isoluminant yarn (or a yarn with no brightness variation), see the blue, green, and gray variegated yarn shown as a skein in Figure 4.1, Top Row, and shown as a swatch in Figure 4.2, Variegated Yarns Section, Top Row. Despite the fantastic variation in color, the texture pattern represented by the folds and undulations is still highly visible and even enlivened by the addition of color. This yarn has very little variation in brightness (as can be seen in the grayscale photo on the right), and consequently the color variation does not conflict with the perception of shadows that arise from the texture. By way of comparison, the variegated yarn shown in Figure 4.1 and Figure 4.2, Bottom Row, has substantial brightness variations that are even more apparent in the grayscale image on the right side. In this case, the brightness variations conflict with the shadow patterns, and the texture pattern of folds and undulations is much more subdued.

Now that we know what we *don't* want in a yarn for certain projects, how do we pick out appropriate isoluminant yarns and pair them with our highly textured projects?

THE GRAYSCALE PHOTO TECHNIQUE

Our study has so far told us that multicolored yarns with minimal variations in brightness make beautiful, cabled crochet projects, in which the texture is highly visible and is even enhanced by the color variations. Finding isoluminant yarn is quite simple. Take a photo of your yarn of interest in grayscale mode or take a color photo and then transform the color photo to grayscale (or black and white). This is easily done by either changing your camera into grayscale mode (e.g., mono mode within the camera settings associated with each photo on the iPhone) or converting a color image into grayscale in programs such as Adobe Photoshop (make a copy of the photo first before converting it to grayscale). Then inspect the grayscale photo of the yarn. Is it a uniform color of gray? Are there any splotches or lines of darkness or brightness? If the grayscale photo of the yarn looks like Figure 4.1 in the upper right corner (a light or medium gray with no lines or splotches), then your project will show texture beautifully. By way of contrast, if the yarn is too dark (as discussed in Chapter 3) or if there is substantial variation in brightness (as can be seen in Figure 4.1, Rows 3 and 4, Right), then you may not be able to see the texture of your pattern very well. Figure 4.2 shows swatches of the yarns shown in Figure 4.1 and demonstrates the decreasing perception of texture associated with increasing variations in brightness.

One of the most difficult challenges in selecting yarns is that most yarns lie somewhere within the wide range between the examples shown in Figure 4.1, Top and Bottom Rows, such as the examples shown in the middle two rows. The perfectly isoluminant yarn (with a set of colors and in a fiber that you love) is not always easy to find. At times I'll select a yarn that is not perfectly isoluminant (such as in Row 2 of Figure 4.1) but still shows some texture, and then spend more time carefully photographing it to better show off the texture.

Original Yarn Color **Yarn Brightness (Black-and-White Images)**

Figure 4.1: Four Variegated Yarn Examples. The four variegated yarns shown are Knit Picks Hand Painted Stroll Yarn in the Celery Seed, Frolic, Mix Tape, and Knight colorways. The images on the left are the original yarn photos, and the images on the right are grayscale versions of the original photo. These four yarns can be also viewed in swatch form (in both color and black and white (grayscale) images) in Figure 4.2.

Natural Yarn (Reference)

Original Yarn Color

**Yarn Lightness
(Grayscale Image)**

Variegated Yarns

Original Yarn Color

**Yarn Lightness
(Grayscale Image)**

Figure 4.2: Swatches of Yarn Examples: Color Variation. The images on the left show five swatches with the same cable texture but made in five different yarn colorways. The left column shows the swatch in each yarn's original color, and the second vertical column shows the swatch when presented in grayscale. The swatch on the top row is a natural yarn color (off-white) and is included as a reference image showing the maximum amount of texture visible in this design. The next four swatches are made with variegated yarns. The first yarn (top row under Variegated Yarns) has no variation in brightness (only variation in color hue), as can be seen in the grayscale image on the right side. By way of contrast, the last swatch (bottom row under Variegated Yarns) is dark in color and has variations in brightness, which makes the pattern nearly invisible. The two middle swatches (second and third rows under Variegated Yarns) have increasing variations in brightness and therefore decreasing cable stitch visibility. Additional uniform yarn swatches of the same cable pattern are shown in Figure 3.1 on page 42. The swatches were made from Knit Picks Hand Painted Stroll Yarn in the Natural, Celery Seed, Frolic, Mix Tape, and Knight colorways (in descending order) with a US size F-5 (3.75 mm) hook. The four yarns in the Variegated Yarn section can also be viewed in skein form (color and black-and-white images) in Figure 4.1.

INSET V: TAKING GRAYSCALE PHOTOS ON THE IPHONE

Grayscale photos can be easily taken on most smartphones by changing the photo settings. For simplicity, we are going to describe the process only for the iPhone, as the iPhone is one of the most popular smartphones worldwide. Taking grayscale photos on your smartphone will make it particularly easy to identify isoluminant yarn (not splotched in grayscale photos). In fact, the smartphones typically show a live feed of the environment while you are framing your photo, so once you set your phone into grayscale mode, you can scan across an entire row of shelves of yarn and find the right one for you.

1. Open the camera application on your iPhone. This is usually an icon of a black camera on the front page of your phone.

2. Press the small upside-down V at the top of your screen (above the image of the photo you are about to take).

Camera Application Icon

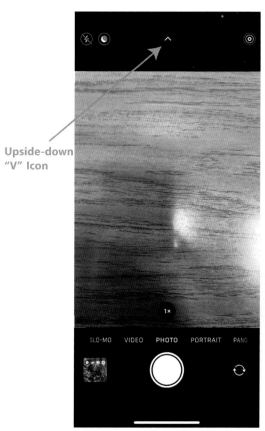

Upside-down "V" Icon

3. You should now see new icons at the bottom of the screen (just above your capture button). All of these icons are buttons to change the settings of your camera. Swipe from right to left across these icons until you reach the last icon, which is of three overlapping rings. Tap the last icon.

4. You should now see a series of small miniature images instead of the icons (left image). Each of these images is a different image capture mode. Swipe from right to left across these images until a white square is around a gray image and the word "Mono" is above it (right image).

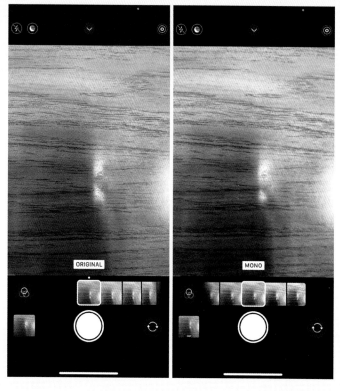

New Icons at the Bottom of the Screen

That's it! Now you should see your main image (the preview of the photo you are going to take) as a gray image. You can take a grayscale image of your yarn, or you can just view the main image as you move your camera across the yarns that you are interested in.

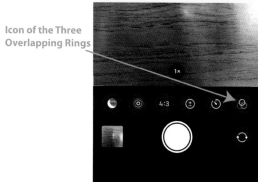

Icon of the Three Overlapping Rings

SUMMARY

Variations in brightness within multicolored yarn conflict with the perception of shadows that generate texture perception. Therefore, to make a crochet project with highly visible texture using multicolored yarn, purchase a yarn that is "isoluminant," such that it varies in hue and saturation but not lightness (brightness). Yarns can be evaluated for isoluminance by taking a grayscale photo and then determining whether the photo is a uniform gray (great for texture projects) or splotchy (bad for texture projects). Yarns with mid-level splotchiness can be used, but if you decide to choose one of these yarns for a highly textured or cabled crochet project, make sure to compensate by taking better photos with excellent lighting and no flash once the project is complete (details are included in Inset IV).

REFERENCES

Bell, Jason, Elena Gheorghiu, and Gokhan Malkoc. 2010. "Chromatic Variations Suppress Suprathreshold Brightness Variations." *Journal of Vision* 10, no. 10 (August): 1–13.

Cavanagh, Patrick. (1987). "Reconstructing the Third Dimension: Interactions between Color, Texture, Motion, Binocular Disparity, and Shape." *Computer Vision, Graphics, and Image Processing* 37, no. 2 (February): 171–95.

Cavanagh, Patrick, and Yvan G. Leclerc. 1989. "Shape from Shadows." *Journal of Experimental Psychology: Human Perception and Performance* 15, no. 1 (February): 3.

Frederick, A. A., Jason Bell, Christian Haddad, and Alysha Bartsch. 2015. "Perceptual Scales for Chromatic and Luminance Blur in Noise Textures." *Journal of Vision* 15, no. 9: 6, 1–10.

Goddard, Erin, and Colin W. G. Clifford. 2013. "A New Type of Change Blindness: Smooth, Isoluminant Color Changes Are Monitored on a Coarse Spatial Scale." *Journal of Vision* 13, no. 5 (April): 20.

Livingstone, Margaret S., and David H. Hubel. 1987. "Psychophysical Evidence for Separate Channels for the Perception of Form, Color, Movement, and Depth." *Journal of Neuroscience* 7, no. 11 (November): 3416–68.

Lüschow, A., and H. C. Nothdurft. 1993. "Pop-Out of Orientation but No Pop-Out of Motion at Isoluminance." *Vision Research* 33, no. 1 (January): 91–104.

Palmer, Stephen E. 1999. *Vision Science: Photons to Phenomenology*. Cambridge, MA: MIT Press.

Sharman, Rebecca J., Paul V. McGraw, and Jonathan W. Peirce. 2015. "Cue Combination of Conflicting Color and Luminance Edges." *i-Perception* 6, no. 6 (December): 2041669515621215.

Wandell, Brian. 1995. *Foundations of Vision*. Sunderland, MA: Sinauer Associates.

Color Gradient Yarns, Speckled Yarns, and Stranded Colorwork

MULTICOLORED YARNS OF OTHER VARIETIES

Chapter 4 focused on textured projects made with multicolored yarns. In this context, the term "multicolored yarns" was used to describe yarns with two or more colors, in which each color segment is about two to five stitches in length. However, there are many other types of colorful yarns available. Two additional types of popular colorful yarn are color gradient yarns and speckled yarns.

Color gradient yarns incorporate slow changes from one solid color to another solid color. These slowly varying color transitions can bridge the entire project length, or they can last for just a few rows, enabling multiple color transitions to occur over the length of one project.

Speckled yarns are typically based on one solid color with a sparse scattering of other colors in very short bursts (typically one stitch or less). These colorful "speckles" often resemble bright sprinkles distributed on the frosting of a cupcake.

In this chapter, we will discuss the use of these two yarn types in textured projects as well as how to select the ideal yarns that will showcase your stitching. We will also discuss the use of stranded colorwork with multicolored yarn, which can be used to make colorful textured projects with yarn that may otherwise obscure texture.

COLOR GRADIENT YARNS

Color gradient yarns have been popularized in the United States and Europe in part by the Scheepjes Whirl yarns, which have multiple slow non-repeating color changes over the course of 1,093 yards (1,000 meters) of yarn. Other gradient yarns of note include YarnArt Flowers, CottonKings Twirl, Freia Fine Handpaints Ombre, Lion Brand Wrap Star, Red Heart It's a Wrap, and Caron Cakes, among numerous alternatives in the United States and abroad. Gradient yarns are most used in crochet for lace shawls in which the project uses precisely one long skein of the color gradient yarn. Shawls of this type have been immensely popular, so much so that the Virus Shawl by Julia Marquardt has been rated the "most popular" Ravelry pattern.

Can these yarns be used for highly textured cable projects? Yes, with a few considerations they can show texture and stitch definition beautifully. The main concern is the overall yarn brightness, as well as the *relative* brightness of each of the colors in the skein. As we discussed in Chapters 3 and 4, yarn should be medium to light brightness in order to display texture effectively. Therefore, confirming that the gradient yarn never transitions to black or charcoal gray levels of brightness is important. In addition, the transitions between the colors should have a minimal change in brightness, as this effect prevents the yarn from getting too dark and the color transition from providing a distraction to your pattern.

For example, consider the yarn skeins in Figure 5.1. The top gradient yarn (top left) when converted to grayscale (black and white; top right) has a relatively consistent gray level from the center out to the cake edge, except for the final color transition. (Note: A cake in this context is a way to wind a yarn skein into a cylinder shape in order to showcase a color gradient.) Therefore, the top gradient yarn should work well with a textured project, especially if the last color transition is excluded. The bottom gradient yarn (bottom left) when converted to grayscale (black and white; bottom right) exhibits several dramatic

Original Yarn Color   **Yarn Brightness (Grayscale Image)**

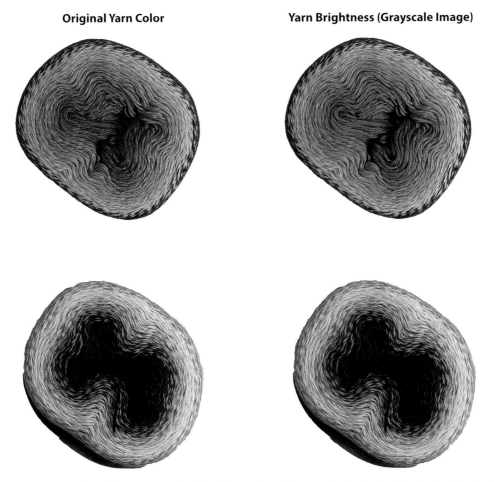

Figure 5.1: Two Examples of Gradient Yarns. The left column shows the yarn skeins (end on) in their original color, and the right column shows the yarn skeins presented in grayscale. The top yarn is Scheepjes Whirl Lemon Cassis Cream (765), and the bottom yarn is Scheepjes Whirl Raspberry Rocky Roads (752). The images on the right are grayscale conversions of the images on the left. Note the near uniform gray level of the Lemon Cassis Cream yarn and the dramatic changes in lightness within the Raspberry Rocky Roads yarn.

transitions from nearly black to nearly white. The bottom yarn would make a textured pattern difficult to see because it includes both a very dark color and a transition between black and white.

This book includes two gradient yarn projects in Chapter 11. These projects are Aran crochet patterns with dense cables and use gradient yarns that are designed to follow the guidelines above.

SPECKLED YARNS

Speckled yarns are a rising trend in hand-painted yarn with growing enthusiasm from small artisanal yarn dyers to large corporate yarn companies (Figure 5.2). Speckled yarns are now available from yarn companies such as Caron (Simply Soft Speckle Yarn), Knit Picks (Hawthorne Speckle Hand Painted), Cascade Yarns (Cascade 200 Superwash

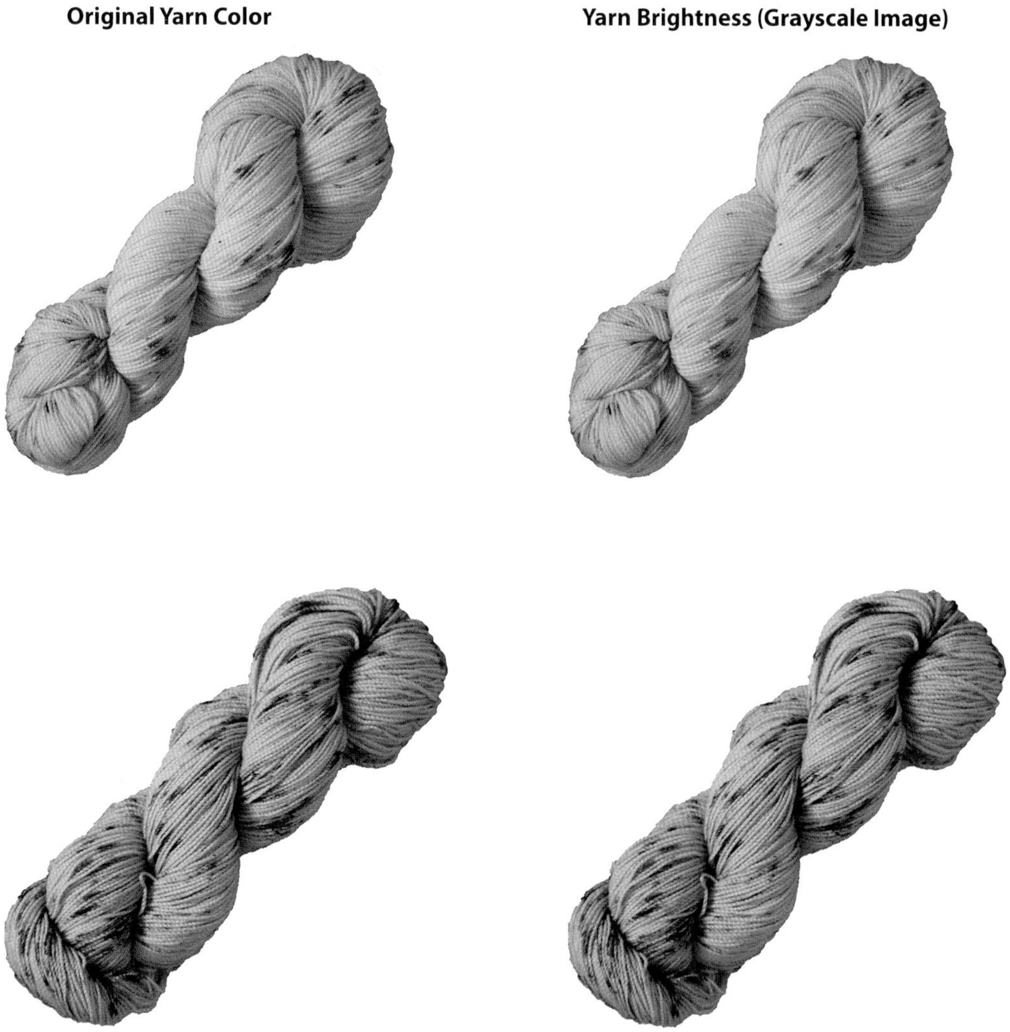

Original Yarn Color   **Yarn Brightness (Grayscale Image)**

Figure 5.2: Two Examples of Speckled Yarns. The yarn in the top row is Knit Picks Hawthorne Speckle Hand Painted in Panettone Speckle, and the yarn in the bottom row is Knit Picks Hawthorne Speckle Hand Painted in Cosmic Speckle. The images on the right are grayscale conversions of the images on the left. Note the near uniform gray level of the Panettone yarn and the dramatic changes in lightness within the Cosmic Speckle yarn.

Aran Splatter), and Plymouth Yarn (Happy Feet 100 Splash). In my opinion, the speckled yarn projects have a birthday cake or starry night ambiance with a dash of inspiration from Stephen Pollock paintings. In other words, they are playful and artsy at the same time.

The main concerns with textured projects that are made with speckled yarn are the brightness of the speckles relative to the background, as well as the density of the speckles. Ideally the speckles would be made with a different color but with the same brightness as the background yarn; however, this is very rarely the case. Therefore, I recommend finding speckled yarn with a minimal brightness change between the speckles and background and with a relatively sparse distribution of speckles.

Two examples of speckled yarn are highlighted in Figure 5.2. The yarn in the top row, shown in the colored image on the left and in the grayscale image on the right, has sparsely distributed speckles with a minimal brightness change relative to the background. By way of contrast, the yarn in the bottom row, shown in the colored image on the left and in the grayscale image on the right, has very dark speckles that are quite dense. Therefore, the top yarn would be reasonable for making a beautiful textured project, but the bottom yarn would likely make a textured project with obscured details.

This book does not include crochet patterns with speckled yarn. However, by using the grayscale photo technique, you will now be empowered to identify the best speckled yarn for your next project.

MERGING SOLID-COLORED AND MULTICOLORED YARNS

Occasionally I fall in love with a multicolored yarn that would likely result in a horrible textured project if used by itself. This is a dilemma, as all the patterns that I write incorporate rich textures and cable motifs because of my enthusiasm for that style. I have found that the best and most beautiful solution to this problem is to do colorwork with a *solid* yarn in combination with that special multicolored yarn.

Colorwork is the use of multiple yarns to make a garment or blanket with a variety of colors or fibers. Stranded colorwork is performed in crochet by making a stitch in one yarn, then dropping that yarn, picking up another yarn, and then proceeding with the next stitch. This technique generates strands of "carried" yarn across the back of the fabric. Most colorwork is performed so that many different solid colors can be used to make a motif on a fabric, including images, words, or geometrical designs. Colorwork can also be used to make textured projects with multicolored yarns that have too much brightness variation for a textured project by themselves (as discussed in Chapter 4). In this case, the multicolored yarn can be used to perform the cable stitches, and a solid yarn can be used for the single or double crochet stitches between the cables (as shown, for example, in Figures 5.3 and 5.4).

Stranded colorwork consequently provides tremendous freedom in design, perhaps at the expense of a bit more work. When selecting yarns, I recommend selecting one highly multicolored yarn for the cables (or texture) and one solid color (such as white) for the background stitches. The yarns can be from different manufacturers; the only constraint is that they should be a similar weight, as otherwise this will change the stitch sizes. When making a colorwork project, I also recommend using a larger hook than you typically would for the yarn you are using. This is because the transition back and forth between the yarns can make the work tighter and reduce the elasticity of the fabric. With a hook that is 0.5 mm larger than usual, some of this elasticity can be restored.

In Chapter 12 there are two projects with stranded colorwork and multicolored yarn that should provide inspiration and guidance in this advanced technique.

Figure 5.4. The Vienna Cable Scarf from Rebecca's Stylings Crochet is an example of Stranded Colorwork and Cables.

Figure 5.3. The Renaissance Rose Cable Scarf from Rebecca's Stylings Crochet is an example of Stranded Colorwork and Cables.

6 *Tips, Colorways, and Swatches*

his book recommends the use of isoluminant yarns to make highly textured projects. We have described a method for identifying these yarns with our grayscale photo technique. But we recognize that there is still a challenge of determining how much brightness variation is too much variation. Of course, the demarcation point between an inconsequential amount of variation and too much variation will depend on the project you are making and your own personal taste.

REVIEW OF YARN SELECTION TIPS

We have discussed many different colorway features that can diminish the perception of texture in your fiber project. Here are key yarn and color properties to keep in mind while shopping for multicolored yarn for a highly textured project:

1. Make sure **the yarn colors are nearly isoluminant** (consistent brightness across the color variations). You can use the grayscale photo technique to test this quality (described in Chapter 4).

2. Make sure that **the colors are not too attention grabbing**. Pastel colors that are in the blue, green, and purple family work the best. Although

you can use bright colors, just be wary of their influence, and swatch your project before you commit (described in Chapter 1).

3. Make sure **the yarn colors are not too dark**. If the yarn is too dark, then it will be more difficult to see shadows from your fabric texture and therefore more difficult to pick out the pattern of the stitching (detailed in Chapter 3).

4. Make sure to **get all of your yarn from the same dye lot**. If the yarn is hand painted and doesn't have dye lots, then check the consistency of the color between skeins by eye (described in Inset II).

In addition, there are other yarn properties that affect the visibility of the texture of your project (discussed in Chapter 3). Here are a few recommendations for yarn type selection:

1. Make sure that **the yarn is not too fuzzy or textured** and therefore will obscure the texture of your stitching (described in Chapter 3).

2. **If possible, buy a yarn with elasticity,** such as animal fiber from sheep, alpacas, rabbits, or goats (if possible, avoid cotton and silk). Fiber with elasticity will make your stitches more even and your cables more bouncy (described in Chapter 3).

For stranded colorwork projects with multicolored yarn and highly textured motifs such as cables, here are a few checklist items to keep in mind (see Chapter 5 for details).

1. Make sure that **your yarns (multicolored or solid colored) are not too different in brightness (lightness)**. If one is very light and the other very dark, it could make the texture details (such as cables) in one of the yarns more difficult to see.

2. However, **for one of your yarns you can choose a multicolored yarn with more variation and brighter colors** than you typically would for a highly textured project.

3. **Use a larger hook than normal** to add back in some fabric elasticity. Stranded colorwork loses some elasticity and is tighter due to the yarn carried or floated on the back side.

4. **Yarns should be of a similar weight** (but can be from different manufacturers). You can get around the yarn weight issue by doubling up a thinner yarn (such as a fingering weight yarn) to match a heavier yarn (such as a worsted weight yarn). If you are using different yarn lines, I recommend making a swatch to confirm that your yarn weights work well together.

THE YARNS USED IN THIS BOOK

I have selected yarns for the projects in this book that appear (to me) to be within the acceptable range of properties for highly textured projects. Therefore, to further inform your yarn decisions, I have included in this chapter examples of all of the yarns used for projects in this book with an accompanying swatch image in color and then in black and white. All of the swatches are extended sc stitches except for the gradient yarns, which have yarn cake photos (because the color transition is too long for a swatch). In addition, select yarns have a photo of the project back side (which is flat with no texture) if the yarn has been discontinued or was not otherwise accessible. Finally, a photo is also included of a finished, highly textured item made with that yarn. I have also included the pattern name and the page numbers for each yarn and item, so that you can easily locate the pattern and further photos of each item or crochet project made with that yarn in Chapters 8–12. Overall, this yarn information and the accompanying photographs should give you an idea of the range of brightness variation (among other properties) that is reasonable and minimally conflicting with crochet texture.

I have listed the yarns by manufacturer type. The manufacturers and dyers of yarn are divided into three different groups: large US brands (available in big-box stores), large online US and international brands, and small independent yarn dyers (boutique and designer brands). These manufacturers' yarn increases successively in price from large US brands on the low end to small independent yarn dyers on the high end. For each brand type listed, I have outlined the benefits of using that type of yarn and the general cost range per skein.

LARGE US BRANDS (AVAILABLE ONLINE AND IN LARGE CRAFT STORES)

The most common yarns in the United States are the yarns offered at craft stores such as JOANN, Michaels, and Hobby Lobby. These large yarn brands are frequently reasonably priced (especially if you use coupons) with a range between $3 and $8 a skein. These yarns are typically dyed in large batches (not hand dyed); however, they can have beautiful colorways that are multicolored. I have selected a few of these yarns for the beginner patterns.

Lion Brand Yarn

Lion Brand Yarn has a wide variety of yarn lines from acrylic to higher-end natural fibers. Their Baby Soft, Vanna's Choice, Wool-Ease, Mandala, and Fisherman's Wool are especially popular. In this book I have used their Baby Soft, Ice Cream, and Mandala Baby yarns, which are all delightfully soft yarns with several isoluminant (or nearly so) colorways.

Baby Soft, Pastel Print: This colorway has some brightness variation; however, the colors are cool and not attention grabbing, so it still works for textured projects.

Figure 6.1. Swatch of Baby Soft in Pastel Print

Figure 6.2. Grayscale swatch of Baby Soft in Pastel Print

Figure 6.3. Egyptian Blue Scarf crocheted with Baby Soft in Pastel Print

Ice Cream Smoothie, Lime: This yarn has subtle color variations, which work well with crochet texture.

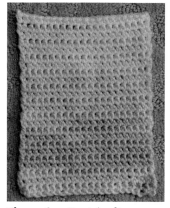 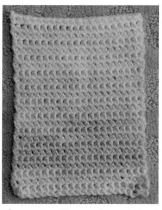

Figure 6.4. Swatch of Ice Cream Smoothie in Lime

Figure 6.5. Grayscale swatch of Ice Cream Smoothie in Lime

Figure 6.6. Kelly Green Shawl crocheted with Ice Cream Smoothie in Lime

Mandala Baby, Diagon Alley: This yarn is nearly isoluminant with nice pastel colors, perfect for a texture project!

 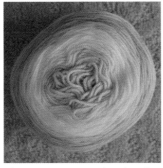

Figure 6.7. Cake of Mandala Baby in Diagon Alley

Figure 6.8. Grayscale cake of Mandala Baby in Diagon Alley

Figure 6.9. Heliotrope Purple Baby Blanket crocheted with Mandala Baby in Diagon Alley

Red Heart by Yarnspirations

In recent years Red Heart has expanded its color offerings, even in the least expensive yarn lines. Many of these colorways are very beautiful gradients of highly saturated hues, and a few of those colorways are also isoluminant. The Super Saver yarn is an acrylic yarn line that is very affordable, and the colors are gorgeous; however, the feel of the yarn is not super soft, so I would not recommend it for a garment with substantial skin contact (like a sweater). It is more suited for scarves, blankets, pillows, and other household items.

Super Saver Stripes, Retro Stripe: While the colors of this yarn are nearly isoluminant, this yarn has neon colors that can be very attention grabbing and therefore can compete with your pattern. Use this type of yarn carefully.

Figure 6.10. Swatch of Super Saver Stripes in Retro Stripe

Figure 6.11. Grayscale swatch of Super Saver Stripes in Retro Stripe

Figure 6.12. Shocking Pink Pillow crocheted with Super Saver Stripes in Retro Stripe

Unforgettable, Meadow: The Unforgettable yarn line is a bit fuzzy, which can make your cable stitches and texture less apparent. The colorway of Meadow varies substantially from skein to skein (even in the same dye lot); be careful in selecting the skeins you use. You should also feel free to remove short stretches of yarn that are not a similar brightness to the rest of the skein. I did not discard any portions of the skein for the swatch or project; however, if I had removed excessively bright or dark stretches, the project's visual appearance could have been a bit more harmonious in the poncho project.

Lily by Yarnspirations

Lily is famous for its Sugar'n Cream cotton yarn line. This cotton yarn is perfect for washcloths, towels, rugs, potholders, and other utilitarian purposes. It is not very soft, but it is durable and comes in a wide variety of single color and multicolored cakes.

Sugar'n Cream, Buttercream: This yarn has subtle color variations that work well with crochet texture.

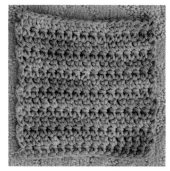

Figure 6.16. Swatch of Sugar'n Cream in Buttercream

Figure 6.17. Grayscale swatch of Sugar'n Cream in Buttercream

Figure 6.13. Swatch of Unforgettable in Meadow

Figure 6.14. Grayscale swatch of Unforgettable in Meadow

Figure 6.18. Imperial Yellow Washcloth crocheted with Sugar'n Cream in Buttercream

Figure 6.15. Sepia Poncho crocheted with Unforgettable in Meadow

LARGE ONLINE US AND INTERNATIONAL BRANDS (AVAILABLE AT ONLINE RETAILERS)

These retailers carry hundreds of types of yarn, with a range from basic acrylic that is as reasonable as the store brands listed above up to the high-end fiber yarn (e.g., merino or cashmere yarn) and hand-painted yarns. This type of retailer is a great option if you would like a wider range of colors or if you need to order many skeins for a large project. If you are interested in trying out that hand-painted yarn at a lower price point than small independent dyers offer, these large online retailers frequently have hand-painted yarn that is more reasonably priced (around $15 a skein).

WeCrochet

WeCrochet is the sister brand of Knit Picks and carries the same yarn lines. Both brands have beautiful yarn, often in very soft fibers (my favorite is the merino yarn). Two of my favorite yarns for making sweaters are Bare Stroll and Bare Swish Fingering.

Stroll Hand Painted, Celery Seed: This yarn has a perfect balance of different colors (green, blue, and white) of similar brightness and a hint of neon green to give it just the right amount of liveliness.

Figure 6.21. Absinthe Scarf crocheted with Stroll Hand Painted in Celery Seed

Stroll, Blue Tweed Tonal: This yarn has both tonal variation and tweed nubs. Tonal is a good option for some color variation but not too much. Tweed yarn, if used, should have only sparse tweed nubs, and the nubs should for the most part have a brightness similar to that of the yarn.

Figure 6.19. Swatch of Stroll Hand Painted in Celery Seed

Figure 6.20. Grayscale swatch of Stroll Hand Painted in Celery Seed

Figure 6.22. Back side of a swatch of Stroll in Blue Tweed Tonal (yarn discontinued)

Figure 6.23. Grayscale swatch of Stroll in Blue Tweed Tonal

Figure 6.24. Cerulean Shawl crocheted with Stroll in Blue Tweed Tonal

Stroll, Seashell Tonal: This tonal pink color is on the edge of brightness variation acceptable with dense cables. However, with the right lighting for your photographs and the right eye-popping cables, it can work great!

Figure 6.25. Swatch of Stroll in Seashell Tonal

Figure 6.26. Grayscale swatch of Stroll in Seashell Tonal

Figure 6.27. Amaranth Cardigan crocheted with Stroll in Seashell Tonal

Muse Aran, Fearless Hand Painted: This yarn has a great color combination (pink, coral, and gold); however, it is not dyed deeply into the yarn (it is a superficial and occasionally weak dye), so there are specks of white that do conflict with the texture.

This is likely because it is both hand painted and a heavier yarn.

Figure 6.28. Swatch of Muse Aran in Fearless Hand Painted

Figure 6.29. Grayscale swatch of Muse Aran in Fearless Hand Painted

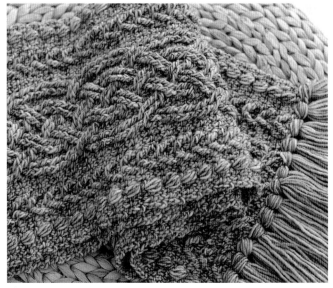

Figure 6.30. Vermilion Shawl crocheted with Muse Aran in Fearless Hand Painted

Scheepjes

Scheepjes is a yarn brand from the Netherlands. It came to my attention when gradient yarns became popular, and its Whirl yarns were both beautiful and frequently used in projects on Ravelry. The yarn is carried at several online retailers such as Webs (https://www.yarn.com/), LoveCrafts (https://www.lovecrafts.com), and Jimmy Beans Wool (https://www.jimmybeanswool

.com). The typical Whirl yarn cake uses cotton yarn as its base, which will showcase a cable a bit less clearly than animal fiber; however, cotton yarn is great for summer blankets and clothes.

Whirl, Lemon Cassis Cream 765: This gradient yarn has a perfect color combination in the center (nearly isoluminant), but a dark ending color. I solved this issue by making the dark color the lace border for the blanket rather than including it in the textured section of the pattern. Always feel free to remove a problematic color from a gradient (particularly at the ends) if that will make your pattern more visible. It is also OK for sections of your item to be less visible if a part of the skein is too dark.

Figure 6.31. Cake of Whirl in Lemon Cassis Cream 765

Figure 6.32. Grayscale cake of Whirl in Lemon Cassis Cream 765

Figure 6.33. Tyrian Purple Blanket crocheted with Whirl in Lemon Cassis Cream 765

SMALL INDEPENDENT YARN DYERS

These yarns are available on Etsy, in small yarn shops, and at yarn, knitting, or crocheting conferences. They are hand dyed in small batches, which can make particularly unique and beautiful yarn, but hand dyeing also tends to make them more expensive due to higher labor costs. Expect to pay $20–$30 per skein for these precious hanks.

Hedgehog Fibres

This moderately sized hand-dyeing yarn company is based in Ireland but ships to small yarn stores around the world. They specialize in multicolored yarns and have many gorgeous colorways.

Merino DK, Pilgrim: This is a beautiful, nearly isoluminant colorway that does not compete with your cables. However, the colorway can be a bit dark.

Figure 6.34. Swatch of Merino DK in Pilgrim

Figure 6.35. Grayscale swatch of Merino DK in Pilgrim

Figure 6.36. Cobalt Pillow crocheted with Merino DK in Pilgrim

Sock Yarn, Down by the River: This colorway has some brightness variation that distracts from the pattern; however, it is within the range of yarns that will work with textured patterns.

Tough Love Sock, Quiet Time: This is a beautiful, nearly isoluminant colorway that does not compete with your cables. However, it is a bit dark, which could slightly obscure the texture in your projects.

Figure 6.37. Back side of swatch of Sock Yarn in Down by the River

Figure 6.38. Grayscale swatch of Sock Yarn in Down by the River

Figure 6.40. Swatch of Tough Love Sock in Quiet Time

Figure 6.41. Grayscale swatch of Tough Love Sock in Quiet Time

Figure 6.39. Terre Verte Scarf crocheted in Sock Yarn in Down by the River

Figure 6.42. Indigo Hat crocheted with Tough Love Sock in Quiet Time

Sweet Georgia

This intermediate-sized hand-dyeing yarn company is based in Oregon. They have many beautiful isoluminant colorways and also have packs of mini skeins in color gradients that are gorgeous.

Figure 6.43. Ultramarine Tote crocheted with Tough Love Sock in Quiet Time

Freia Fine Handpaints

Freia specializes in color gradient yarns and has many of the most beautiful and continuous gradients I have found anywhere.

Ombre Merino Lace, Flare 19-1: This yarn is very dark at the end of the cake (outer edge for the cake photo below), but given that the color change is very gradual, it can be used carefully.

Figure 6.44. Cake of Ombre Merino Lace in Flare 19-1. *Image courtesy of Freia Fibers*

Figure 6.45. Grayscale cake of Ombre Merino Lace in Flare 19-1. *Image courtesy of Freia Fibers*

Figure 6.46. Archil Scarf crocheted with Ombre Merino Lace in Flare 19-1

Spincycle Yarns

This yarn dyer has the beautiful and unique effect of using plies of different colors in their yarn so that you can see the twist of the yarn itself. This style is less common in hand-painted yarn and has the appearance of being handspun. It can also make beautiful effects in your finished items, if the yarn is still relatively isoluminant.

Dyed in the Wool, Salty Dog: This colorway has a good brightness uniformity with only a couple of bright and dark spots.

Figure 6.47. Skein of Dyed in the Wool in Salty Dog. *Image courtesy of Spincycle Yarns*

Figure 6.48. Grayscale skein of Dyed in the Wool in Salty Dog. *Image courtesy of Spincycle Yarns*

Figure 6.49. Orpiment Shawl crocheted with Dyed in the Wool in Salty Dog

Figure 6.50. Verdigris Scarf crocheted with Dyed in the Wool in Salty Dog

Fiberstory

Fiberstory is a small yarn-dyeing brand based in Michigan, and it has some beautiful colorways. But note that they often sell out of colorways, so your favorite may not always be available.

CORE Worsted, Bouquet: This colorway is a bit dark but mostly uniform in brightness.

Figure 6.51. Swatch of CORE Worsted in Bouquet

Figure 6.52. Grayscale swatch of CORE Worsted in Bouquet

Figure 6.53. Violet Fingerless Gloves crocheted with CORE Worsted in Bouquet

PART 2

Twenty Crochet Patterns with Multicolored and Gradient Yarns

7 *Introduction to the Patterns*

This chapter provides the stitch definitions for the patterns in Chapters 8 through 12, as well as other helpful hints and conventions for making the items in this book.

PATTERN NAMES

To continue the focus on color perception in this book, I have named each of the patterns after historical hues and/or color pigments. If you are interested in the history of colors and how they have shaped botany, fashion, architecture, and art, I recommend reading *The Secret Lives of Color* by Kassia St. Clair.

I am personally fascinated by the evolution of pigments that St. Clair details. In my view, a society's obsessed use or willful rejection of vibrant colors is a valuable reflection on a culture's sensibility and identity. In addition, as St. Clair highlights, the manufacture of inexpensive pigments (used on fabric, plastic, and paper products) is a modern phenomenon and primarily due to our ability to produce saturated color pigments resulting from advancements in chemistry. So the next time you are watching historical dramas with clothing in vibrant colors (I am looking at you, *Bridgerton*), think about how the seemingly simple choice of a bright, colorful wardrobe

for a character of interest can signal an unexpected cultural modernity to the audience.

Note: For experts on colors, I am aware that my pattern's sample items or garments do not always exactly match the color that they are named for. However, I did choose the color-based pattern names so that one or more of the colors in the pattern's sample item is in the same color family.

SKILL LEVELS FOR EACH PATTERN

The patterns are labeled by the estimated skill level required to make them. I have included descriptions of the skills required for each level here.

- Beginner: The crocheter should be able to make single and double crochet stitches and add increases and decreases to these stitches. They should be able to make post stitches and begin to do cable stitches.
- Intermediate: The crocheter should have the skills of a beginner and also be able to work with longer, more complex cable motifs.
- Advanced: The crocheter should have the skills of an intermediate and also be able to shape garments by altering cable motifs to fit. In addition, in

the experienced patterns of Chapter 12, the crocheter should be able to do colorwork with post stitches and cables.

STITCH DESCRIPTIONS

Single, Double, and Puff Crochet Stitches

Extended Single Crochet (esc) (moves right to left): Insert hook in next stitch, yarn over and pull through, yarn over, pull through 1 loop, yarn over, and pull through 2 loops. Note: This is an extended version of the traditional sc.

Single Crochet Decrease (Dec): Insert hook in next stitch, yarn over and pull through, insert hook in the next stitch, yarn over and pull through, yarn over, pull through 2 loops, yarn over, and pull through 2 loops. Note: This is an extended version of the traditional Dec stitch.

Single Crochet Increase (Inc): Make 2 esc stitches (details above) in the next stitch. Note: This is an extended version of the traditional Inc stitch.

Reverse sc (moves left to right): Insert hook into the stitch to the right of the chain, yarn over and pull through, yarn over, pull through 1 loop, yarn over, and pull through 2 loops.

Double Crochet (dc): Yarn over, insert hook in next stitch, yarn over and pull through (yarn over and pull through 2 loops) twice.

Dc 2 Together (dc2tog): Yarn over, insert hook in next stitch, yarn over and pull through, yarn over, and pull through 2 loops. Yarn over, insert hook in next stitch, yarn over and pull through, yarn over, and pull through 2 loops. Yarn over and pull through 3 loops on hook.

Puff Stitch: [Yarn over, insert your hook into the gap between stitches, yarn over, and pull up a loop] four times. Yarn over and pull through all 11 loops on your hook. Yarn over and pull through to secure the stitch.

Front and Back Post Stitches

Double Crochet Front Post Stitch (FPS): Yarn over, insert hook around next stitch (insert from front to back, and then back to front), yarn over and pull through (yarn over and pull through 2 loops) twice.

Double Crochet Back Post Stitch (BPS): Yarn over, insert hook around next stitch (insert from back to front, and then front to back), yarn over and pull through (yarn over and pull through 2 loops) twice.

Decrease Front Post Double Crochet (DecDFPS): Yarn over, insert hook around the next stitch (like a front post stitch), yarn over and pull through, yarn over, and pull through 2 loops. Yarn over, insert hook around the next stitch (like a front post stitch) and pull through, yarn over, and pull through 2 loops. Yarn over and pull through 3 loops on hook.

Bridging Decrease Front Post Double Crochet (BDecDFPS): Yarn over, insert hook around the next stitch (like a front post stitch), yarn over and pull through, yarn over, and pull through 2 loops. Skip an esc stitch, then yarn over, insert hook around the next stitch (like a front post stitch) and pull through, yarn over, and pull through 2 loops. Yarn over and pull through 3 loops on hook.

Decrease Back Post Double Crochet (DecDBPS): Yarn over, insert hook around the next stitch (like a back post stitch), yarn over and pull through, yarn over, and pull through 2 loops. Yarn over, insert hook around the next stitch (like a back post stitch) and pull through, yarn over, and pull through 2 loops. Yarn over and pull through 3 loops on hook.

Triple Crochet Front Post Stitch (TFPS): Yarn over twice, insert hook around next stitch (insert from front to back, and then back to front), yarn over and pull through, yarn over, pull through 1 loop, (yarn over and pull through 2 loops) 3 times. Note: This is an extended version of the traditional post stitch. A regular post stitch will also work, but your work will be a little tighter.

Traditional Cable Stitches

2-Cross Front Cable Stitch (2CF): Skip a stitch, TFPS in the next stitch, TFPS in the skipped stitch. Note: The TFPS in the skipped stitch should be worked in front of the first TFPS. (Two crossed stitches)

2-Cross Back Cable Stitch (2CB): Skip a stitch, TFPS in the next stitch, TFPS in the skipped stitch. Note: The TFPS in the skipped stitch should be worked behind the first TFPS. (Two crossed stitches)

4-Cross Front Cable Stitch (4CF): Skip 2 stitches, TFPS in the next 2 stitches, TFPS in the skipped stitches. Note: The TFPS in the skipped stitches should be worked in front of the first 2 TFPS. (Four crossed stitches)

4-Cross Back Cable Stitch (4CB): Skip 2 stitches, TFPS in the next 2 stitches, TFPS in the skipped stitches. Note: The TFPS in the skipped stitches should be worked behind the first 2 TFPS. (Four crossed stitches)

6-Cross Front Cable Stitch (6CF): Skip 3 stitches, TFPS in the next 3 stitches, TFPS in the skipped stitches. Note: The TFPS in the skipped stitches should be worked in front of the first 3 TFPS. (Six crossed stitches)

6-Cross Back Cable Stitch (6CB): Skip 3 stitches, TFPS in the next 3 stitches, TFPS in the skipped stitches. Note: The TFPS in the skipped stitches should be worked behind the first 3 TFPS. (Six crossed stitches)

8-Cross Front Cable Stitch (8CF): Skip 4 stitches, TFPS in the next 4 stitches, TFPS in the skipped stitches. Note: The TFPS in the skipped stitches should be worked in front of the first 4 TFPS. (Eight crossed stitches)

8-Cross Back Cable Stitch (8CB): Skip four 4, TFPS in the next 4 stitches, TFPS in the skipped stitches. Note: The TFPS in the skipped stitches should be worked behind the first 4 TFPS. (Eight crossed stitches)

Twist Stitches

Twist Back Stitch (TBS): Skip a stitch, TFPS in the next stitch, single crochet in the skipped stitch. Note: The single crochet in the skipped stitch should be worked behind the TFPS. (Two crossed stitches)

Twist Front Stitch (TFS): Skip a stitch, single crochet in the next stitch, TFPS crochet in the skipped stitch. Note: The TFPS crochet in the skipped stitch should be worked in front of the single crochet. (Two crossed stitches)

Cable Stitches that Bridge over Single Crochet Stitches

Occasionally cable stitches need to be made that bridge over single crochet stitches, effectively skipping the single crochets. These cable stitches are described below.

Bridging 2-Cross Front Cable Stitch (B2CF): Skip a stitch, TFPS in the next stitch, TFPS in the skipped stitch. Note: The TFPS in the skipped stitch should be worked in front of the first TFPS. The single crochet stitches between the post stitches are skipped—they do not have stitches made into them. (Two crossed stitches)

Bridging 2-Cross Back Cable Stitch (B2CB): Skip a stitch, TFPS in the next stitch, TFPS in the skipped stitch. Note: The TFPS in the skipped stitch should be worked behind the first TFPS. The single crochet stitches between the post stitches are skipped—they do not have stitches made into them. (Two crossed stitches)

Bridging 4-Cross Front Cable Stitch (B4CF): Skip 2 post stitches and 2 single crochet stitches, TFPS in the next 2 post stitches, TFPS in the skipped 2 post stitches. Note: The TFPS in the skipped stitches should be worked in front of the first 2 TFPS. The single crochet stitches between the post stitches are skipped—they do not have stitches made into them. (Four crossed stitches)

Bridging 4-Cross Back Cable Stitch (B4CB): Skip 2 post stitches and 2 single crochet stitches, TFPS in the next 2 post stitches, TFPS in the skipped 2 post stitches. Note: The TFPS in the skipped stitches should be worked behind the first 2 TFPS. The single crochet stitches between the post stitches are skipped—they do not have stitches made into them. (Four crossed stitches)

Bridging 6-Cross Front Cable Stitch (B6CF): Skip 3 post stitches and 2 single crochet stitches, TFPS in the next 3 post stitches, TFPS in the skipped 3 post stitches. Note: The TFPS in the skipped stitches should be worked in front of the first 3 TFPS. The single crochet stitches between the post stitches are skipped—they do not have stitches made into them. (Six crossed stitches)

Bridging 6-Cross Back Cable Stitch (B6CB): Skip 3 post stitches and 2 single crochet stitches, TFPS in the next 3 post stitches, TFPS in the skipped 3 post stitches. Note: The TFPS in the skipped stitches should be worked behind the first 3 TFPS. The single crochet stitches between the post stitches are skipped—they do not have stitches made into them. (Six crossed stitches)

Shell and Clover Stitches

Shell Stitch: (3 dc, chain 3, 3 dc) in the same stitch from the previous row.

Large Shell Stitch: (4 dc, chain 3, 4 dc) in the same stitch from the previous row.

Clover Stitch: (Dc2tog, chain 3, dc2tog, chain 3, dc2tog) in the same stitch from the previous row.

ADDITIONAL TERMINOLOGY AND OTHER CONVENTIONS

Extended Stitches

Many of the stitches used in these patterns are extended in length. The single crochet stitch used is extended so that it is the optimal height to match the cable stitch and post-stitch heights. In addition, the post stitches within the cables are extended so that the cable stitches are looser and therefore show more texture. Make sure that you read the stitch descriptions and understand how the extended stitches are used in the patterns before beginning your crochet project.

Adding Single Crochet Stitches Between Cable Stitches

Single crochet stitches are often added between cable stitches to spread out the cable stitches laterally. When you are asked to do this in the pattern, it will state, "Add 2 esc stitches between the next 2 stitches" (see tutorial in Figure 7.1). The single crochet stitch is always added between two post stitches (either alone or within cables) to add additional single crochets and move two cables or cable threads apart. Since post stitches are worked on top of (or around) stitches in the previous row, work in the space between the post stitches to add any stitches between them. To add the single crochet stitch, you just find the space between the two post stitches (or post stitches within a cable), and you make one or two sc stitches (depending on the instructions) into that gap or space between the stitches.

Twist (TBS and TFS) Stitches

The TBS and TFS are two-stitch pseudo-cables, or twist stitches (as discussed in Chapter 2). These stitches are often confusing for beginners, so I recommend viewing the video tutorial at Rebecca's Stylings Crochet on YouTube. In general, for the TBS stitch you skip a stitch and then make a front post stitch. Then you work behind that post stitch and make an esc in the stitch you skipped. The sc is not a post stitch, so you would make it into the skipped stitch like you would normally do. The TFS is the same but worked in the opposite order; you skip a stitch, make a normal sc stitch, and then make the post stitch in front of the sc stitch (back into the stitch you skipped). So both twist stitches are

Adding Extended Stitches Between the Next Two Stitches
A Guided Tutorial

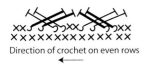

Direction of crochet on even rows ←

Step 1: View the example cable motif we will be using for this tutorial. It has two cable stitches and extended sc stitches in between the cables.

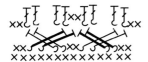

Step 2: We will now perform the back-side row of the cable motif (row 3) with back post stitches and extended sc stitches.

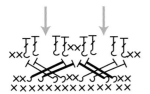

Step 3: We will now discuss the next row (row 4) of this cable motif. To make row 4, you will be adding the extended sc stitches between the post stitches. To do that, you will make two extended sc stitches where each of the blue arrows are pointed.

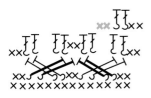

Step 4: Let's start the 4th row: You first make the 2 extended sc stitches, and then make two front post stitches. Next you would be adding two sc stitches between the next two stitches. The added esc stitches (in blue) are made between the post stitches of row 3.

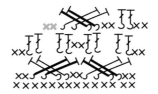

Step 5: Let's continue with the 4th row. Next you make a Bridging 4CF stitch (B4CF) using the next two post stitches, skipping the next two esc stitches, and using the next two post stitches (see video tutorial on B4CF stitch). Again we now add two esc stitches between the next two stitches. These 2 esc stitches (in blue) are between the post stitches of the previous row.

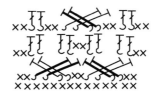

Step 6: We can now finish row 4 by making two front post stitches and two esc stitches.

This example cable motif and guided instruction highlights where to place the esc stitches (in blue) when they are added between post stitches. Hopefully the step-by-step diagrams and instructions clarified how to add esc stitches to spread out cable motifs and post stitch designs.

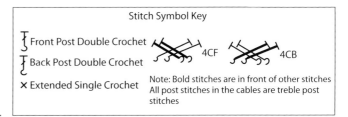

Stitch Symbol Key

Front Post Double Crochet

Back Post Double Crochet

✕ Extended Single Crochet

4CF

4CB

Note: Bold stitches are in front of other stitches
All post stitches in the cables are treble post stitches

Figure 7.1: Adding Extended Stitches Between the Next Two Stitches—A Guided Tutorial

two-cross cable stitches but with one of the stitches an sc stitch. An additional note: When you are in the next front-facing row after the first TBS TFS, you should work the post stitches of those new TBS and TFS into the central two sc stitches between the TBS and TFS of the previous row. You basically want to make a new "V" with every other row so that the V's are layered one on top of each other. Look at the image of the pattern and watch the YouTube video for additional guidance.

Counting Chains at the Beginning of Pattern Rows

The beginning chain of each row is not counted as a stitch. In the first row, the number of stitches and the chain are listed in the written pattern at the end of the row. In each subsequent row of the pattern, the chain is added on the left or right side in addition to the stitches in the stitch diagram. In the written pattern, the chain is listed in addition to stitches for the main pattern.

Left-Handed Crocheters

I am left-handed (although I learned to crochet right-handed), and I know that it can be challenging to find patterns and support for left-handed crocheting. The patterns in this book are left-right symmetric and therefore can be made as is by left-handed crocheters without a substantial difference in the appearance of the finished product. The only difference in the crocheted items if you make the patterns left-handed is that the cable stitches will be in the opposite direction (i.e., left-leaning instead of right-leaning or vice versa). However, this difference is not noticeable and will not substantially change the appearance of the finished item. The reason for this result is that the important aspect of the crochet cables is the relationship of the cable direction in one row relative to the following rows. As long as the pattern of cable directions (such as alternating cable directions from row to row) is maintained, the overall appearance will be nearly identical between right-handed and left-handed crocheted items.

VIDEO TUTORIALS

The Rebecca's Stylings YouTube Channel has video tutorials for cable stitches as well as for twist stitches. I highly recommend that you view the video tutorials if you are new to making cable stitches.

STITCH DIAGRAMS

Stitch diagrams are provided for most of the patterns. These diagrams can be used in concert with the written pattern also provided. A key is provided for each stitch diagram, and the symbols used are consistent throughout the book.

GAUGE

Gauge is the number of stitches per inch. Gauge can change with the yarn, the hook, and the tension (how tightly you pull the yarn) you use for each crochet project. For this reason, I highly recommend that you check your gauge before starting any garment, such as hats, sweaters, and gloves, to make sure that you are on track in terms of fit. To check the gauge, simply make a crochet swatch with extended single crochet stitches and then measure the number of stitches per one or two inches and check whether it matches the gauge in the pattern. If your gauge does not match, consider using a different hook or yarn to better align with the project gauge.

8 Crochet Patterns with Multicolored Yarns: Beginner Patterns

The first chapter of patterns has beginner-level Aran-style stitches with multicolored yarns. The items included range from baby blankets to scarves, pillows, and dishcloths. All of the items are made in a rectangular shape with only basic fabric joining for select projects. Most of the yarns in this chapter are also easily accessible in the United States at major craft retail stores. The yarn used is in most cases acrylic, which is reasonably priced for a beginner. Hopefully this chapter will convince you that beautiful, multicolored cabled projects can be affordable and accessible to all.

As with all of the patterns in this book, my comments on the multicolored yarn used in each pattern can be found in Chapter 6. These comments focus on the yarn's brightness variation and suitability for textured projects. In addition, Chapter 6 includes images of the swatch (or skein) of the yarn used, in both color and black and white. For stitch descriptions, additional pattern instructions, and notes, refer to Chapter 7.

Egyptian Blue Scarf (Unisex, Beginner)

Materials

2 skeins of Lion Brand Yarn Baby Soft in Pastel Print (367 yd./335.6 m and 4 oz./113.4 g net weight per skein; 60% acrylic and 40% nylon; light weight #3)

Hook

US size 7 (4.5 mm) crochet hook

Scarf Dimensions

4.5 in. (11.4 cm) wide by 57 in. (144.8 cm) long (excluding tassels)

Gauge

9 esc stitches x 8.5 esc rows = 2 in. x 2 in. (5.1 cm x 5.1 cm)

Crochet Stitch Video Tutorials

4-Cross Front Cable Stitch (4CF): "Four Cross Front Crochet Cable Stitch Tutorial," https://www.youtube.com/watch?v=rzuMC6mB68w &t=1s

4-Cross Back Cable Stitch (4CB): "Four Cross Back Crochet Cable Stitch Tutorial," https://www.youtube.com/watch?v=EGBMJaXAcEQ &t=35s

Stitch Diagram

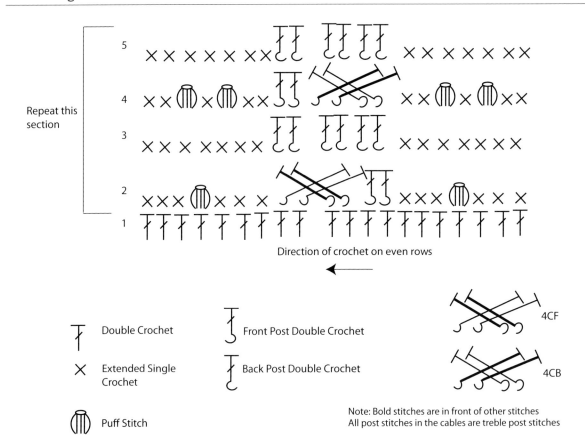

Repeat this section

Direction of crochet on even rows

Double Crochet

Extended Single Crochet

Puff Stitch

Front Post Double Crochet

Back Post Double Crochet

4CF

4CB

Note: Bold stitches are in front of other stitches
All post stitches in the cables are treble post stitches

INSTRUCTIONS

Row 1: Chain 23 (including starting loop), dc in fourth chain from hook, and dc across. (20 dc, 1 chain)

Row 2: Chain 2, turn, 3 esc, puff stitch, 3 esc, 2 FPS, 4CF, 3 esc, puff stitch, 3 esc.

Row 3: Chain 2, turn, 3 esc, make an esc into the puff stitch in the previous row (Row 2), 3 esc, 6 BPS, 3 esc, make an esc into the puff stitch in the previous row (Row 2), 3 esc.

Row 4: Chain 2, turn, 2 esc, puff stitch, esc, puff stitch, 2 esc, 4CB, 2 FPS, 2 esc, puff stitch, esc, puff stitch, 2 esc.

Row 5: Chain 2, turn, 2 esc, make an esc into the puff stitch in the previous row (Row 4), esc, make an esc into the puff stitch in the previous row (Row 4), 2 esc, 6 BPS, 2 esc, make an esc into the puff stitch in the previous row (Row 4), esc, make an esc into the puff stitch in the previous row (Row 4), 2 esc.

Rows 6–197: Repeat Rows 2–5 forty-eight times.

Rows 198 and 199: Repeat Rows 2 and 3 once.

Tie off yarn.

Weave in any loose yarn ends.

Tassel Instructions

1. Cut yarn segments (10 segments per tassel) about 9 in. (22.9 cm) in length.

2. Align the 10 segments (1 tassel) and fold them in half.

3. Take the loop at the half mark of the tassel and insert it into the scarf edge (from the front of the scarf to the back).

4. Take the ends of the yarn segments and pull them through the loop (pull tight).

5. Make and place 7 total tassels on each end of the scarf, equally spaced.

6. Trim tassel ends to make them even.

Shocking Pink Pillow (Beginner)

Materials

- 3 skeins of Red Heart Super Saver Stripes in Retro Stripe (236 yd./215.8 m and 5 oz./141.8 g net weight per skein; 100% acrylic; medium weight #4)
- 15 in. x 15 in. (38.1 cm x 38.1 cm) pillow insert

Hook

US H-8 (5.0 mm) crochet hook

Pillow Dimensions

15 in. x 15 in. (38.1 cm x 38.1 cm)

Gauge

7.5 esc stitches x 6.5 esc rows = 2 in. x 2 in. (5.1 cm x 5.1 cm)

Crochet Stitch Video Tutorials

 *6-Cross Front Cable Stitch* (6CF): "Six Cross Front Crochet Cable Stitch Tutorial," https://www.youtube.com/watch?v=znjRYYXoRXY

 *6-Cross Back Cable Stitch* (6CB): "Six Cross Back Crochet Cable Stitch Tutorial," https://www.youtube.com/watch?v=Ldx84gbKVKA&t=1s

Stitch Diagram

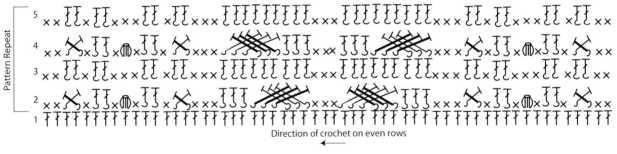

Direction of crochet on even rows

Puff Stitch | Double Crochet | Front Post Double Crochet
Extended Single Crochet | Back Post Double Crochet
6CF | 6CB | 2CF

Note: Bold stitches are in front of other stitches
All post stitches in the cables are treble post stitches

INSTRUCTIONS

Make two of the following rectangles.

Row 1: Chain 60 (including starting loop), dc in fourth chain from hook, and dc across. (57 dc, 1 chain)

Row 2: Chain 2, turn, 2 esc, [2CF, esc, FPS, FPS, esc, puff stitch, esc, FPS, FPS, esc, 2CF], 3 esc, 3 FPS, 6CF, 3 esc, 6CB, 3 FPS, 3 esc, repeat instructions in [ ] once, 2 esc.

Row 3: Chain 2, turn, 2 esc, [BPS, BPS, esc, BPS, BPS, esc, make an esc into the puff stitch in the previous row, esc, BPS, BPS, esc, BPS, BPS], 3 esc, 9 BPS, 3 esc, 9 BPS, 3 esc, repeat instructions in [ ] once, 2 esc.

Row 4: Chain 2, turn, 2 esc, [2CF, esc, FPS, FPS, esc, puff stitch, esc, FPS, FPS, esc, 2CF], 3 esc, 6CB, 3 FPS, 3 esc, 3 FPS, 6CF, 3 esc, repeat instructions in [ ] once, 2 esc.

Row 5: Chain 2, turn, 2 esc, [BPS, BPS, esc, BPS, BPS, esc, make an esc into the puff stitch in the previous row, esc, BPS, BPS, esc, BPS, BPS], 3 esc, 9 BPS, 3 esc, 9 BPS, 3 esc, repeat instructions in [ ] once, 2 esc.

Rows 6–37: Repeat Rows 2–5 eight times.

Rows 38 and 39: Repeat Rows 2 and 3 once.

Tie off yarn.

Pillow Assembly

You should now have 2 pillow sides (2 rectangles) and a pillow form/insert. The instructions below will tell you how to assemble the 2 pillow sides around the pillow insert.

1. Check that your pillow rectangles are about 15 in. (38.1 cm) wide by 15 in. (38.1 cm) tall. If they are slightly smaller than they need to be, either block the squares or add a single crochet row to the top, bottom, or sides. Alternatively, you can buy a pillow insert of a different size that matches your as-fabricated pillow covers.

2. Place the 2 pillow sides facing outward (back sides facing each other). Attach your yarn. [Crochet join* across 1 edge. At the corner make 3 crochet join stitches.] Repeat instructions in [ ]

_____

* A crochet join is simply an esc stitch but worked through 2 fabrics rather than into 1 chain or fabric.

twice. You should have 3 out of 4 of the sides joined/sewed together.

3. Place the pillow form inside the pillow covering. Then continue your pillow edge joining. Crochet join across the last edge. At the final corner, make three crochet join stitches. Slip stitch with starting chain. Tie off yarn.

Tassel Instructions

Make 4 tassels from the yarn using the instructions below and tie each tassel to each corner of the pillow.

1. Cut yarn segments (12 segments per tassel) about 9 in. (22.9 cm) in length.

2. Align 11 segments (1 tassel), place 1 yarn segment across the 11 segments at their midway point, and tie it into a knot. Fold the 11 segments in half.

3. Cut a new yarn segment (same length), and wind it around the 11 segments about ½ in. (1.3 cm) from the folded end. Use your hook to pull the loose end of the new yarn segment through your yarn wound around the folded tassel and into the tassel end.

4. Trim tassel ends to make them even.

Kelly Green Shawl (Unisex, Beginner)

Materials

5 skeins of Lion Brand Ice Cream Smoothie in Lime (219 yd./200.3 m and 3 oz./85.1 g net weight per skein; 100% acrylic; light weight #3)

Hook

US size H-8 (5.0 mm) crochet hook

Shawl Dimensions

9.75 in. (24.8 cm) wide by 58 in. (147.3 cm) long (excluding tassels)

Gauge

8.5 esc stitches x 7.5 esc rows = 2 in. x 2 in. (5.1 cm x 5.1 cm)

Crochet Stitch Video Tutorials

4-Cross Front Cable Stitch (4CF): "Four Cross Front Crochet Cable Stitch Tutorial," https://www.youtube.com/watch?v=rzuMC6mB68w&t=1s

6-Cross Front Cable Stitch (6CF): "Six Cross Front Crochet Cable Stitch Tutorial," https://www.youtube.com/watch?v=znjRYYXoRXY

Stitch Diagram

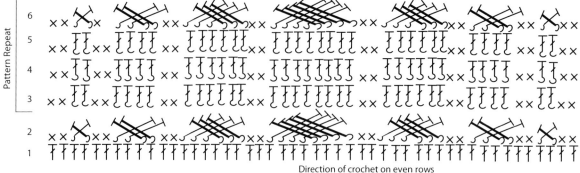

Direction of crochet on even rows

Double Crochet

Extended Single Crochet

Front Post Double Crochet

Back Post Double Crochet

8CF   6CF   4CF   2CF

Note: Bold stitches are in front of other stitches
All post stitches in the cables are treble post stitches

INSTRUCTIONS

Row 1: Chain 51 (including starting loop), dc in fourth chain from hook, and dc across. (48 dc, 1 chain)

Row 2: Chain 2, turn, 2 esc, 2CF, 2 esc, 4CF, 2 esc, 6CF, 2 esc, 8CF, 2 esc, 6CF, 2 esc, 4CF, 2 esc, 2CF, 2 esc.

Row 3: Chain 2, turn, 2 esc, 2 BPS, 2 esc, 4 BPS, 2 esc, 6 BPS, 2 esc, 8 BPS, 2 esc, 6 BPS, 2 esc, 4 BPS, 2 esc, 2 BPS, 2 esc.

Row 4: Chain 2, turn, 2 esc, 2 FPS, 2 esc, 4 FPS, 2 esc, 6 FPS, 2 esc, 8 FPS, 2 esc, 6 FPS, 2 esc, 4 FPS, 2 esc, 2 FPS, 2 esc.

Row 5: Chain 2, turn, 2 esc, 2 BPS, 2 esc, 4 BPS, 2 esc, 6 BPS, 2 esc, 8 BPS, 2 esc, 6 BPS, 2 esc, 4 BPS, 2 esc, 2 BPS, 2 esc.

Row 6: Chain 2, turn, 2 esc, 2CF, 2 esc, 4CF, 2 esc, 6CF, 2 esc, 8CF, 2 esc, 6CF, 2 esc, 4CF, 2 esc, 2CF, 2 esc.

Rows 7–174: Repeat Rows 3–6 forty-two times.

Row 175: Repeat Row 3.

Tie off yarn.

Weave in any loose yarn ends.

Tassel Instructions

1. Cut yarn segments (10 segments per tassel) about 9 in. (22.9 cm) in length.
2. Align the 10 segments (1 tassel) and fold them in half.
3. Take the loop at the half mark of the tassels and insert it in the shawl edge (from the front of the shawl to the back).
4. Take the ends of the yarn segments and pull them through the loop (pull tight).
5. Place 13 tassels on each end of the shawl, equally spaced.
6. Trim tassel ends to make them even.

Heliotrope Purple Baby Blanket (Beginner)

Materials

4 skeins of Lion Brand Mandala Baby in Diagon Alley (590 yd./539.5 cm) and 5.3 oz./150.3 g net weight per skein; 100% acrylic; light weight #3)

Hook

US size H-8 (5.0 mm) crochet hook

Blanket Dimensions

31.5 in. (80 cm) wide by 33 in. (83.8 cm) long

Gauge

8 esc stitches x 8 esc rows = 2 in. x 2 in. (5.1 cm x 5.1 cm)

Crochet Stitch Video Tutorials

4-Cross Front Cable Stitch (4CF): "Four Cross Front Crochet Cable Stitch Tutorial," https://www.youtube.com/watch?v=rzuMC6mB68w&t=1s

4-Cross Back Cable Stitch (4CB): "Four Cross Back Crochet Cable Stitch Tutorial," https://www.youtube.com/watch?v=EGBMJaXAcEQ&t=35s

6-Cross Front Cable Stitch (6CF): "Six Cross Front Crochet Cable Stitch Tutorial," https://www.youtube.com/watch?v=znjRYYXoRXY

6-Cross Back Cable Stitch (6CB): "Six Cross Back Crochet Cable Stitch Tutorial," https://www.youtube.com/watch?v=Ldx84gbKVKA&t=1s

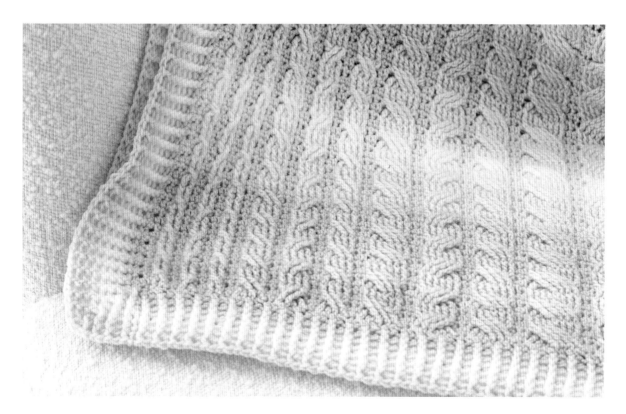

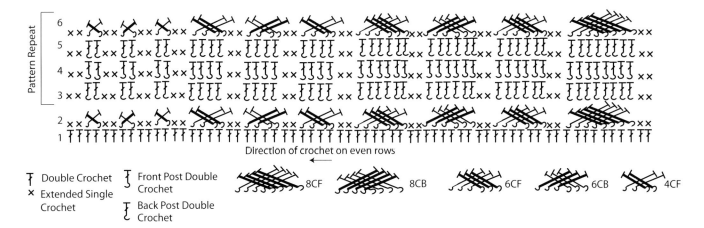

INSTRUCTIONS

Note: To make the color transitions continuous when you transition from one skein to the next skein, you may need to unravel the new skein to the color transition that your previous skein ended on. Then you can return to unraveled yarn when you reach the appropriate color transition (usually at the end of the new skein).

Blanket Body

Row 1: Chain 143 (including starting loop), dc in fourth chain from hook, and dc across. (140 dc, 1 chain)

Row 2: Chain 2, turn, 2 esc, 2CF, 2 esc, 2CB, 2 esc, 2CF, 2 esc, 4CF, 2 esc, 4CB, 2 esc, 4CF, 2 esc, 6CF, 2 esc, 6CB, 2 esc, 6CF, 2 esc, 8CF, 2 esc, 8CB, 2 esc, 8CF, 2 esc, 6CF, 2 esc, 6CB, 2 esc, 6CF, 2 esc, 4CF, 2 esc, 4CB, 2 esc, 4CF, 2 esc, 2CF, 2 esc, 2CB, 2 esc, 2CF, 2 esc.

Row 3: Chain 2, turn, [2 esc, 2 BPS] three times, [2 esc, 4 BPS] three times, [2 esc, 6 BPS] three times, 2 esc, 8 BPS, 2 esc, 8 BPS, 2 esc, 8 BPS, [2 esc, 6 BPS] three times, [2 esc, 4 BPS] three times, [2 esc, 2 BPS] three times, 2 esc.

Row 4: Chain 2, turn, [2 esc, 2 FPS] three times, [2 esc, 4 FPS] three times, [2 esc, 6 FPS] three times, 2 esc, 8 FPS, 2 esc, 8 FPS, 2 esc, 8 FPS, [2 esc, 6 FPS] three times, [2 esc, 4 FPS] three times, [2 esc, 2 FPS] three times, 2 esc.

Row 5: Chain 2, turn, [2 esc, 2 BPS] three times, [2 esc, 4 BPS] three times, [2 esc, 6 BPS] three times, 2 esc, 8 BPS, 2 esc, 8 BPS, 2 esc, 8 BPS, [2 esc, 6 BPS] three times, [2 esc, 4 BPS] three times, [2 esc, 2 BPS] three times, 2 esc.

Row 6: Chain 2, turn, 2 esc, 2CF, 2 esc, 2CB, 2 esc, 2CF, 2 esc, 4CF, 2 esc, 4CB, 2 esc, 4CF, 2 esc, 6CF, 2 esc, 6CB, 2 esc, 6CF, 2 esc, 8CF, 2 esc, 8CB, 2 esc, 8CF, 2 esc, 6CF, 2 esc, 6CB, 2 esc, 6CF, 2 esc, 4CF, 2 esc, 4CB, 2 esc, 4CF, 2 esc, 2CF, 2 esc, 2CB, 2 esc, 2CF, 2 esc.

Rows 7–106: Repeat Rows 3–6 twenty-five times.

Row 107: Repeat Row 3.

Tie off yarn.

Weave in any loose yarn ends.

Blanket Border

Note: Use the extra yarn from the blanket body for the blanket border. You can start the border on any color, but try to make color transitions within the border appear continuous for the best appearance.

Round 1: Attach yarn to the edge of the blanket (at the end of a row), chain 3 and then sc evenly around the blanket border, with three single crochets in each corner. Slip stitch with beginning chain.

Round 2: Chain 2, {[FPS, BPS]. Repeat instructions in [ ] until you reach a corner. In the single stitch

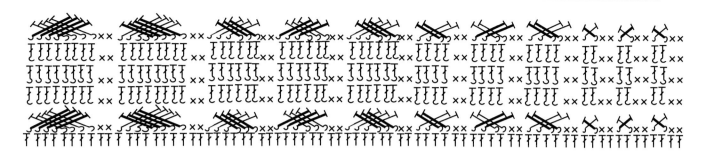

 4CB ✕ 2CF ✕ 2CB

Note: Bold stitches are in front of other stitches
All post stitches in the cables are treble post stitches

on the corner perform the following stitches if the previous stitch was a BPS: (FPS, BPS, FPS); and the following stitches if the previous stitch was an FPS: (BPS, FPS, BPS). Note: All of the stitches in ( ) are performed into one stitch; this expands the ribbing at the corner.} Repeat instructions within { } three times. Slip stitch with beginning chain.

Repeat Round 2 *without turning* until the ribbed edging is the width you prefer. I repeated it 6 times.

Imperial Yellow Washcloth (Beginner)

Materials for One Washcloth

1 skein of Lily Sugar'n Cream in Buttercream (143 yd./130.8 m and 3 oz./85.1 g net weight per skein; 100% cotton; medium weight #4)

Hook

US size I-9 (5.5 mm) crochet hook

Washcloth Dimensions

8.5 in. (21.6 cm) wide by 8.8 in. (22.2 cm) tall

Gauge

6 esc stitches x 5.5 esc rows = 2 in. x 2 in. (5.1 cm x 5.1 cm)

Stitch Diagram

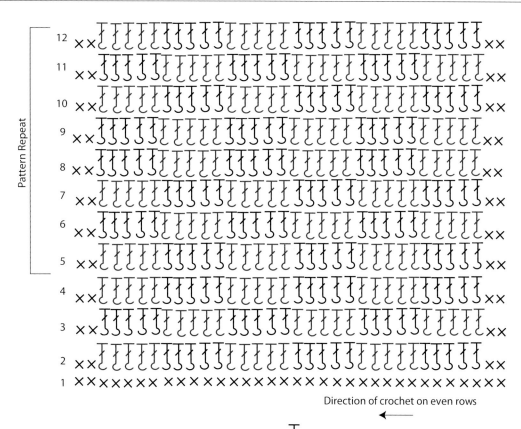

Direction of crochet on even rows

⟵

X Extended Single Crochet

⌡ Front Post Double Crochet

⌡ Back Post Double Crochet
(colored red only for visualization purposes)

INSTRUCTIONS FOR ONE WASHCLOTH

Row 1: Chain 36 (including starting loop), esc in third chain from hook, and esc across. (34 esc, 1 chain)

Rows 2–4: Chain 2, turn, 2 esc, [5 FPS, 5 BPS] three times, 2 esc.

Rows 5–8: Chain 2, turn, 2 esc, [5 BPS, 5 FPS] three times, 2 esc.

Rows 9–12: Chain 2, turn, 2 esc, [5 FPS, 5 BPS] three times, 2 esc.

Rows 13–20: Repeat Rows 5–12 once.

Rows 21–24: Repeat Rows 5–8 once.

Tie off yarn.

Weave in any loose yarn ends.

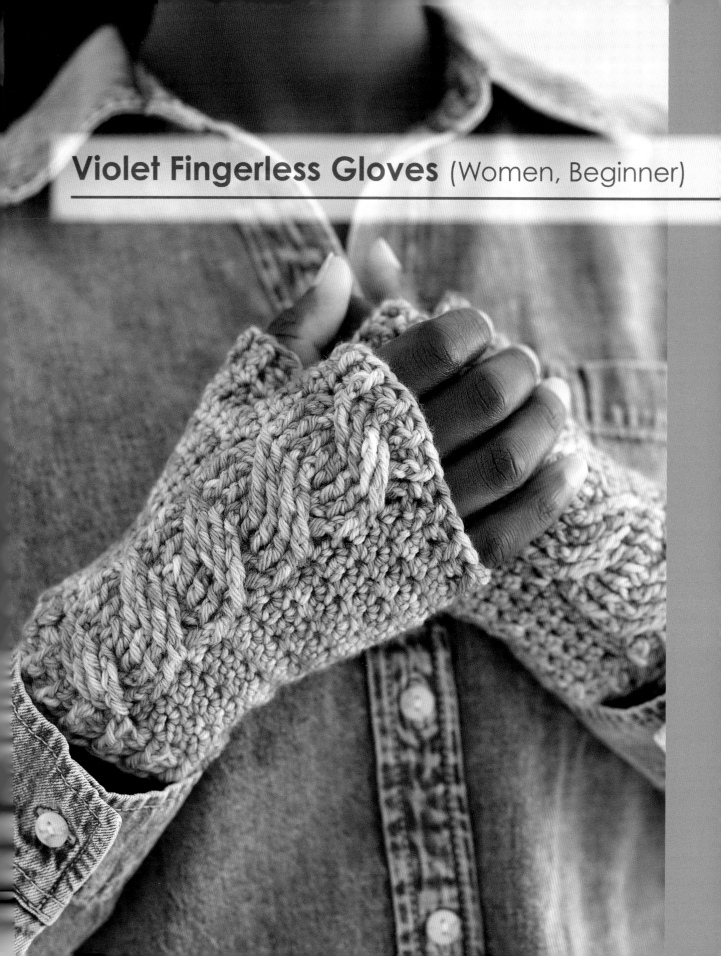

Violet Fingerless Gloves (Women, Beginner)

Materials

1 skein of Fiberstory CORE Worsted in Bouquet (218 yd./199.3 m and 3.5 oz./100 g net weight per skein; 100% superwash Merino wool; medium weight #4)

Hook

US size H-8 (5.0 mm) crochet hook

Women's Glove Dimensions

3.5 in. (8.9 cm) wide at wrist by 6.5 in. (16.5 cm) long

Gauge

8 stitches x 7.5 rows = 2 in. x 2 in. (5.1 cm x 5.1 cm)

INSTRUCTIONS

Left Hand Glove

Glove Body

Round 1: Chain 30 (including starting loop), slip stitch with starting chain. Chain 2, esc around, slip stitch with starting chain. (30 esc, 1 chain)

Round 2: Chain 2, turn, 11 esc, 8CF, 11 esc. Slip stitch with starting chain.

Round 3: Chain 2, turn, 11 esc, 8 BPS, 11 esc. Slip stitch with starting chain.

Round 4: Chain 2, turn, 11 esc, 8 FPS, 11 esc. Slip stitch with starting chain.

Round 5: Chain 2, turn, 11 esc, 8 BPS, 11 esc. Slip stitch with starting chain.

Rounds 6–9: Repeat Rounds 2–5 once.

Round 10: Chain 2, turn, Inc, 3 esc, Inc, 3 esc, Inc, 2 esc, 8CF, 11 esc. Slip stitch with starting chain.

Round 11: Chain 2, turn, 11 esc, 8 BPS, 14 esc. Slip stitch with starting chain.

Round 12: Chain 2, turn, [3 esc, inc] three times, 2 esc, 8 FPS, 11 esc. Slip stitch with starting chain.

Round 13: Chain 2, turn, 11 esc, 8 BPS, 17 esc. Slip stitch with starting chain.

Round 14: Chain 2, turn, [3 esc, inc] four times, 1 esc, 8CF, 11 esc. Slip stitch with starting chain.

Round 15: Chain 2, turn, 11 esc, 8 BPS, 21 esc. Slip stitch with starting chain.

Glove Fingers and Finger Edging

We will now divide our glove into the finger and thumb and then continue with the finger section of the glove. Do not cut the yarn; continue from the previous round.

Round 16: Chain 2, turn, 3 esc, Inc, 2 esc, skip 11 esc stitches, 4 esc, 8 FPS, 11 esc. Slip stitch with starting chain.

Round 17: Chain 2, turn, 11 esc, 8 BPS, 11 esc. Slip stitch with starting chain.

Round 18: Chain 2, turn, 11 esc, 8CF, 11 esc. Slip stitch with starting chain.

Round 19: Chain 2, turn, 11 esc, 8 BPS, 11 esc. Slip stitch with starting chain.

Round 20: Chain 2, turn, [FPS, BPS] 15 times. Slip stitch with starting chain.

Tie off yarn.

Glove Thumb Edging

Reattach your yarn to Round 15 (the row before you transitioned to the finger section of the glove) at the thumb opening. We will now add an edging to the opening for the thumb.

Round 1: Chain 2, turn, 4 esc, Inc, 6 esc. Slip stitch with starting chain.

Round 2: Chain 2, turn, [FPS, BPS] 6 times. Slip stitch with starting chain.

Tie off yarn.

Glove Wrist Edging

Reattach your yarn to Round 1 (the chain base). We will now add the edging at the base of the glove that goes around the wrist.

Round 1: Chain 2, turn, [FPS, BPS] 15 times. Slip stitch with starting chain.

Round 2: Chain 2, *do not turn*, [FPS, BPS] 15 times. Slip stitch with starting chain.

Tie off yarn.

Weave in any loose yarn ends.

Right Hand Glove

Glove Body

Rounds 1–9: Repeat the instructions for the Left Hand Glove Rounds 1–9.

Round 10: Chain 2, turn, 11 esc, 8CF, 2 esc, Inc, 3 esc, Inc, 3 esc, Inc. Slip stitch with starting chain.

Round 11: Chain 2, turn, 14 esc, 8 BPS, 11 esc. Slip stitch with starting chain.

Round 12: Chain 2, turn, 11 esc, 8 FPS, 2 esc, [Inc, 3 esc] three times. Slip stitch with starting chain.

Round 13: Chain 2, turn, 17 esc, 8 BPS, 11 esc. Slip stitch with starting chain.

Round 14: Chain 2, turn, 11 esc, 8CF, 1 esc, [Inc, 3 esc] four times. Slip stitch with starting chain.

Round 15: Chain 2, turn, 21 esc, 8 BPS, 11 esc. Slip stitch with starting chain.

Glove Fingers and Finger Edging

We will now divide our glove into the finger and thumb and then continue with the finger section of the glove. Do not cut the yarn; continue from the previous round.

Round 16: Chain 2, turn, 11 esc, 8 FPS, 4 esc, skip 11 esc stitches, 2 esc, Inc, 3 esc. Slip stitch with starting chain.

Round 17: Chain 2, turn, 11 esc, 8 BPS, 11 esc. Slip stitch with starting chain.

Round 18: Chain 2, turn, 11 esc, 8CF, 11 esc. Slip stitch with starting chain.

Round 19: Chain 2, turn, 11 esc, 8 BPS, 11 esc. Slip stitch with starting chain.

Round 20: Chain 2, turn, [FPS, BPS] 15 times. Slip stitch with starting chain.

Tie off yarn.

Glove Thumb Edging and Wrist Edging

Follow the instructions for the Left Hand Glove Thumb Edging and Wrist Edging.

Cobalt Pillow (Beginner)

Materials

- 3 skeins of Hedgehog Fibres Merino DK in Pilgrim (218.7 yd./200 m and 3.5 oz./100 g net weight per skein; 100% Merino wool; light weight #3)
- 15 in. x 15 in. (38.1 cm x 38.1 cm) pillow form

Hook

US size 7 (4.5 mm) crochet hook

Pillow Dimensions

15 in. x 15 in. (38.1 cm x 38.1 cm)

Gauge

8.5 esc stitches x 8 esc rows = 2 in. x 2 in. (5.1 cm x 5.1 cm)

Crochet Stitch Video Tutorials

4-Cross Front Cable Stitch (4CF): "Four Cross Front Crochet Cable Stitch Tutorial," https://www.youtube.com/watch?v=rzuMC6mB68w&t=1s

4-Cross Back Cable Stitch (4CB): "Four Cross Back Crochet Cable Stitch Tutorial," https://www.youtube.com/watch?v=EGBMJaXAcEQ&t=35s

Stitch Diagram

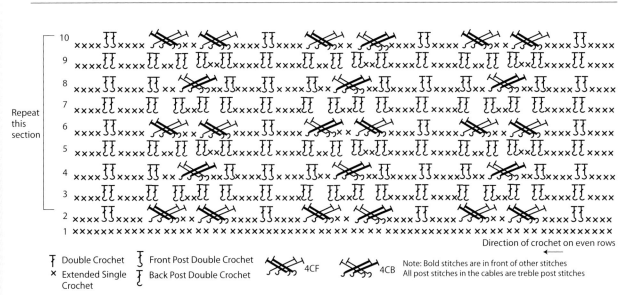

Repeat this section

Direction of crochet on even rows ←

⊤ Double Crochet	Front Post Double Crochet
✗ Extended Single Crochet	Back Post Double Crochet

4CF   4CB

Note: Bold stitches are in front of other stitches
All post stitches in the cables are treble post stitches

INSTRUCTIONS

Make two of the following rectangles.

Row 1: Chain 72 (including starting loop), esc in the third chain from hook, and esc across. (70 esc, 1 chain)

Row 2: Chain 2, turn, [4 esc, 2 FPS, 4 esc, 4CF, 2 esc, 4CF, 4 esc, 2 FPS, 4 esc], 4CB, 2 esc, 4CF, repeat instructions in [ ] once.

Row 3: Chain 2, turn, [4 esc, 2 BPS, 4 esc, 4 BPS, 2 esc, 4 BPS] three times, 4 esc, 2 BPS, 4 esc.

Row 4: Chain 2, turn, [4 esc, 2 FPS, 4 esc, 2 FPS, add 2 esc stitches between the next 2 stitches, B4CB, add 2 esc stitches between the next 2 stitches, 2 FPS] three times, 4 esc, 2 FPS, 4 esc.

Row 5: Chain 2, turn, [4 esc, 2 BPS, 4 esc, 2 BPS, 2 esc, 4 BPS, 2 esc, 2 BPS] three times, 4 esc, 2 BPS, 4 esc.

Row 6: Chain 2, turn, [4 esc, 2 FPS, 4 esc, B4CF, add 2 esc stitches between the next 2 stitches, B4CF, 4 esc, 2 FPS, 4 esc], B4CF, add 2 esc stitches between the next 2 stitches, B4CB, repeat instructions in [ ] once.

Row 7: Repeat Row 3.

Row 8: Repeat Row 4.

Row 9: Repeat Row 5.

Row 10: Chain 2, turn, [4 esc, 2 FPS, 4 esc, B4CF, add 2 esc stitches between the next 2 stitches, B4CF, 4 esc, 2 FPS, 4 esc], B4CB, add 2 esc stitches between the next 2 stitches, B4CF, repeat instructions in [ ] once.

Rows 11–50: Repeat Rows 3–10 five times.

Rows 51–55: Repeat Rows 3–7 once.

Tie off yarn.

Pillow Assembly

You should now have 2 pillow sides (2 rectangles) and a pillow form/insert. The instructions below will tell you how to assemble the 2 pillow sides around the pillow insert.

1. Check that your pillow rectangles are about 15 in. (38.1 cm) wide by 15 in. (38.1 cm) tall. If they are slightly too small, either block the squares or add a single crochet row to the top, bottom, or sides. Alternatively, you can buy a pillow insert of a different size that matches your pillow cover.

2. Place the 2 pillow sides facing outward (back sides facing each other). Attach your yarn. [Crochet join* across 1 edge. At the corner make 3 crochet join stitches.] Repeat instructions in [ ] twice. You should have 3 out of 4 of the sides joined/sewed together.

3. Place the pillow form inside the pillow covering. Then continue your pillow edge joining. Crochet join across the last edge. At the final corner make 3 crochet join stitches. Slip stitch with starting chain. Tie off yarn.

Weave in any loose yarn ends.

---

* A crochet join is simply an esc stitch but worked through 2 fabrics rather than into 1 chain or fabric.

Crochet Patterns with Multicolored Yarns: Accessories

9

*T*his chapter continues with multicolored yarns but with more advanced cable techniques decorating a variety of accessories. The chapter includes scarves and hats for women and men as well as a champagne gift tote. The two hat patterns in this chapter introduce the shaping of the crocheted fabric with cable motifs. However, if you are newer to crochet, the two scarf patterns have no shaping and are a great introduction to more intricate cable designs. Overall, the cable designs in this chapter are more complex than those in Chapter 8, dramatically shifting and morphing as they progress into different intricate motifs.

As with all of the patterns in this book, my comments on the multicolored yarn used in each pattern can be located in Chapter 6. These comments focus on the yarn's brightness variation and suitability for textured projects. In addition, Chapter 6 includes images of the swatch (or skein) of the yarn used in both color and black and white. For stitch descriptions, additional pattern instructions, and notes, refer to Chapter 7.

Indigo Hat (Women, Intermediate)

Materials

1 skein of SweetGeorgia Yarns Tough Love Sock in Quiet Time (425 yd./ 388.6 m and 4 oz./113.4 g net weight per skein; 80% superwash Merino wool and 20% nylon; super fine yarn weight #1)

Hook

US size G-6 (4.0 mm) crochet hook

Women's Hat Dimensions

9.25 in. (23.5 cm) wide by 8.5 in. (21.6 cm) long

Gauge

10.5 esc stitches x 10 esc rows = 2 in. x 2 in. (5.1 cm x 5.1 cm)

Crochet Stitch Video Tutorials

4-Cross Front Cable Stitch (4CF): "Four Cross Front Crochet Cable Stitch Tutorial," https://www.youtube.com/watch?v=rzuMC6mB68w&t=1s

4-Cross Back Cable Stitch (4CB): "Four Cross Back Crochet Cable Stitch Tutorial," https://www.youtube.com/watch?v=EGBMJaXAcEQ&t=35s

Stitch Diagram

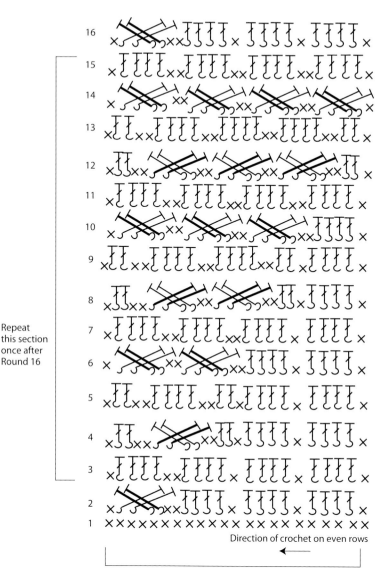

16
15
14
13
12
11
10
9
8
7
6
5
4
3
2
1

Repeat this section once after Round 16

Direction of crochet on even rows

Crochet this section a total of five times

⌐Ƭ Front Post Double Crochet

Ƭ Back Post Double Crochet

✕ Extended Single Crochet

4CF

4CB

Note: Bold stitches are in front of other stitches
All post stitches in the cables are treble post stitches

INSTRUCTIONS

Round 1: Chain 106 (including starting loop), slip stitch with starting chain. Chain 2, esc around, slip stitch with starting chain. (106 esc, 1 chain)

Round 2: Chain 2, turn, esc, ([4 FPS, esc] three times, esc, 4CF, esc) five times. Slip stitch with starting chain.

Round 3: Chain 2, turn, (esc, 4 BPS, 2 esc, [4 BPS, esc] twice, 4 BPS) five times, esc. Slip stitch with starting chain.

Round 4: Chain 2, turn, esc, ([4 FPS, esc] twice, 2 FPS, add 2 esc stitches between the next 2 stitches, B4CB, add 2 esc stitches between the next 2 stitches, 2 FPS, esc) five times. Slip stitch with starting chain.

Round 5: Chain 2, turn, (esc, 2 BPS, 2 esc, 4 BPS, 2 esc, 2 BPS, esc, 4 BPS, esc, 4 BPS) five times, esc. Slip stitch with starting chain.

Round 6: Chain 2, turn, esc, (4 FPS, esc, 4 FPS, make 2 esc in the next stitch, B4CF, add 2 esc stitches between the next 2 stitches, B4CF, esc) five times. Slip stitch with starting chain.

Round 7: Chain 2, turn, (esc, 4 BPS, 2 esc, 4 BPS, 2 esc, 4 BPS, esc, 4 BPS) five times, esc. Slip stitch with starting chain.

Round 8: Chain 2, turn, esc, (4 FPS, esc, 2 FPS, add 2 esc stitches between the next 2 stitches, [B4CB, add 2 esc stitches between the next 2 stitches] twice, 2 FPS, esc) five times. Slip stitch with starting chain.

Round 9: Chain 2, turn, (esc, 2 BPS, 2 esc, 4 BPS, 2 esc, 4 BPS, 2 esc, 2 BPS, esc, 4 BPS) five times, esc. Slip stitch with starting chain.

Round 10: Chain 2, turn, esc, (4 FPS, make 2 esc in the next stitch, [B4CF, add 2 esc stitches between the next two stitches] twice, B4CF, esc) five times. Slip stitch with starting chain.

Round 11: Chain 2, turn, (esc, 4 BPS, [2 esc, 4 BPS] three times) five times, esc. Slip stitch with starting chain.

Round 12: Chain 2, turn, esc, (2 FPS, add 2 esc stitches between the next 2 stitches, [B4CB, add 2 esc stitches between the next 2 stitches] three times, 2 FPS, esc) five times. Slip stitch with starting chain.

Round 13: Chain 2, turn, (esc, 2 BPS, [2 esc, 4 BPS] three times, 2 esc, 2 BPS) five times, esc. Slip stitch with starting chain.

Round 14: Chain 2, turn, esc, ([B4CF, add 2 esc stitches between the next 2 stitches] three times, B4CF, esc) five times. Slip stitch with starting chain.

Round 15: Chain 2, turn, (esc, [4 BPS, 2 esc] three times, 4 BPS) five times, esc. Slip stitch with starting chain.

Round 16: Chain 2, turn, esc, (4 FPS, esc, skip a stitch, 4 FPS, esc, skip a stitch, 4 FPS, 2 esc, 4CF, esc) five times. Slip stitch with starting chain.

Rounds 17–29: Repeat Rounds 3–15.

Round 30: Chain 2, turn, (esc, [FPS, DecDFPS, FPS, Dec] three times, FPS, DecDFPS, FPS) five times, esc. Slip stitch with starting chain.

Round 31: Chain 2, turn, (esc, [DecDBPS, BPS, esc] three times, DecDBPS, BPS) five times, esc. Slip stitch with starting chain.

Round 32: Chain 2, turn, (esc, [DecDFPS, esc] three times, DecDFPS) five times, esc. Slip stitch with starting chain.

Round 33: Chain 2, turn, esc in each stitch. Slip stitch with starting chain. (41 esc stitches)

Round 34: Chain 2, turn, [2 esc, Dec] 10 times, esc. Slip stitch with starting chain.

Round 35: Chain 2, turn, esc in each stitch. Slip stitch with starting chain. (31 esc stitches)

Round 36: Chain 2, turn, [esc, Dec] 10 times, esc. Slip stitch with starting chain.

Round 37: Chain 2, turn, esc in each stitch. Slip stitch with starting chain. (21 esc stitches)

Round 38: Chain 2, turn, [Dec] 10 times, esc. Slip stitch with starting chain.

Round 39: Chain 2, turn, [Dec] 5 times, esc. Slip stitch with starting chain.

Make a slip stitch across the hole at the top of the hat to close it.

Tie off yarn.

Finishing

Reattach your yarn to the bottom of the hat. Chain 2, reverse single crochet in each stitch around the hat. Slip stitch with starting chain.

Tie off yarn.

Weave in any loose yarn ends.

Make a pom-pom from the remaining yarn and attach it to the top of the hat.

Terre Verte Scarf (Unisex, Intermediate)

Materials

2 skeins of Hedgehog Fibres Sock Yarn in Down by the River (437.5 yd./400 m and 3.5 oz./100 g net weight per skein; 90% Merino wool and 10% nylon; super fine weight #1)

Hook

US size E-4 (3.5 mm) crochet hook

Dimensions

4 in. (10.2 cm) wide by 59 in. (149.9 cm) long (excluding tassels)

Crochet Stitch Video Tutorials

 *6-Cross Front Cable Stitch* (6CF): "Six Cross Front Crochet Cable Stitch Tutorial," https://www.youtube.com/watch?v=znjRYYXoRXY

 *6-Cross Back Cable Stitch* (6CB): "Six Cross Back Crochet Cable Stitch Tutorial," https://www.youtube.com/watch?v=Ldx84gbKVKA&t=1s

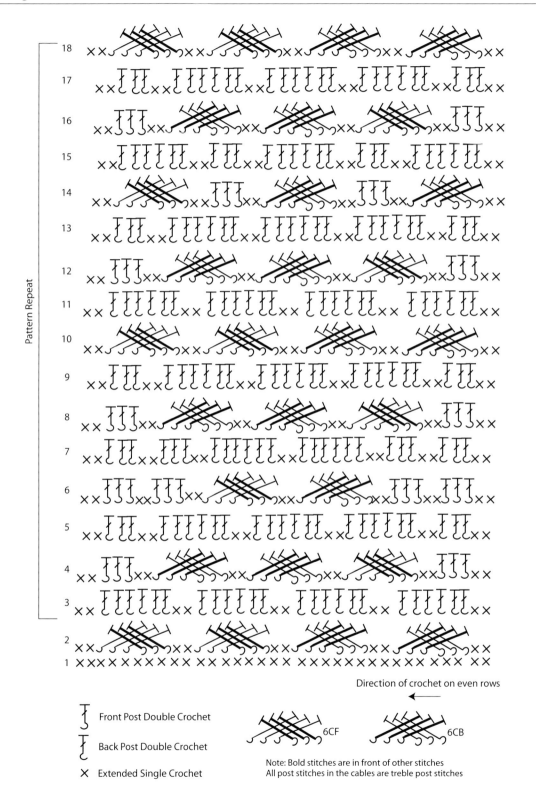

Direction of crochet on even rows

⌐ Front Post Double Crochet

⌐ Back Post Double Crochet

X Extended Single Crochet

6CF

6CB

Note: Bold stitches are in front of other stitches
All post stitches in the cables are treble post stitches

INSTRUCTIONS

Row 1: Chain 36 (including starting loop), esc in the third chain from hook, and esc across. (34 esc, 1 chain)

Row 2: Chain 2, turn, [2 esc, 6CB] twice, [2 esc, 6CF] twice, 2 esc.

Row 3: Chain 2, turn, [2 esc, 6 BPS] four times, 2 esc.

Row 4: Chain 2, turn, 2 esc, 3 FPS, add 2 esc between the next 2 stitches, B6CF, [add 2 esc between the next 2 stitches, B6CB] twice, add 2 esc between the next 2 stitches, 3 FPS, 2 esc.

Row 5: Chain 2, turn, 2 esc, 3 BPS, [2 esc, 6 BPS] three times, 2 esc, 3 BPS, 2 esc.

Row 6: Chain 2, turn, [2 esc, 3 FPS] twice, add 2 esc between the next 2 stitches, B6CB, add 2 esc between the next 2 stitches, B6CF, add 2 esc between the next 2 stitches, (3 FPS, 2 esc) twice.

Row 7: Chain 2, turn, [2 esc, 3 BPS] three times, 3 BPS, 2 esc, 6 BPS, repeat instructions in [ ] twice, 2 esc.

Row 8: Chain 2, turn, 2 esc, 3 FPS, 2 esc, B6CF, add 2 esc between the next 2 stitches, B6CB, add 2 esc between the next 2 stitches, B6CB, 2 esc, 3 FPS, 2 esc.

Row 9: Chain 2, turn, 2 esc, 3 BPS, [2 esc, 6 BPS] three times, 2 esc, 3 BPS, 2 esc.

Row 10: Chain 2, turn, 2 esc, [B6CB, add 2 esc between the next 2 stitches] twice, B6CF, add 2 esc between the next 2 stitches, B6CF, 2 esc.

Row 11: Chain 2, turn, [2 esc, 6 BPS] four times, 2 esc.

Row 12: Chain 2, turn, 2 esc, 3 FPS, add 2 esc between the next 2 stitches, B6CF, [add 2 esc between the next 2 stitches, B6CB] twice, add 2 esc between the next 2 stitches, 3 FPS, 2 esc.

Row 13: Chain 2, turn, 2 esc, 3 BPS, [2 esc, 6 BPS] three times, 2 esc, 3 BPS, 2 esc.

Row 14: Chain 2, turn, 2 esc, B6CB, add 2 esc between the next 2 stitches, 3 FPS, 2 esc, 6CB, 2 esc, 3 FPS, add 2 esc between the next 2 stitches, B6CF, 2 esc.

Row 15: Chain 2, turn, [2 esc, 6 BPS, 2 esc, 3 BPS] twice, 2 esc, 6 BPS, 2 esc.

Row 16: Chain 2, turn, 2 esc, 3 FPS, add 2 esc between the next 2 stitches, B6CF, 2 esc, 6CB, 2 esc, B6CB, add 2 esc between the next 2 stitches, 3 FPS, 2 esc.

Row 17: Chain 2, turn, 2 esc, 3 BPS, [2 esc, 6 BPS] three times, 2 esc, 3 BPS, 2 esc.

Row 18: Chain 2, turn, 2 esc, [B6CB, add 2 esc between the next 2 stitches] twice, B6CF, add 2 esc between the next 2 stitches, B6CF, 2 esc.

Rows 19–242: Repeat Rows 3–18 fourteen times.

Rows 243–251: Repeat Rows 3–11 once.

Tie off yarn.

Weave in any loose yarn ends.

Tassel Instructions

1. Cut yarn segments (12 segments per tassel) about 9 in. (22.9 cm) in length.

2. Align the 12 segments (1 tassel) and fold them in half.

3. Take the loop at the half mark of the tassel and insert it into the scarf edge (from the front of the scarf to the back).

4. Take the ends of the yarn segments and pull them through the loop (pull tight).

5. Make and place 9 tassels on each end of the scarf, equally spaced.

6. Trim tassel ends to make them even.

Ultramarine Champagne Tote (Intermediate)

Materials

- 1 skein of SweetGeorgia Yarns Tough Love Sock in Quiet Time (425 yd./388.6 m and 4 oz./ 113.4 g net weight per skein; 80% superwash Merino wool and 20% nylon; super fine weight #1)
- Fabric and Pellon Extra-Firm Stabilizer for lining (optional)
- Ribbon for decoration (optional)

Hook

US size G-6 (4.0 mm) crochet hook

Dimensions

12 in. (30.5 cm) tall by 5 in. (12.7 cm) diameter (of cylinder base)

Gauge

10.5 esc stitches x 10 esc rows = 2 in. x 2 in. (5.1 cm x 5.1 cm)

Crochet Stitch Video Tutorials

4-Cross Front Cable Stitch (4CF): "Four Cross Front Crochet Cable Stitch Tutorial," https://www.youtube.com/watch?v=rzuMC6mB68w&t=1s

4-Cross Back Cable Stitch (4CB): "Four Cross Back Crochet Cable Stitch Tutorial," https://www.youtube.com/watch?v=EGBMJaXAcEQ&t=35s

Stitch Diagram

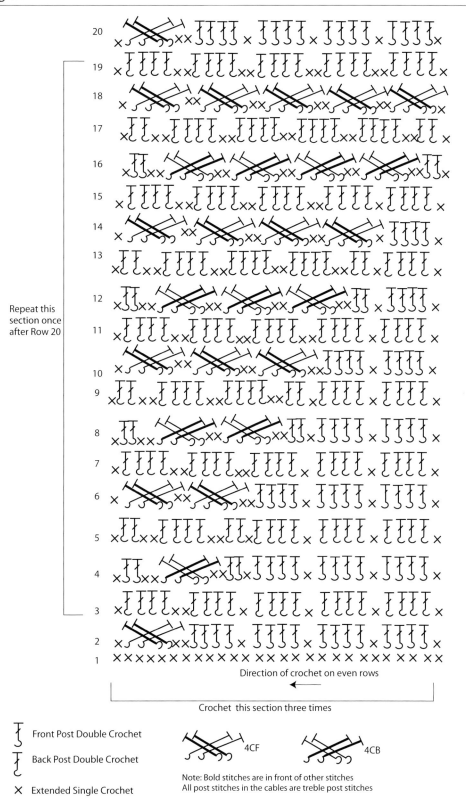

Repeat this section once after Row 20

Direction of crochet on even rows

Crochet this section three times

Front Post Double Crochet

Back Post Double Crochet

X Extended Single Crochet

4CF

4CB

Note: Bold stitches are in front of other stitches
All post stitches in the cables are treble post stitches

INSTRUCTIONS

Body of Tote

The body of the tote is a crocheted rectangle, which will be joined on one side to form a cylinder (make one).

Row 1: Chain 81 (including starting loop), esc in the third chain from hook, and esc across. (79 esc, 1 chain)

Row 2: Chain 2, turn, esc, ([4 FPS, esc] 4 times. esc, 4CF, esc) three times.

Row 3: Chain 2, turn, (esc, 4 BPS, 2 esc, [4 BPS, esc] three times, 4 BPS) three times, esc.

Row 4: Chain 2, turn, esc, ([4 FPS, esc] three times, 2 FPS, add 2 esc stitches between the next 2 stitches, B4CB, add 2 esc stitches between the next 2 stitches, 2 FPS, esc) three times.

Row 5: Chain 2, turn, (esc, 2 BPS, 2 esc, 4 BPS, 2 esc, 2 BPS, esc, [4 BPS, esc] twice, 4 BPS) three times, esc.

Row 6: Chain 2, turn, esc, ([4 FPS, esc] twice, 4 FPS, make 2 esc in the next stitch, B4CF, add 2 esc stitches between the next 2 stitches, B4CF, esc) three times.

Row 7: Chain 2, turn, (esc, [4 BPS, 2 esc] twice, [4BPS, esc] twice, 4 BPS) three times, esc.

Row 8: Chain 2, turn, esc, ([4 FPS, esc] twice, 2 FPS, add 2 esc stitches between the next 2 stitches, [B4CB, add 2 esc stitches between the next 2 stitches] twice, 2 FPS, esc) three times.

Row 9: Chain 2, turn, (esc, 2 BPS, 2 esc, [4 BPS, 2 esc] twice, 2 BPS, esc, 4 BPS, esc, 4 BPS) three times, esc.

Row 10: Chain 2, turn, esc, (4 FPS, esc, 4 FPS, make 2 esc in the next stitch, [B4CF, add 2 esc stitches between the next 2 stitches] twice, B4CF, esc) three times.

Row 11: Chain 2, turn, (esc, 4 BPS, [2 esc, 4 BPS] three times, esc, 4 BPS) three times, esc.

Row 12: Chain 2, turn, esc, (4 FPS, esc, 2 FPS, add 2 esc stitches between the next 2 stitches, [B4CB, add 2 esc stitches between the next 2 stitches] three times, 2 FPS, esc) three times.

Row 13: Chain 2, turn, (esc, 2 BPS, [2 esc, 4 BPS] three times, 2 esc, 2 BPS, esc, 4 BPS) three times, esc.

Row 14: Chain 2, turn, esc, (4 FPS, esc, [B4CF, add 2 esc stitches between the next 2 stitches] three times, B4CF, esc) three times.

Row 15: Chain 2, turn, (esc, [4 BPS, 2 esc] three times, 4 BPS, esc, 4 BPS) three times, esc.

Row 16: Chain 2, turn, esc, (2 FPS, [add 2 esc stitches between the next 2 stitches, B4CB] four times, add 2 esc stitches between the next 2 stitches, 2 FPS, esc) three times.

Row 17: Chain 2, turn, (esc, 2 BPS, [2 esc, 4 BPS] four times, 2 esc, 2 BPS) three times, esc.

Row 18: Chain 2, turn, esc, ([B4CF, add 2 esc stitches between the next 2 stitches] four times, B4CF, esc) three times.

Row 19: Chain 2, turn, (esc, [4 BPS, 2 esc] four times, 4 BPS) three times, esc.

Row 20: Chain 2, turn, esc, (4 FPS, [esc, skip a stitch, 4 FPS] three times, 2 esc, 4CF, esc) three times.

Rows 21–37: Repeat Rows 3–19 once.

Row 38: Chain 2, turn, esc, (4 FPS, [esc, skip a stitch, 4 FPS] four times, esc) three times.

Row 39: Chain 2, turn, [esc, 4 BPS] fifteen times, esc.

Row 40: Chain 2, turn, [esc, 4 FPS] fifteen times, esc.

Rows 41–56: Repeat Rows 39–40 eight times.

Tie off yarn.

Weave in any loose yarn ends.

Fabric and Pellon Lining (Optional)

Cut a rectangle of fabric that is 1 in. (2.5 cm) longer and 1 in. (2.5 cm) wider than the crocheted rectangle made above. Cut a length of Pellon fabric reinforcer that is approximately the size of the rectangle made above. Pin the fabric over the Pellon fabric with about a ½ in. (1.3 cm) folded over on each side. Pin the Pellon with the fabric covering it to the back side of the crocheted rectangle above. Using a needle and thread, sew the Pellon and fabric onto the back side of the crocheted rectangle.

Bottom of Tote

The bottom is a crocheted disk (make one).

Round 1: Chain 4 (including starting loop). Working in the starting loop, make 9 dc stitches. Slip stitch with starting chain.

Round 2: Chain 2, turn, dc twice in each stitch. Slip stitch with starting chain.

Round 3: Chain 2, turn, [dc, dc twice in the next stitch] nine times. Slip stitch with starting chain.

Round 4: Chain 2, turn, [2 dc, dc twice in the next stitch] nine times. Slip stitch with starting chain.

Round 5: Chain 2, turn, [3 dc, dc twice in the next stitch] nine times. Slip stitch with starting chain.

Round 6: Chain 2, turn, [4 dc, dc twice in the next stitch] nine times. Slip stitch with starting chain.

Round 7: Chain 2, turn, [5 dc, dc twice in the next stitch] nine times. Slip stitch with starting chain.

Tie off yarn.

Weave in any loose yarn ends.

Assembly of Tote

Sew (join) the 2 sides of the rectangle together (to form a cylinder) from Row 1 up to Row 37 (the 2 green arrows in the diagram). The remainder of the rectangle can remain open to showcase the top of the bottle in the bag.

Next, you will crochet join the bottom edge of the rectangle to the crocheted disk finished in the previous step (the two orange arrows in the diagram). Before you start the join, make sure that your disk is the same size as the bottom of the crocheted rectangle (now a cylinder). If the sizes do not match, either take out a row from the crocheted disk to make it smaller or add a row to make the disk larger. Next,

perform the crochet join by inserting your hook into both fabrics with the front sides facing you (the disk edge and the rectangle bottom) and chaining 2, and then make an esc stitch by inserting your hook into the next stitch in both fabrics. Continue this joining esc stitch until you join the whole disk to the bottom of the rectangle, and then slip stitch with the starting chain. Tie off yarn.

Finally, add a ribbon (if desired) by weaving it through the stitches at the top of the bag and tying a bow on the front (see photo for reference). The ribbon can be used to cinch the top of the tote to the wine bottle, and it adds a beautiful bow to the gift.

Tote Assembly Instructions

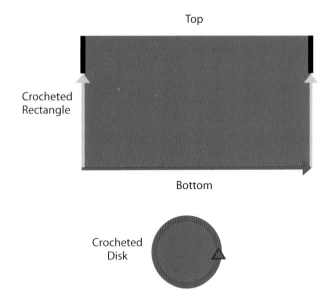

Diagram Key

➤ Sew together the green arrow sections on the crocheted rectangle (Note: Do not sew the top, black edge sections)

➤ Crochet join the orange arrow section on the bottom of crocheted rectangle to the edge of the crocheted disk (orange arrow)

See instructions for more details

Top

Crocheted Rectangle

Bottom

Crocheted Disk

Absinthe Scarf (Unisex, Intermediate)

Materials

2 skeins of WeCrochet/Knit Picks Stroll Hand Painted in Celery Seed (462 yd./422.5 m and 3.5 oz./100 g net weight per skein; 75% fine superwash Merino wool and 25% nylon; super fine weight #1)

Hook

US size F-5 (3.75 mm) crochet hook

Dimensions

4.5 in. (11.4 cm) wide by 56 in. (142.2 cm) long (excluding tassels)

Gauge

11 esc stitches x 11 esc rows = 2 in. x 2 in. (5.1 cm x 5.1 cm)

Crochet Stitch Video Tutorials

4-Cross Front Cable Stitch (4CF): "Four Cross Front Crochet Cable Stitch Tutorial," https://www.youtube.com/watch?v=rzuMC6mB68w &t=1s

4-Cross Back Cable Stitch (4CB): "Four Cross Back Crochet Cable Stitch Tutorial," https://www.youtube.com/watch?v=EGBMJaXAcEQ &t=35s

Stitch Diagram

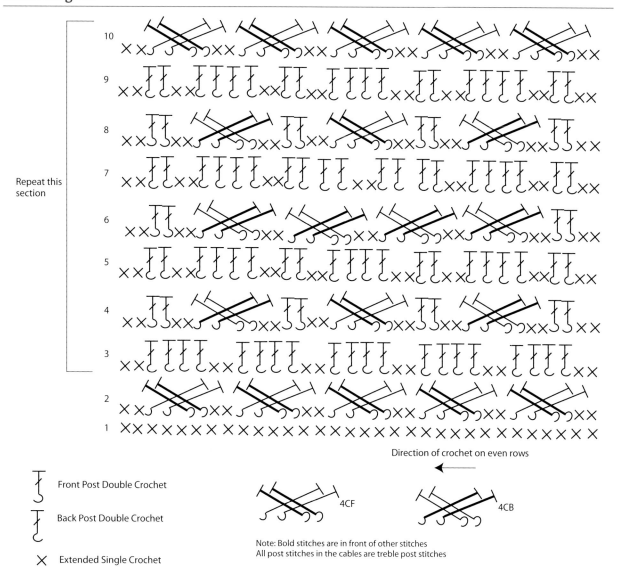

10
9
8
7
6
5
4
3
2
1

Repeat this section

Direction of crochet on even rows

4CF

4CB

Note: Bold stitches are in front of other stitches
All post stitches in the cables are treble post stitches

Front Post Double Crochet

Back Post Double Crochet

X   Extended Single Crochet

INSTRUCTIONS

Row 1: Chain 34 (including starting loop), esc in the third chain from hook, and esc across. (32 esc, 1 chain)

Row 2: Chain 2, turn, [2 esc, 4CF] five times, 2 esc.

Row 3: Chain 2, turn, [2 esc, 4 BPS] five times, 2 esc.

Row 4: Chain 2, turn, [2 esc, 2 FPS, add 2 esc stitches between the next 2 stitches, B4CB, add 2 esc stitches between the next 2 stitches, 2 FPS, 2 esc], 4CF, repeat instructions in [ ] once.

Row 5: Chain 2, turn, [2 esc, 2 BPS, 2 esc, 4 BPS, 2 esc, 2 BPS, 2 esc], 4 BPS, repeat instructions in [ ] once.

Row 6: Chain 2, turn, 2 esc, 2 FPS, 2 esc, 4CB, 2 esc, B4CB, add 2 esc stitches between the next 2 stitches, B4CB, 2 esc, 4CB, 2 esc, 2 FPS, 2 esc.

Row 7: Chain 2, turn, 2 esc, 2 BPS, [2 esc, 4 BPS] four times, 2 esc, 2 BPS, 2 esc.

Row 8: Chain 2, turn, 2 esc, 2 FPS, 2 esc, 4CB, 2 esc, 2 FPS, add 2 esc stitches between the next 2 stitches, B4CF, add 2 esc stitches between the next 2 stitches, 2 FPS, 2 esc, 4CB, 2 esc, 2 FPS, 2 esc.

Row 9: Chain 2, turn, 2 esc, 2 BPS, [2 esc, 4 BPS, 2 esc, 2 BPS] three times, 2 esc.

Row 10: Chain 2, turn, [2 esc, B4CF, add 2 esc stitches between the next 2 stitches, B4CF, 2 esc], 4CF, repeat instructions in [ ] once.

Rows 11–250: Repeat Rows 3–10 thirty times.

Row 251: Repeat Row 3.

Tie off yarn.

Weave in any loose yarn ends.

Tassel Instructions

1. Cut yarn segments (12 segments per tassel) about 9 in. (22.9 cm) in length.

2. Align the 12 segments (1 tassel) and fold them in half.

3. Take the loop at the half mark of the tassel and insert it into the scarf edge (from the front of the scarf to the back).

4. Take the ends of the yarn segments and pull them through the loop (pull tight).

5. Make and place 9 tassels on each end of the scarf, equally spaced.

6. Trim tassel ends to make them even.

Absinthe Hat (Unisex, Experienced)

Materials

1 skein of WeCrochet/Knit Picks Stroll Hand Painted in Celery Seed (462 yd./422.5 m and 3.5 oz./100 g net weight per skein; 75% fine superwash Merino wool and 25% nylon; super fine weight #1)

Hook

US size F-5 (3.75 mm) crochet hook

Hat Dimensions

11.5 in. (29.2 cm) wide by 7.3 in. (18.4 cm) long
Note: These dimensions are for the fitted hat style. This pattern also has instructions for the slouchy hat style, which will have a length of about 9 in. (22.9 cm).

Gauge

11 esc stitches x 11 esc rows = 2 in. x 2 in. (5.1 cm x 5.1 cm)

Crochet Stitch Video Tutorials

4-Cross Front Cable Stitch (4CF): "Four Cross Front Crochet Cable Stitch Tutorial," https://www.youtube.com/watch?v=rzuMC6mB68w&t=1s

4-Cross Back Cable Stitch (4CB): "Four Cross Back Crochet Cable Stitch Tutorial," https://www.youtube.com/watch?v=EGBMJaXAcEQ&t=35s

Stitch Diagram

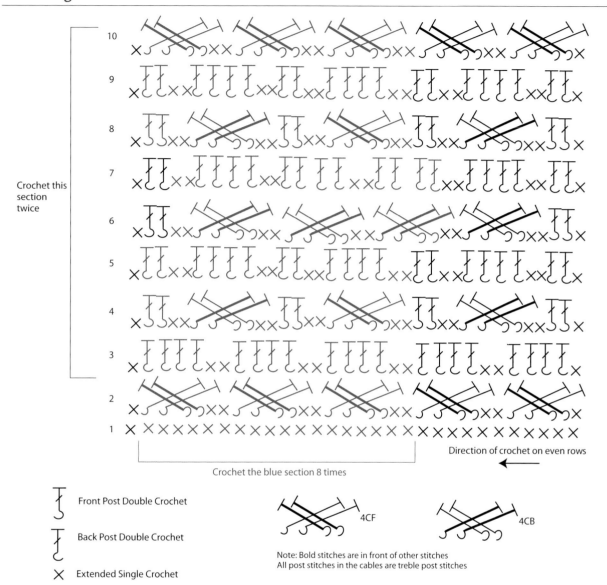

Crochet this section twice

Crochet the blue section 8 times

Direction of crochet on even rows

Front Post Double Crochet

Back Post Double Crochet

X Extended Single Crochet

4CF

4CB

Note: Bold stitches are in front of other stitches
All post stitches in the cables are treble post stitches

INSTRUCTIONS

Round 1: Chain 156 (including starting loop), slip stitch with starting chain. Chain 2, esc around, slip stitch with starting chain. (156 esc, 1 chain)

Round 2: Chain 2, turn, esc, [4CF, 2 esc] 25 times, 4CF, esc. Slip stitch with starting chain.

Round 3: Chain 2, turn, esc, [4 BPS, 2 esc] 25 times, 4 BPS, esc. Slip stitch with starting chain.

Round 4: Chain 2, turn, esc, 2 FPS, add 2 esc stitches between the next 2 stitches, B4CB, add 2 esc stitches between the next 2 stitches, 2 FPS, [2 esc, 4CF, 2 esc, 2 FPS, add 2 esc stitches between the next 2 stitches, B4CB, add 2 esc stitches between the next 2 stitches, 2 FPS] eight times, esc. Slip stitch with starting chain.

Round 5: Chain 2, turn, esc, [2 BPS, 2 esc, 4 BPS, 2 esc, 2 BPS, 2 esc, 4 BPS, 2 esc] eight times, 2 BPS, 2 esc, 4 BPS, 2 esc, 2 BPS, esc. Slip stitch with starting chain.

Round 6: Chain 2, turn, esc, 2 FPS, 2 esc, 4CB, 2 esc, [B4CB, add 2 esc stitches between the next 2 stitches, B4CB, 2 esc, 4CB, 2 esc] eight times, 2 FPS, esc. Slip stitch with starting chain.

Round 7: Chain 2, turn, esc, 2 BPS, [2 esc, 4 BPS, 2 esc, 4 BPS, 2 esc, 4 BPS] eight times, 2 esc, 4 BPS, 2 esc, 2 BPS, esc. Slip stitch with starting chain.

Round 8: Chain 2, turn, esc, 2 FPS, 2 esc, 4CB, 2 esc, 2 FPS, [add 2 esc stitches between the next 2 stitches, B4CF, add 2 esc stitches between the next 2 stitches, 2 FPS, 2 esc, 4CB, 2 esc, 2 FPS] eight times, esc. Slip stitch with starting chain.

Round 9: Chain 2, turn, esc, [2 BPS, 2 esc, 4 BPS, 2 esc, 2 BPS, 2 esc, 4 BPS, 2 esc] eight times, 2 BPS, 2 esc, 4 BPS, 2 esc, 2 BPS, esc. Slip stitch with starting chain.

Round 10: Chain 2, turn, esc, B4CF, add 2 esc stitches between the next 2 stitches, B4CF, [2 esc, 4CF, 2 esc, B4CF, add 2 esc stitches between the next 2 stitches, B4CF] eight times, esc. Slip stitch with starting chain.

Rounds 11–18: Repeat Rounds 3–10 once.

Note: For a slouchy-style hat, add one additional repeat of Rounds 3–10. This will add about 1.75 in. (4.5 cm) to the hat length.

Round 19: Chain 2, turn, esc, [DecDBPS, DecDBPS, 2 esc] 25 times, DecDBPS, DecDBPS, esc. Slip stitch with starting chain.

Round 20: Chain 2, turn, esc, FPS, add 2 esc stitches between the next 2 stitches, B2CB, add 2 esc stitches between the next 2 stitches, FPS, [2 esc, 2CF, 2 esc, FPS, add 2 esc stitches between the next 2 stitches, B2CB, add 2 esc stitches between the next 2 stitches, FPS] eight times, esc. Slip stitch with starting chain.

Round 21: Chain 2, turn, esc, [BPS, 2 esc, 2 BPS, 2 esc, BPS, 2 esc, 2 BPS, 2 esc] eight times, BPS, 2 esc, 2 BPS, 2 esc, BPS, esc. Slip stitch with starting chain.

Round 22: Chain 2, turn, esc, FPS, 2 esc, 2CB, 2 esc, [B2CB, add 2 esc stitches between the next 2 stitches, B2CB, 2 esc, 2CB, 2 esc] eight times, FPS, esc. Slip stitch with starting chain.

Round 23: Chain 2, turn, esc, BPS, [2 esc, 2 BPS, 2 esc, 2 BPS, 2 esc, 2 BPS] eight times, 2 esc, 2 BPS, 2 esc, BPS, esc. Slip stitch with starting chain.

Round 24: Chain 2, turn, esc, FPS, 2 esc, 2CB, 2 esc, FPS, [add 2 esc stitches between the next 2 stitches, B2CF, add 2 esc stitches between the next 2 stitches, FPS, 2 esc, 2CB, 2 esc, FPS] eight times, esc. Slip stitch with starting chain.

Round 25: Chain 2, turn, esc, [BPS, 2 esc, 2 BPS, 2 esc, BPS, 2 esc, 2 BPS, 2 esc] eight times, BPS, 2 esc, 2 BPS, 2 esc, BPS, esc. Slip stitch with starting chain.

Round 26: Chain 2, turn, esc, B2CF, add 2 esc stitches between the next 2 stitches, B2CF, [2 esc, 2CF, 2 esc, B2CF, add 2 esc stitches between the next 2 stitches, B2CF] eight times, esc. Slip stitch with starting chain.

Round 27: Chain 2, turn, esc, [2 BPS, Dec] 25 times, 2 BPS, esc. Slip stitch with starting chain.

Round 28: Chain 2, turn, esc, FPS, add 1 esc stitch between the next 2 stitches, B2CB, add 1 esc stitch between the next 2 stitches, FPS, [esc, 2CF, esc, FPS, add 1 esc stitch between the next 2 stitches, B2CB, add 1 esc stitch between the next 2 stitches, FPS] eight times, esc. Slip stitch with starting chain.

Round 29: Chain 2, turn, esc, [BPS, esc, 2 BPS, esc, BPS, esc, 2 BPS, esc] eight times, BPS, esc, 2 BPS, esc, BPS, esc. Slip stitch with starting chain.

Round 30: Chain 2, turn, esc, FPS, esc, 2CB, esc, [B2CB, add 1 esc stitch between the next 2 stitches, B2CB, esc, 2CB, esc] eight times, FPS, esc. Slip stitch with starting chain.

Round 31: Chain 2, turn, esc, BPS, [esc, DecDBPS, esc, DecDBPS, esc, DecDBPS] eight times, esc, DecDBPS, esc, BPS, esc. Slip stitch with starting chain.

Round 32: Chain 2, turn, esc, [FPS, esc, BDecDFPS, esc] nine times.

Round 33: Chain 2, turn, esc, [BPS, esc] eighteen times.

Round 34: Chain 2, turn, esc, [FPS, esc] eighteen times.

Round 35: Chain 2, turn, esc, [BPS, esc] eighteen times.

Round 36: Chain 2, turn, esc, [BDecDFPS, esc] nine times.

Round 37: Chain 2, turn, esc, 9 Dec.

Sew the hole at the top of the hat closed.

Tie off yarn.

Weave in any loose yarn ends.

Finishing

Reattach your yarn to the bottom of the hat. Chain 2, reverse single crochet in each stitch around the hat. Slip stitch with starting chain.

Tie off yarn.

Weave in any loose yarn ends.

10 Crochet Patterns with Multicolored Yarns: Clothing

This chapter describes the use of multi-colored yarn to make articles of clothing, from shawls to sweaters. The first three patterns are for two shawls and a poncho; all of these patterns have no shaping of the crochet fabric. While the shawls and poncho are listed as intermediate level due to their intricate cable design, they are on the easier end of the intermediate range if you have some familiarity with cable stitches. The final pattern in this chapter is a women's cardigan pattern that has both shaping and detailed cables, which make it an advanced pattern.

As with all of the patterns in this book, my comments on the multicolored yarn used in each pattern are in Chapter 6. These comments focus on the yarn's brightness variation and suitability for textured projects. In addition, Chapter 6 has an image of the swatch (or skein) of the yarn used in both color and black and white. For stitch descriptions, additional pattern instructions, and notes, refer to Chapter 7.

Vermilion Shawl (Unisex, Intermediate)

Materials

7 skeins of WeCrochet/Knit Picks Muse Aran in Fearless Hand Painted (114 yd./104.2 m per skein and 3.5 oz./100 g net weight per skein; 100% superwash Merino wool; medium weight #4)

Hook

US size J-10 (6.0 mm) crochet hook

Shawl Dimensions

11.5 in. (29.2 cm) wide by 55.5 in. (141 cm) long (excluding tassels)

Gauge

6.5 esc stitches x 6 esc rows = 2 in. x 2 in. (5.1 cm x 5.1 cm)

Crochet Stitch Video Tutorials

4-Cross Front Cable Stitch (4CF): "Four Cross Front Crochet Cable Stitch Tutorial," https://www.youtube.com/watch?v=rzuMC6mB68w &t=1s

4-Cross Back Cable Stitch (4CB): "Four Cross Back Crochet Cable Stitch Tutorial," https://www.youtube.com/watch?v=EGBMJaXAcEQ &t=35s

Twist Stitches (TBS and TFS): "Crochet Twist Front and Twist Back Cable Stitch Tutorial," https://www.youtube .com/watch?v=0dIDgHCA7DU

Stitch Diagram

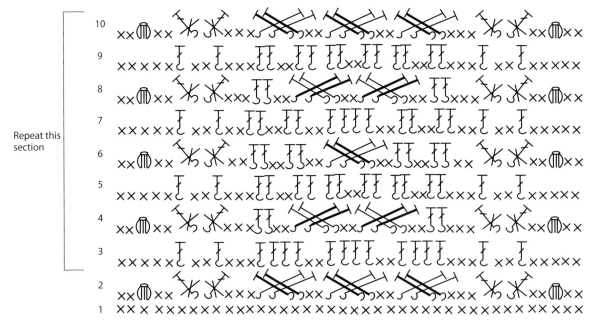

Repeat this section

Direction of crochet on even rows

Front Post Double Crochet

Back Post Double Crochet

X   Extended Single Crochet

Puff Stitch

4CF

4CB

TBS

TFS

Note: Bold stitches are in front of other stitches
All post stitches in the cables are treble post stitches

INSTRUCTIONS

Row 1: Chain 42 (including starting loop), esc in the third chain from hook, and esc across. (40 esc, 1 chain)

Row 2: Chain 2, turn, 2 esc, puff stitch, 2 esc, TBS, TFS, 3 esc, [4CF, 2 esc] three times, esc, TBS, TFS, 2 esc, puff stitch, 2 esc.

Row 3: Chain 2, turn, 2 esc, esc into puff stitch in previous row, 2 esc, BPS, 2 esc, BPS, 3 esc, [4 BPS, 2 esc] three times, esc, BPS, 2 esc, BPS, 2 esc, esc into puff stitch in previous row, 2 esc.

Row 4: Chain 2, turn, 2 esc, puff stitch, 2 esc, TBS, TFS, 3 esc, 2 FPS, [add 2 esc stitches between the next 2 stitches, B4CB] twice, add 2 esc stitches between the next 2 stitches, 2 FPS, 3 esc, TBS, TFS, 2 esc, puff stitch, 2 esc.

Row 5: Chain 2, turn, 2 esc, esc into puff stitch in previous row, 2 esc, BPS, 2 esc, BPS, 3 esc, 2 BPS, 2 esc, [4 BPS, 2 esc] twice, 2 BPS, 3 esc, BPS, 2 esc, BPS, 2 esc, esc into puff stitch in previous row, 2 esc.

Row 6: Chain 2, turn, 2 esc, puff stitch, 2 esc, TBS, TFS, 2 esc, skip an esc stitch, 2 FPS, 2 esc, 2 FPS, add 2 esc stitches between the next 2 stitches, B4CF, add 2 esc stitches between the next 2 stitches, 2 FPS, 2 esc, 2 FPS, skip an esc stitch, 2 esc, TBS, TFS, 2 esc, puff stitch, 2 esc.

Row 7: Chain 2, turn, 2 esc, esc into puff stitch in previous row, [2 esc, BPS] twice, 2 esc, [2 BPS, 2 esc] twice, 4 BPS, 2 esc, [2 BPS, 2 esc] twice, [BPS, 2 esc] twice, esc into puff stitch in previous row, 2 esc.

Row 8: Chain 2, turn, 2 esc, puff stitch, 2 esc, TBS, TFS, esc, make 2 esc in the next stitch, 2 FPS, 2 esc,

B4CB, add 2 esc stitches between the next 2 stitches, B4CB, 2 esc, 2 FPS, make 2 esc in the next stitch, esc, TBS, TFS, 2 esc, puff stitch, 2 esc.

Row 9: Repeat Row 5.

Row 10: Chain 2, turn, 2 esc, puff stitch, 2 esc, TBS, TFS, 3 esc, [B4CF, add 2 esc stitches between the next 2 stitches] twice, B4CF, 3 esc, TBS, TFS, 2 esc, puff stitch, 2 esc.

Rows 11–138: Repeat Rows 3–10 sixteen times.

Row 139: Repeat Row 3 once.

Tie off yarn.

Weave in any loose yarn ends.

Tassel Instructions

1. Cut yarn segments (10 segments per tassel) about 9 in. (22.9 cm) in length.
2. Align the 10 segments (1 tassel) and fold them in half.
3. Take the loop at the half mark of the tassel and insert it into the shawl edge (from the front of the shawl to the back).
4. Take the ends of the yarn segments and pull them through the loop (pull tight).
5. Make and place 15 tassels on each end of the shawl, equally spaced.
6. Trim tassel ends to make them even.

Cerulean Shawl (Unisex, Intermediate)

Materials

2 skeins of WeCrochet/Knit Picks, Stroll in Blue Tweed Tonal (462 yd./422.5 m per skein and 3.5 oz./100 g net weight per skein; 65% fine superwash Merino wool, 25% nylon, and 10% Donegal; super fine weight #1)

Hook

US size F-5 (3.75 mm) crochet hook

Shawl Dimensions

6.5 in. (16.5 cm) wide by 58 in. (147.3 cm) long

Crochet Stitch Video Tutorials

 *4-Cross Front Cable Stitch* (4CF): "Four Cross Front Crochet Cable Stitch Tutorial," https://www.youtube.com/watch?v=rzuMC6mB68w&t=1s

 *4-Cross Back Cable Stitch* (4CB): "Four Cross Back Crochet Cable Stitch Tutorial," https://www.youtube.com/watch?v=EGBMJaXAcEQ&t=35s

Stitch Diagram

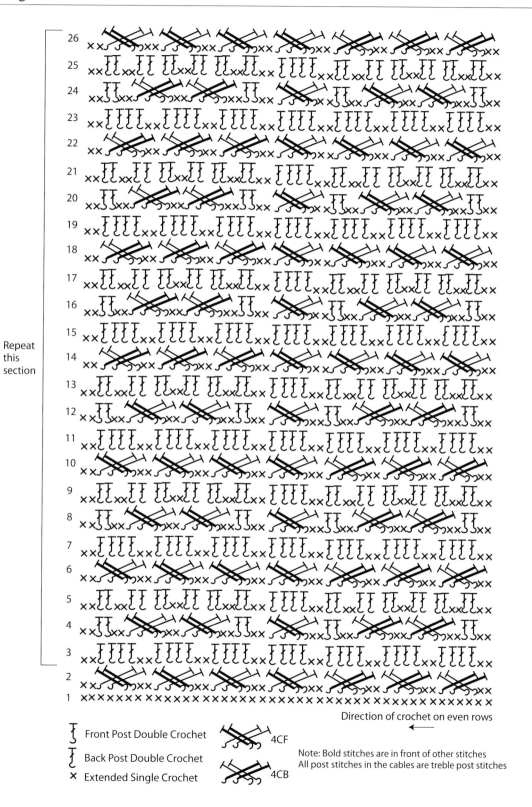

Repeat this section

Direction of crochet on even rows
←

Front Post Double Crochet

Back Post Double Crochet

× Extended Single Crochet

4CF

4CB

Note: Bold stitches are in front of other stitches
All post stitches in the cables are treble post stitches

INSTRUCTIONS

Row 1: Chain 46 (including starting loop), esc in the third chain from hook, and esc across. (44 esc, 1 chain)

Row 2: Chain 2, turn, 2 esc, [4CB, 2 esc] three times, [4CF, 2 esc] four times.

Row 3: Chain 2, turn, 2 esc, [4 BPS, 2 esc] seven times.

Row 4: Chain 2, turn, 2 esc, 2 FPS, [add 2 esc stitches between the next 2 stitches, B4CB] twice, add 2 esc stitches between the next 2 stitches. 2 FPS, 2 esc, 4CF, 2 esc, 2 FPS, [add 2 esc stitches between the next 2 stitches, B4CF] twice, add 2 esc stitches between the next 2 stitches, 2 FPS, 2 esc.

Row 5: Chain 2, turn, 2 esc, 2 BPS, [2 esc, 4 BPS] twice, 2 esc, 2 BPS, 2 esc, 4 BPS, 2 esc, 2 BPS, [2 esc, 4 BPS] twice, 2 esc, 2 BPS, 2 esc.

Row 6: Chain 2, turn, 2 esc, [B4CB, add 2 esc stitches between the next 2 stitches] twice, B4CB, 2 esc, 4CF, 2 esc, [B4CF, add 2 esc stitches between the next 2 stitches] twice, B4CF, 2 esc.

Rows 7–10: Repeat Rows 3–6 once.

Rows 11–13: Repeat Rows 3–5 once.

Row 14: Chain 2, turn, 2 esc, [B4CF, add 2 esc stitches between the next 2 stitches] twice, B4CF, 2 esc, 4CF, 2 esc, [B4CB, add 2 esc stitches between the next 2 stitches] twice, B4CB, 2 esc.

Row 15: Repeat Row 3.

Row 16: Chain 2, turn, 2 esc, 2 FPS, [add 2 esc stitches between the next 2 stitches, B4CF] twice, add 2 esc stitches between the next 2 stitches, 2 FPS, 2 esc, 4CF, 2 esc, 2 FPS, [add 2 esc stitches between the next 2 stitches, B4CB] twice, add 2 esc stitches between the next 2 stitches. 2 FPS, 2 esc.

Row 17: Repeat Row 5.

Rows 18–25: Repeat Rows 14–17 twice.

Row 26: Repeat Row 6.

Rows 27–218: Repeat Rows 3–26 eight times.

Rows 219–238: Repeat Rows 3–22 once.

Tie off yarn.

Weave in any loose yarn ends.

Sepia Poncho (Women, Intermediate)

Materials

- 8 skeins of Red Heart Unforgettable in Meadow (270 yd./246.9 m per skein and 3.5 oz./100 g net weight per skein; 100% acrylic; medium weight #4)
- 2 buttons (25 mm Stitched Leather Buttons by Skacel)

Hook

US size H-8 (5.0 mm) crochet hook

Poncho Dimensions

Women's Small–Women's Large: 34 in. (86.4 cm) wide by 31 in. (78.7 cm) long

Women's Plus Sized (1X–3X): 38 in. (96.5 cm) wide by 36.5 in. (92.7 cm) long

Note: Plus size adds 3 cable stitches to the rectangle widths (one pattern repeat in blue in the stitch diagram on page 139), which is about 3.5 in. (8.9 cm) wide. In addition, this size adds 3.5 in. (8.9 cm) to the long rectangle length.

Gauge

8.5 esc stitches x 8 esc rows = 2 in. x 2 in. (5.1 cm x 5.1 cm)

Crochet Stitch Video Tutorials

4-Cross Front Cable Stitch (4CF): "Four Cross Front Crochet Cable Stitch Tutorial," https://www.youtube.com/watch?v=rzuMC6mB68w&t=1s

4-Cross Back Cable Stitch (4CB): "Four Cross Back Crochet Cable Stitch Tutorial," https://www.youtube.com/watch?v=EGBMJaXAcEQ&t=35s

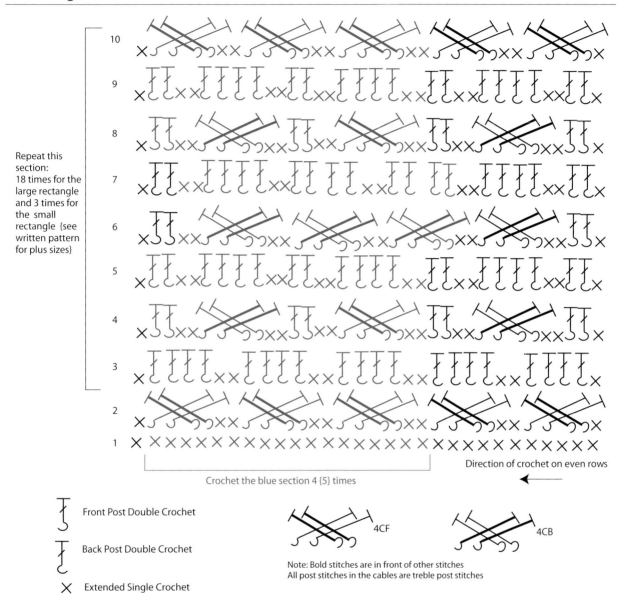

Repeat this section: 18 times for the large rectangle and 3 times for the small rectangle {see written pattern for plus sizes}

Crochet the blue section 4 {5} times

Direction of crochet on even rows

Front Post Double Crochet

Back Post Double Crochet

✕ Extended Single Crochet

4CF

4CB

Note: Bold stitches are in front of other stitches
All post stitches in the cables are treble post stitches

INSTRUCTIONS

The main pattern is written for the Women's Small–Women's Large poncho size. The Plus-Sized poncho has additional repeats relative to the main pattern; therefore, the number of stitches or repeats for the Plus-Sized poncho is listed in braces { } when they are different from the main pattern.

Part I: Large Rectangle

Make 1 large rectangle. These instructions detail the first part of the poncho. This is a very long rectangle that will drape diagonally across the front and onto the back of the poncho.

Row 1: Chain 86 {104} (including starting loop), esc in the third chain from hook, and esc across. (84 {102} esc, 1 chain)

Row 2: Chain 2, turn, esc, 4CF, 2 esc, 4CF, [2 esc, 4CF, 2 esc, 4CF, 2 esc, 4CF] 4 {5} times, esc.

Row 3: Chain 2, turn, esc, [4 BPS, 2 esc, 4 BPS, 2 esc, 4 BPS, 2 esc] 4 {5} times, 4 BPS, 2 esc, 4 BPS, esc.

Row 4: Chain 2, turn, esc, 2 FPS, add 2 esc stitches between the next 2 stitches, B4CB, add 2 esc stitches between the next 2 stitches, 2 FPS, [2 esc, 4CF, 2 esc, 2 FPS, add 2 esc stitches between the next 2 stitches, B4CB, add 2 esc stitches between the next 2 stitches, 2 FPS] 4 {5} times, esc.

Row 5: Chain 2, turn, esc, [2 BPS, 2 esc, 4 BPS, 2 esc, 2 BPS, 2 esc, 4 BPS, 2 esc] 4 {5} times, 2 BPS, 2 esc, 4 BPS, 2 esc, 2 BPS, esc.

Row 6: Chain 2, turn, esc, 2 FPS, 2 esc, 4CB, 2 esc, [B4CB, add 2 esc stitches between the next 2 stitches, B4CB, 2 esc, 4CB, 2 esc] 4 {5} times, 2 FPS, esc.

Row 7: Chain 2, turn, esc, 2 BPS, [2 esc, 4 BPS, 2 esc, 4 BPS, 2 esc, 4 BPS] 4 {5} times, 2 esc, 4 BPS, 2 esc, 2 BPS, esc.

Row 8: Chain 2, turn, esc, 2 FPS, 2 esc, 4CB, 2 esc, 2 FPS, [add 2 esc stitches between the next 2 stitches, B4CF, add 2 esc stitches between the next 2 stitches, 2 FPS, 2 esc, 4CB, 2 esc, 2 FPS] 4 {5} times, esc.

Row 9: Chain 2, turn, esc, [2 BPS, 2 esc, 4 BPS, 2 esc, 2 BPS, 2 esc, 4 BPS, 2 esc] 4 {5} times, 2 BPS, 2 esc, 4 BPS, 2 esc, 2 BPS, esc.

Row 10: Chain 2, turn, esc, B4CF, add 2 esc stitches between the next 2 stitches, B4CF, [2 esc, 4CF, 2 esc, B4CF, add 2 esc stitches between the next 2 stitches, B4CF] 4 {5} times, esc.

Women's Small–Large Only:

Rows 11–154: Repeat Rows 3–10 eighteen times.

Row 155: Repeat Row 3.

Women's Plus-Sized Only:

Rows 11–162: Repeat Rows 3–10 nineteen times.

Rows 163–165: Repeat Rows 3–5 once.

Note: Check that your long rectangle has the following ratio:

> Full length of the long rectangle = (2 x the width of the long rectangle) + 10 in. (25.4 cm)

This relationship will allow you to have a notch at the neckline that is 5 in. (12.7 cm) on each side (see Poncho Assembly Diagram below). The long rectangle in the example garment is 48 in. (121.9 cm) long and 19 in. (48.3 cm) wide for the Women's Small–Large size. The Plus-Sized long rectangle should be 55 in. (139.7 cm) long and 22.5 in. (57.2 cm) wide. Your long rectangle can be a different size; just make sure that it matches the formula above. However, if your long rectangle is the wrong length (relative to the width), you can fix this issue by adding or subtracting rows to the rectangle. You can also make the notch for the neck larger by adding rows (just make sure to add the same number of rows to the small rectangle).

Tie off yarn.

Weave in any loose yarn ends.

Poncho Assembly Diagram

Step 1

Steps 2 and 3

Poncho Part II

Poncho Part I

Part II: Small Rectangle

Make 1 small rectangle. These instructions detail the second part of the poncho, a short rectangle that covers the other shoulder and connects the 2 sides of the first rectangle. For assembly instructions, see below.

Rows 1–10: Work Rows 1–10 of Part I Instructions for Large Rectangle.

Rows 11–34: Repeat Rows 3–10 of Part I Instructions three times.

Row 35: Repeat Row 3.

Note: Check that your short rectangle has the following dimensions:

> Length: 10 in. (25.4 cm). Width: Should be the same width as the long rectangle. If your short rectangle is the wrong length, you can fix this issue by adding or subtracting rows.

Tie off yarn.

Weave in any loose yarn ends.

Poncho Assembly Instructions

When you have completed the 2 rectangles, follow the instructions on the right and the Poncho Assembly Diagram on the previous page to assemble them into a poncho.

1. Fold over the Part 1: Large Rectangle so that it is folded perfectly in half with all the edges lined up. (Note: The diagram on the previous page does not show the rectangle perfectly folded in order to show both the front and the back of the rectangle.)

2. Fold the Part II: Small Rectangle in half. Align the folded Small Rectangle diagonally to the Large Rectangle. The neck (the notch at top) should be about 5 in. (12.7 cm) on each side.

3. Sew or crochet join the seam between the two rectangle parts. Note: There are two seams: one on the front side, and one on the back side. The seam is presented as a thin black arrow in the poncho diagram.

4. Attach the yarn to the outer edge of the poncho, chain 2 and then reverse sc around the outer edge. Slip stitch with beginning chain. Tie off yarn.

5. Attach the yarn to the edge of the neckline of the poncho, chain 2, and then reverse sc around the inner edge. Slip stitch with beginning chain. Tie off yarn.

6. Sew the buttons to the poncho in the desired position (see images for reference).

Amaranth Cardigan (Women, Experienced)

Materials

- 6 skeins of WeCrochet/Knit Picks Stroll in Seashell Tonal (462 yd./422.5 m per skein and 3.5 oz./100 g net weight per skein; 75% fine superwash Merino wool, and 25% nylon; super fine weight #1) (you might need an extra skein or two of yarn for the larger sizes)
- 5 buttons matching or complementing the color of your yarn

Hook

US size G-6 (4.0 mm) crochet hook

Sweater Dimensions

Notes on sizing:

- There is no shaping for the body of the sweater. Therefore, this sweater can also be made for men if the dimensions are the appropriate size.
- The sizes are made by changing the gauge of the yarn for the sweater. Look below for the gauge differences for the different sizes. You can then reference and match the crochet gauge listed on the labels of most commercial yarn. Note: The larger sizes will also be heavier and warmer.

Women's Small (shown in photo): 18 in. (45.7 cm) wide lying flat (double for circumference) and 22 in. (55.9 cm) long

Women's Medium: 19.5 in. (49.5 cm) wide lying flat (double for circumference) and 25 in. (63.5 cm) long

Women's Large: 21.5 in. (54.6 cm) wide lying flat (double for circumference) and 26 in. (66 cm) long

Gauge

Women's Small: 11.5 esc stitches x 10 esc rows = 2 in. x 2 in. (5.1 cm x 5.1 cm)

Women's Medium: 10.5 esc stitches x 9 esc rows = 2 in. x 2 in. (5.1 cm x 5.1 cm)

Women's Large: 9.5 esc stitches x 8 esc rows = 2 in. x 2 in. (5.1 cm x 5.1 cm)

Crochet Stitch Video Tutorials

4-Cross Front Cable Stitch (4CF): "Four Cross Front Crochet Cable Stitch Tutorial," https://www.youtube.com/watch?v=rzuMC6mB68w&t=1s

4-Cross Back Cable Stitch (4CB): "Four Cross Back Crochet Cable Stitch Tutorial," https://www.youtube.com/watch?v=EGBMJaXAcEQ&t=35s

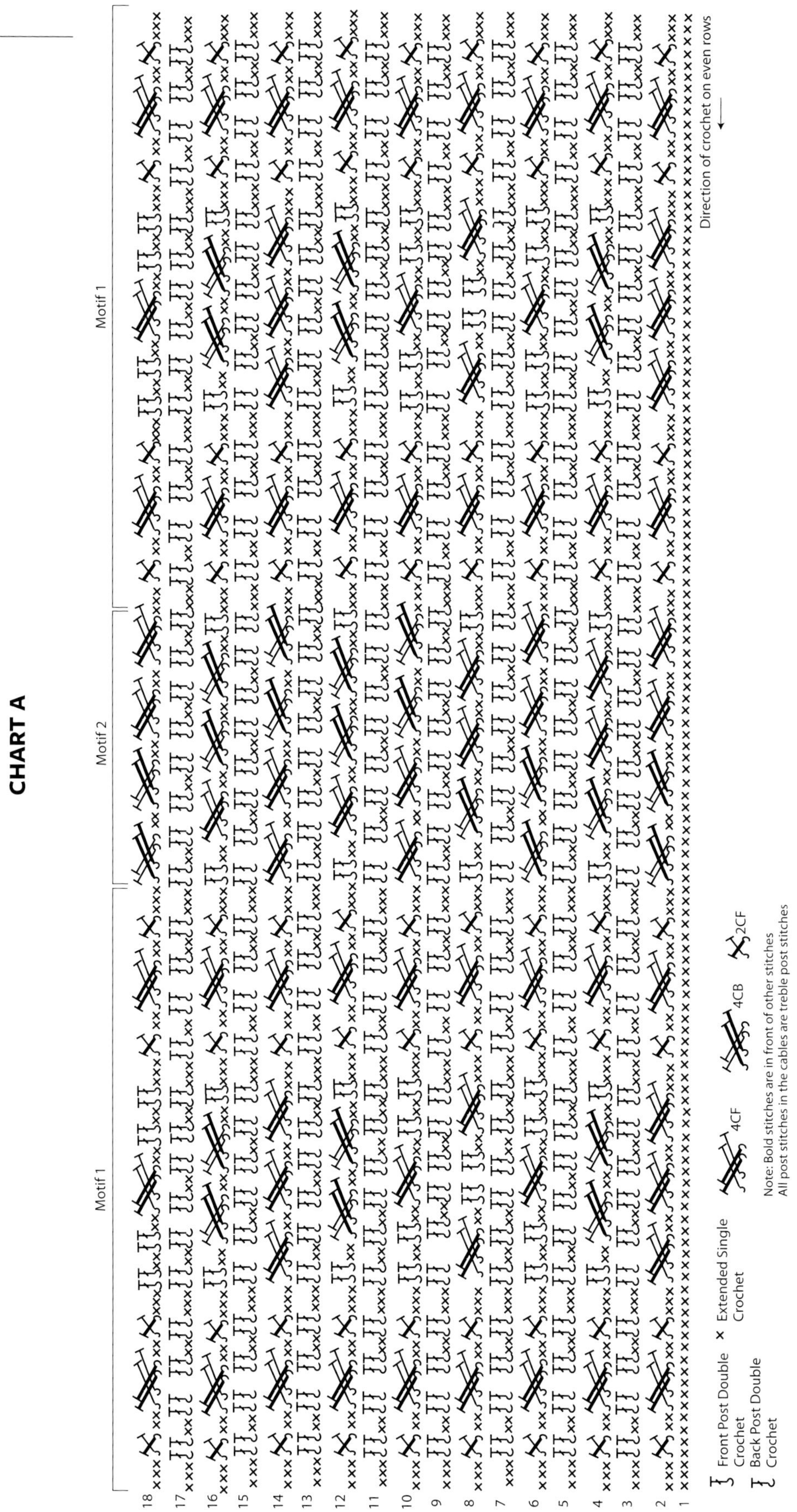

CHART A

Motif 1   Motif 2   Motif 1

Direction of crochet on even rows

18
17
16
15
14
13
12
11
10
9
8
7
6
5
4
3
2
1

╎ Front Post Double
╎ Crochet

╎ Back Post Double
╎ Crochet

× Extended Single
  Crochet

4CF   4CB   2CF

Note: Bold stitches are in front of other stitches
All post stitches in the cables are treble post stitches

145

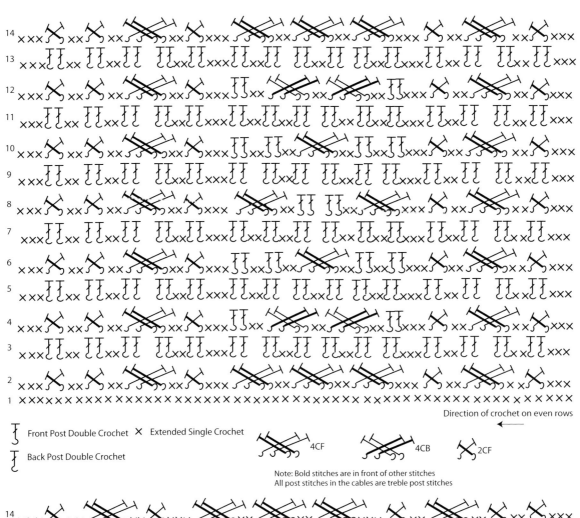

Direction of crochet on even rows

Front Post Double Crochet   ✕ Extended Single Crochet

Back Post Double Crochet

4CF   4CB   2CF

Note: Bold stitches are in front of other stitches
All post stitches in the cables are treble post stitches

CHART C

CHART D

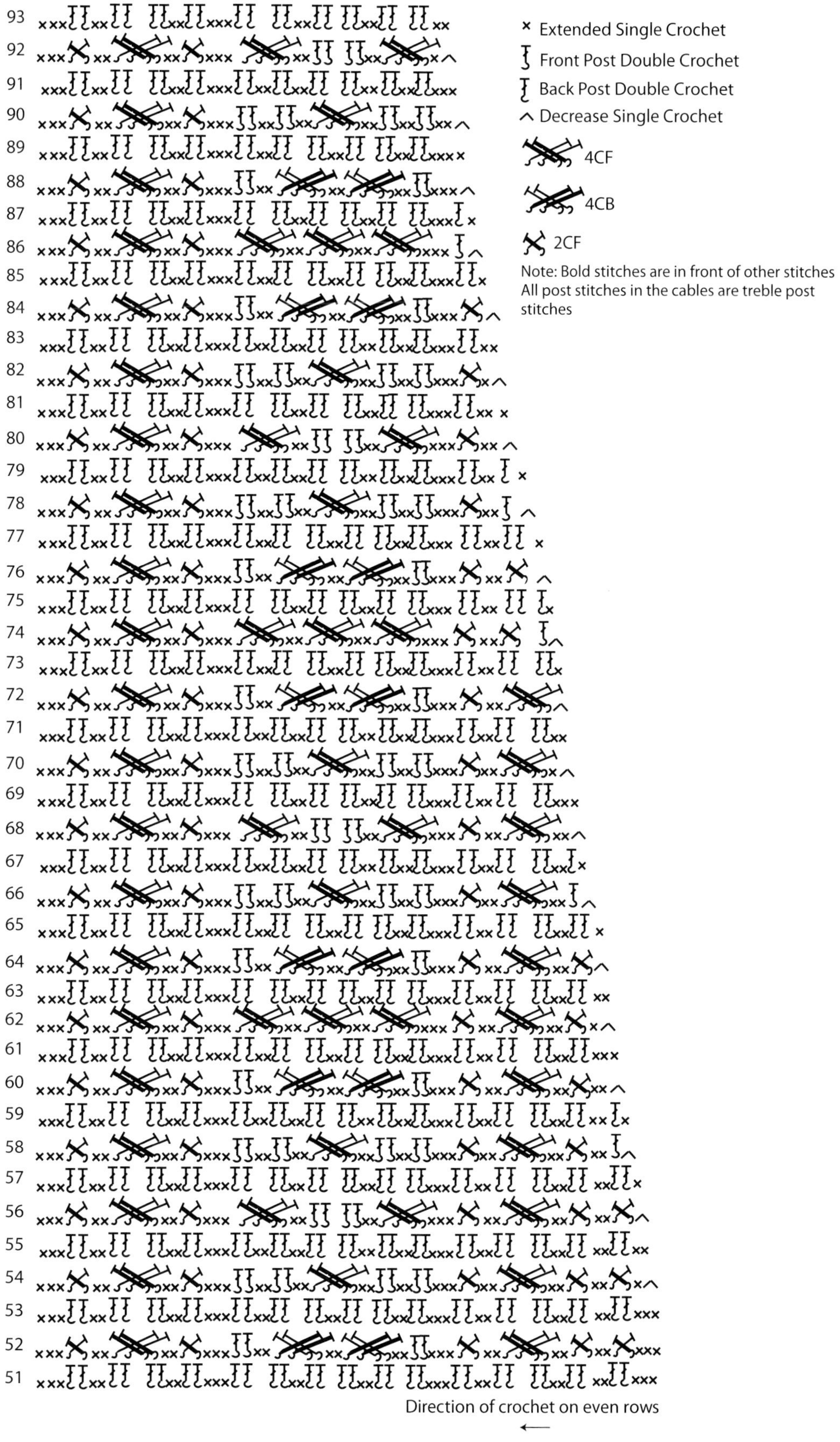

93
92
91
90
89
88
87
86
85
84
83
82
81
80
79
78
77
76
75
74
73
72
71
70
69
68
67
66
65
64
63
62
61
60
59
58
57
56
55
54
53
52
51

× Extended Single Crochet

Ʃ Front Post Double Crochet

Ɩ Back Post Double Crochet

∧ Decrease Single Crochet

4CF

4CB

2CF

Note: Bold stitches are in front of other stitches
All post stitches in the cables are treble post stitches

Direction of crochet on even rows
←

Crochet Patterns with Multicolored Yarns: Clothing ⌒ **147**

Direction of crochet on even rows
⟵

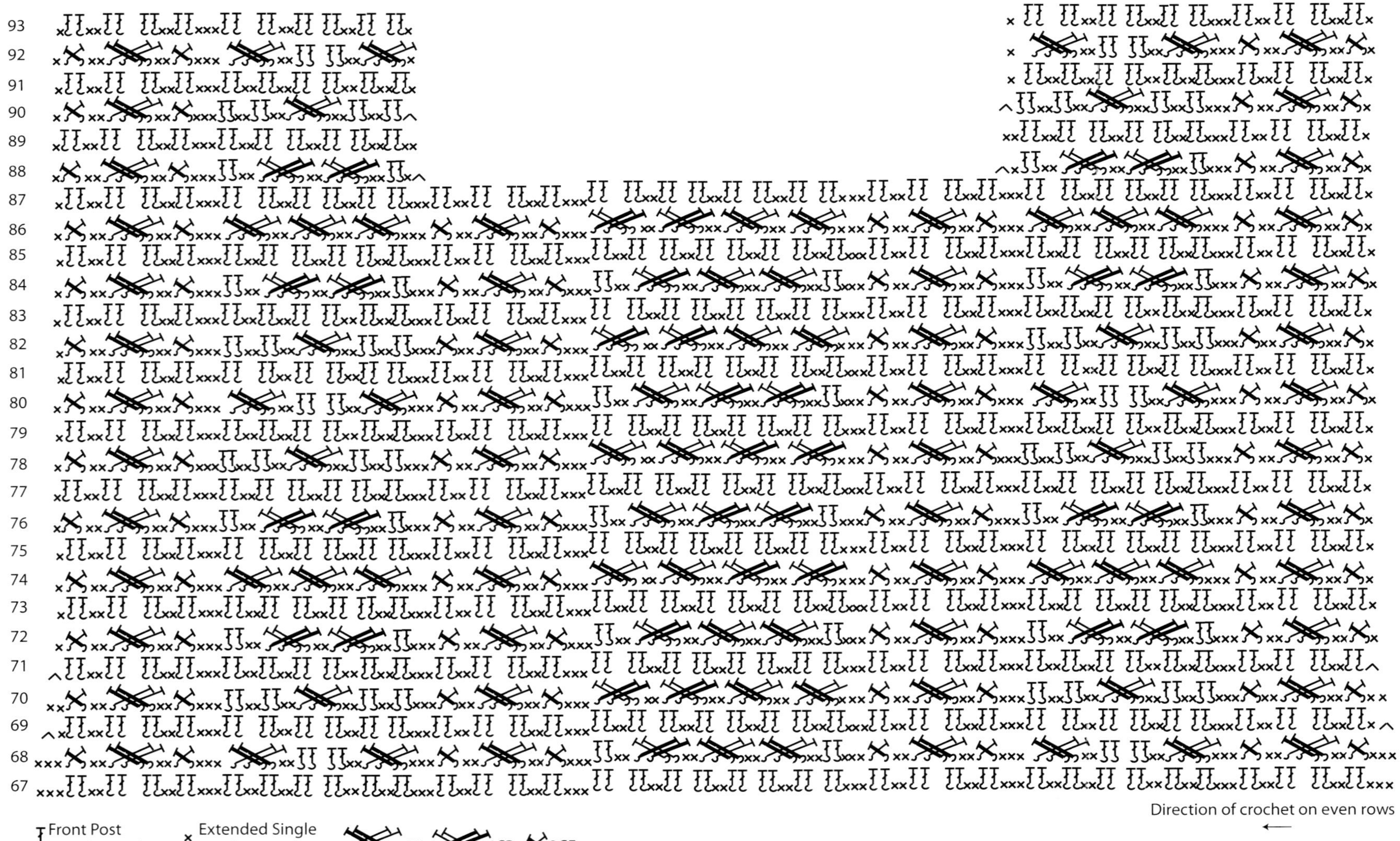

{ Front Post Double Crochet

{ Back Post Double Crochet

× Extended Single Crochet

⟨ Decrease Single Crochet

4CF   4CB   2CF

Note: Bold stitches are in front of other stitches
All post stitches in the cables are treble post stitches

INSTRUCTIONS

Sweater Front Left Side

Make one of the front side of the sweater left side. See Charts C and D.

Row 1: Chain 58 (including starting loop), esc in the third chain from hook, and esc across. (56 esc, 1 chain)

Row 2: Chain 2, turn, 3 esc, [2CF, 2 esc] twice, 4CF, 2 esc, 2CF, 3 esc, 4CF, [2 esc, 4CF] twice, 3 esc, 2CF, 2 esc, 4CF, 2 esc, 2CF, 3 esc.

Row 3: Chain 2, turn, 3 esc, 2 BPS, 2 esc, 4 BPS, 2 esc, 2 BPS, 3 esc, 4 BPS, 2 esc, 4 BPS, 2 esc, 4 BPS, 3 esc, 2 BPS, 2 esc, 4 BPS, [2 esc, 2 BPS] twice, 3 esc.

Row 4: Chain 2, turn, 3 esc, [2CF, 2 esc] twice, 4CF, 2 esc, 2CF, 3 esc, 2 FPS, [add 2 esc stitches between the next 2 stitches, B4CB] twice, add 2 esc stitches between the next 2 stitches, 2 FPS, 3 esc, 2CF, 2 esc, 4CF, 2 esc, 2CF, 3 esc.

Row 5: Chain 2, turn, 3 esc, 2 BPS, 2 esc, 4 BPS, 2 esc, 2 BPS, 3 esc, 2 BPS, [2 esc, 4 BPS] twice, 2 esc, 2 BPS, 3 esc, 2 BPS, 2 esc, 4 BPS, [2 esc, 2BPS] twice, 3 esc.

Row 6: Chain 2, turn, 3 esc, 2CF, 2 esc, 2CF, 2 esc, 4CF, 2 esc, 2CF, 3 esc, 2 FPS, 2 esc, 2 FPS, add 2 esc stitches between the next 2 stitches, B4CF, add 2 esc stitches between the next 2 stitches, 2 FPS, 2 esc, 2 FPS, 3 esc, 2CF, 2 esc, 4CF, 2 esc, 2CF, 3 esc.

Row 7: Chain 2, turn, 3 esc, 2 BPS, 2 esc, 4 BPS, 2 esc, 2 BPS, 3 esc, [2 BPS, 2 esc] twice, 4 BPS, 2 esc, 2 BPS, 2 esc, 2 BPS, 3 esc, 2 BPS, 2 esc, 4 BPS, 2 esc, 2 BPS, 2 esc, 2 BPS, 3 esc.

Row 8: Chain 2, turn, 3 esc, [2CF, 2 esc] twice, 4CF, 2 esc, 2CF, 3 esc, B4CF, 2 esc, 4 FPS, 2 esc, B4CF, 3 esc, 2CF, 2 esc, 4CF, 2 esc, 2CF, 3 esc.

Row 9: Chain 2, turn, 3 esc, 2 BPS, 2 esc, 4 BPS, 2 esc, 2 BPS, 3 esc, [4 BPS, 2 esc] twice, 4 BPS, 3 esc, 2 BPS, 2 esc, 4 BPS, 2 esc, 2 BPS, 2 esc, 2 BPS, 3 esc.

Row 10: Chain 2, turn, 3 esc, 2CF, 2 esc, 2CF, 2 esc, 4CF, 2 esc, 2CF, 3 esc, [2 FPS, add 2 esc stitches between the next 2 stitches], 2 FPS, 2 esc, 4CF, 2 esc, repeat instructions in [ ] once, 2 FPS, 3 esc, 2CF, 2 esc, 4CF, 2 esc, 2CF, 3 esc.

Row 11: Chain 2, turn, 3 esc, 2 BPS, 2 esc, 4 BPS, 2 esc, 2 BPS, 3 esc, [2 BPS, 2 esc] twice, 4 BPS, 2 esc, repeat instructions in [ ] once, 2 BPS, 3 esc, 2 BPS, 2 esc, 4 BPS, 2 esc, 2 BPS, 2 esc, 2 BPS, 3 esc.

Row 12: Chain 2, turn, 3 esc, [2CF, 2 esc] twice, 4CF, 2 esc, 2CF, 3 esc, 2 FPS, 2 esc, B4CB, add 2 esc stitches between the next 2 stitches, B4CB, 2 esc, 2 FPS, 3 esc, 2CF, 2 esc, 4CF, 2 esc, 2CF, 3 esc.

Row 13: Chain 2, turn, 3 esc, 2 BPS, 2 esc, 4 BPS, 2 esc, 2 BPS, 3 esc, 2 BPS, [2 esc, 4 BPS] twice, 2 esc, 2 BPS, 3 esc, 2 BPS, 2 esc, 4 BPS, [2 esc, 2 BPS] twice, 3 esc.

Row 14: Chain 2, turn, 3 esc, 2CF, 2 esc, 2CF, 2 esc, 4CF, 2 esc, 2CF, 3 esc, [B4CF, add 2 esc stitches between the next 2 stitches] twice, B4CF, 3 esc, 2CF, 2 esc, 4CF, 2 esc, 2CF, 3 esc.

Rows 15–50: Repeat Rows 3–14 three times.

Row 51: Chain 2, turn, 3 esc, 2 BPS, 2 esc, 4 BPS, 2 esc, 2 BPS, 3 esc, 4 BPS, [2 esc, 4 BPS] twice, 3 esc, 2 BPS, 2 esc, 4 BPS, [2 esc, 2 BPS] twice, 3 esc.

Row 52: Chain 2, turn, 3 esc, 2CF, 2 esc, 2CF, 2 esc, 4CF, 2 esc, 2CF, 3 esc, 2 FPS, [add 2 esc stitches between the next 2 stitches, B4CB] twice, add 2 esc stitches between the next 2 stitches, 2 FPS, 3 esc, 2CF, 2 esc, 4CF, 2 esc, 2CF, 3 esc.

Row 53: Chain 2, turn, 3 esc, 2 BPS, 2 esc, 4 BPS, 2 esc, 2 BPS, 3 esc, 2 BPS, [2 esc, 4 BPS] twice, 2 esc, 2 BPS, 3 esc, 2 BPS, 2 esc, 4 BPS, [2 esc, 2 BPS] twice, 3 esc.

Row 54: Chain 2, turn, Dec, esc, 2CF, 2 esc, 2CF, 2 esc, 4CF, 2 esc, 2CF, 3 esc, 2 FPS, 2 esc, 2 FPS, add 2 esc stitches between the next 2 stitches, B4CF, add 2 esc stitches between the next 2 stitches, 2 FPS, 2 esc, 2 FPS, 3 esc, 2CF, 2 esc, 4CF, 2 esc, 2CF, 3 esc.

Row 55: Chain 2, turn, 3 esc, 2 BPS, 2 esc, 4 BPS, 2 esc, 2 BPS, 3 esc, 2 BPS, 2 esc, 2 BPS, 2 esc, 4 BPS, [2 esc, 2 BPS] twice, 3 esc, 2 BPS, 2 esc, 4 BPS, 2 esc, [2 BPS, 2 esc] twice.

Row 56: Chain 2, turn, Dec, [2CF, 2 esc] twice, 4CF, 2 esc, 2CF, 3 esc, B4CF, 2 esc, 4 FPS, 2 esc, B4CF, 3 esc, 2CF, 2 esc, 4CF, 2 esc, 2CF, 3 esc.

Row 57: Chain 2, turn, 3 esc, 2 BPS, 2 esc, 4 BPS, 2 esc, 2 BPS, 3 esc, 4 BPS, [2 esc, 4 BPS] twice, 3 esc, 2 BPS, 2 esc, 4 BPS, 2 esc, [2 esc, 2 BPS] twice.

Row 58: Chain 2, turn, Dec in esc and post stitch, FPS, 2 esc, 2CF, 2 esc, 4CF, 2 esc, 2CF, 3 esc, [2 FPS, add 2 esc stitches between the next 2 stitches], 2 FPS, 2 esc, 4CF, 2 esc, repeat instructions in [ ] once, 2 FPS, 3 esc, 2CF, 2 esc, 4CF, 2 esc, 2CF, 3 esc.

Row 59: Chain 2, turn, 3 esc, 2 BPS, 2 esc, 4 BPS, 2 esc, 2 BPS, 3 esc, [2 BPS, 2 esc] twice, 4 BPS, 2 esc, repeat instructions in [ ] once, 2 BPS, 3 esc, 2 BPS, 2 esc, 4 BPS, 2 esc, 2 BPS, 2 esc, BPS, esc.

Row 60: Chain 2, turn, Dec in esc and post stitch, 2 esc, 2CF, 2 esc, 4CF, 2 esc, 2CF, 3 esc, 2 FPS, 2 esc, B4CB, add 2 esc stitches between the next 2 stitches, B4CB, 2 esc, 2 FPS, 3 esc, 2CF, 2 esc, 4CF, 2 esc, 2CF, 3 esc.

Row 61: Chain 2, turn, 3 esc, 2 BPS, 2 esc, [4 BPS, 2 esc, 2 BPS, 3 esc, 2 BPS, 2 esc, 4 BPS, 2 esc] twice, 2 BPS, 3 esc.

Row 62: Chain 2, turn, Dec, esc, 2CF, 2 esc, 4CF, 2 esc, 2CF, 3 esc, [B4CF, add 2 esc stitches between the next 2 stitches] twice, B4CF, 3 esc, 2CF, 2 esc, 4CF, 2 esc, 2CF, 3 esc.

Row 63: Chain 2, turn, 3 esc, 2 BPS, 2 esc, 4 BPS, 2 esc, 2 BPS, 3 esc, 4 BPS, 2 esc, 4 BPS, 2 esc, 4 BPS, 3 esc, 2 BPS, 2 esc, 4 BPS, 2 esc, 2 BPS, 2 esc.

Row 64: Chain 2, turn, Dec, 2CF, 2 esc, 4CF, 2 esc, 2CF, 3 esc, 2 FPS, [add 2 esc stitches between the next 2 stitches, B4CB] twice, add 2 esc stitches between the next 2 stitches, 2 FPS, 3 esc, 2CF, 2 esc, 4CF, 2 esc, 2CF, 3 esc.

Row 65: Chain 2, turn, 3 esc, 2 BPS, 2 esc, 4 BPS, 2 esc, 2 BPS, 3 esc, 2 BPS, [2 esc, 4 BPS] twice, 2 esc, 2 BPS, 3 esc, 2 BPS, 2 esc, 4 BPS, 2 esc, 2 BPS, esc.

Row 66: Chain 2, turn, Dec in esc and post stitch, FPS, 2 esc, 4CF, 2 esc, 2CF, 3 esc, 2 FPS, 2 esc, 2 FPS, add 2 esc stitches between the next 2 stitches, B4CF, add 2 esc stitches between the next 2 stitches, 2 FPS, 2 esc, 2 FPS, 3 esc, 2CF, 2 esc, 4CF, 2 esc, 2CF, 3 esc.

Row 67: Chain 2, turn, 3 esc, 2 BPS, 2 esc, 4 BPS, 2 esc, 2 BPS, 3 esc, 2 BPS, 2 esc, 2 BPS, 2 esc, 4 BPS, 2 esc, 2 BPS, 2 esc, 2 BPS, 3 esc, 2 BPS, 2 esc, 4 BPS, 2 esc, BPS, esc.

Row 68: Chain 2, turn, Dec in esc and post stitch, 2 esc, 4CF, 2 esc, 2CF, 3 esc, B4CF, 2 esc, 4 FPS, 2 esc, B4CF, 3 esc, 2CF, 2 esc, 4CF, 2 esc, 2CF, 3 esc.

Row 69: Chain 2, turn, 3 esc, 2 BPS, 2 esc, 4 BPS, 2 esc, 2 BPS, 3 esc, 4 BPS, [2 esc, 4 BPS] twice, 3 esc, 2 BPS, 2 esc, 4 BPS, 3 esc.

Row 70: Chain 2, turn, Dec, esc, 4CF, 2 esc, 2CF, 3 esc, [2 FPS, add 2 esc stitches between the next 2 stitches], 2 FPS, 2 esc, B4CF, 2 esc, repeat instructions in [ ] once, 2 FPS, 3 esc, 2CF, 2 esc, 4CF, 2 esc, 2CF, 3 esc.

Row 71: Chain 2, turn, 3 esc, 2 BPS, 2 esc, 4 BPS, 2 esc, 2 BPS, 3 esc, [2 BPS, 2 esc] twice, 4 BPS, 2 esc, repeat instructions in [ ] once, 2 BPS, 3 esc, 2 BPS, 2 esc, 4 BPS, 2 esc.

Row 72: Chain 2, turn, Dec, 4CF, 2 esc, 2CF, 3 esc, 2 FPS, 2 esc, B4CB, add 2 esc stitches between the next 2 stitches, B4CB, 2 esc, 2 FPS, 3 esc, 2CF, 2 esc, 4CF, 2 esc, 2CF, 3 esc.

Row 73: Chain 2, turn, 3 esc, 2 BPS, 2 esc, 4 BPS, 2 esc, 2 BPS, 3 esc, 2 BPS, [2 esc, 4 BPS] twice, 2 esc, 2 BPS, 3 esc, 2 BPS, 2 esc, 4 BPS, esc.

Row 74: Chain 2, turn, Dec in esc and post stitch, FPS, 2CF, 2 esc, 2CF, 3 esc, [B4CF, add 2 esc stitches between the next 2 stitches] twice, B4CF, 3 esc, 2CF, 2 esc, 4CF, 2 esc, 2CF, 3 esc.

Row 75: Chain 2, turn, 3 esc, 2 BPS, 2 esc, 4 BPS, 2 esc, 2 BPS, 3 esc, 4 BPS, [2 esc, 4 BPS] twice, 3 esc, 2 BPS, 2 esc, 3 BPS, esc.

Row 76: Chain 2, turn, Dec in esc and post stitch, 2CF, 2 esc, 2CF, 3 esc, 2 FPS, [add 2 esc stitches between the next 2 stitches, B4CB] twice, add 2 esc stitches between the next 2 stitches, 2 FPS, 3 esc, 2CF, 2 esc, 4CF, 2 esc, 2CF, 3 esc.

Row 77: Chain 2, turn, 3 esc, 2 BPS, 2 esc, 4 BPS, 2 esc, 2 BPS, 3 esc, 2 BPS, [2 esc, 4 BPS] twice, 2 esc, 2 BPS, 3 esc, 2 BPS, 2 esc, 2 BPS, esc.

Row 78: Chain 2, turn, Dec in esc and post stitch, FPS, 2 esc, 2CF, 3 esc, 2 FPS, 2 esc, 2 FPS, add 2 esc stitches between the next 2 stitches, B4CF, add 2 esc stitches between the next 2 stitches, 2 FPS, 2 esc, 2 FPS, 3 esc, 2CF, 2 esc, 4CF, 2 esc, 2CF, 3 esc.

Row 79: Chain 2, turn, 3 esc, 2 BPS, 2 esc, 4 BPS, 2 esc, 2 BPS, 3 esc, 2 BPS, 2 esc, 2 BPS, 2 esc, 4 BPS, [2 esc, 2 BPS] twice, 3 esc, 2 BPS, 2 esc, BPS, esc.

Row 80: Chain 2, turn, Dec in esc and post stitch, 2 esc, 2CF, 3 esc, B4CF, 2 esc, 4 FPS, 2 esc, B4CF, 3 esc, 2CF, 2 esc, 4CF, 2 esc, 2CF, 3 esc.

Row 81: Chain 2, turn, 3 esc, 2 BPS, 2 esc, 4 BPS, 2 esc, 2 BPS, 3 esc, 4 BPS, [2 esc, 4 BPS] twice, 3 esc, 2 BPS, 3 esc.

Row 82: Chain 2, turn, Dec, esc, 2CF, 3 esc, [2 FPS, add 2 esc stitches between the next 2 stitches], 2 FPS, 2 esc, B4CF, 2 esc, repeat instructions in [ ] once, 2 FPS, 3 esc, 2CF, 2 esc, 4CF, 2 esc, 2CF, 3 esc.

Row 83: Chain 2, turn, 3 esc, 2 BPS, 2 esc, 4 BPS, 2 esc, 2 BPS, 3 esc, [2 BPS, 2 esc] twice, 4 BPS, 2 esc, repeat instructions in [ ] once, 2 BPS, 3 esc, repeat instructions in [ ] once.

Row 84: Chain 2, turn, Dec, 2CF, 3 esc, 2 FPS, 2 esc, B4CB, add 2 esc stitches between the next 2 stitches, B4CB, 2 esc, 2 FPS, 3 esc, 2CF, 2 esc, 4CF, 2 esc, 2CF, 3 esc.

Row 85: Chain 2, turn, 3 esc, 2 BPS, 2 esc, 4 BPS, 2 esc, 2 BPS, 3 esc, 2 BPS, [2 esc, 4 BPS] twice, 2 esc, 2 BPS, 3 esc, 2 BPS, esc.

Row 86: Chain 2, turn, Dec in esc and post stitch, FPS, 3 esc, [B4CF, add 2 esc stitches between the next 2 stitches] twice, B4CF, 3 esc, 2CF, 2 esc, 4CF, 2 esc, 2CF, 3 esc.

Row 87: Chain 2, turn, 3 esc, 2 BPS, 2 esc, 4 BPS, 2 esc, 2 BPS, 3 esc, 4 BPS, [2 esc, 4 BPS] twice, 3 esc, BPS, esc.

Row 88: Chain 2, turn, Dec in esc and post stitch, 3 esc, 2 FPS, [add 2 esc stitches between the next 2 stitches, B4CB] twice, add 2 esc stitches between the next 2 stitches, 2 FPS, 3 esc, 2CF, 2 esc, 4CF, 2 esc, 2CF, 3 esc.

Row 89: Chain 2, turn, 3 esc, 2 BPS, 2 esc, 4 BPS, 2 esc, 2 BPS, 3 esc, 2 BPS, [2 esc, 4 BPS] twice, 2 esc, 2 BPS, 4 esc.

Row 90: Chain 2, turn, Dec, [2 esc, 2 FPS] twice, add 2 esc stitches between the next 2 stitches, B4CF, add 2 esc stitches between the next 2 stitches, 2 FPS, 2 esc, 2 FPS, 3 esc, 2CF, 2 esc, 4CF, 2 esc, 2CF, 3 esc.

Row 91: Chain 2, turn, 3 esc, 2 BPS, 2 esc, 4 BPS, 2 esc, 2 BPS, 3 esc, [2 BPS, 2 esc] twice, 4 BPS, [2 esc, 2 BPS] twice, 3 esc.

Row 92: Chain 2, turn, Dec, esc, B4CF, 2 esc, 4 FPS, 2 esc, B4CF, 3 esc, 2CF, 2 esc, 4CF, 2 esc, 2CF, 3 esc.

Row 93: Chain 2, turn, 3 esc, 2 BPS, 2 esc, 4 BPS, 2 esc, 2 BPS, 3 esc, [4 BPS, 2 esc] three times.

Tie off yarn.

Sweater Front Right Side

Make 1 of the right side of the sweater front. Refer to Chart B for Rows 1–14. Note: For the remaining rows, you can use the diagram for the front left side (Chart D), but move across the rows in the opposite direction. In other words, on the even rows move left to right in the diagram, although you are still making the even rows right to left in real life. This simply reverses the stitch order (i.e., the mirror image of left front side), which is the difference between the left and right front sides.

Row 1: Chain 58 (including starting loop), esc in the third chain from hook, and esc across. (56 esc, 1 chain)

Row 2: Chain 2, turn, 3 esc, 2CF, 2 esc, 4CF, 2 esc, 2CF, 3 esc, 4CF, [2 esc, 4CF] twice, 3 esc, 2CF, 2 esc, 4CF, [2 esc, 2CF] twice, 3 esc.

Row 3: Chain 2, turn, 3 esc, [2 BPS, 2 esc] twice, 4 BPS, 2 esc, 2 BPS, 3 esc, [4 BPS, 2 esc] three times, esc, 2 BPS, 2 esc, 4 BPS, 2 esc, 2 BPS, 3 esc.

Row 4: Chain 2, turn, 3 esc, 2CF, 2 esc, 4CF, 2 esc, 2CF, 3 esc, 2 FPS, [add 2 esc stitches between the next 2 stitches, B4CB] twice, add 2 esc stitches between the next 2 stitches, 2 FPS, 3 esc, 2CF, 2 esc, 4CF, [2 esc, 2CF] twice, 3 esc.

Row 5: Chain 2, turn, 3 esc, 2 BPS, 2 esc, 2 BPS, 2 esc, 4 BPS, 2 esc, 2 BPS, 3 esc, 2 BPS, [2 esc, 4 BPS] twice, 2 esc, 2 BPS, 3 esc, 2 BPS, 2 esc, 4 BPS, 2 esc, 2 BPS, 3 esc.

Row 6: Chain 2, turn, 3 esc, 2CF, 2 esc, 4CF, 2 esc, 2CF, 3 esc, 2 FPS, 2 esc, 2 FPS, add 2 esc stitches between the next 2 stitches, B4CF, add 2 esc stitches between the next 2 stitches, 2 FPS, 2 esc, 2 FPS, 3 esc, 2CF, 2 esc, 4CF, 2 esc, 2CF, 2 esc, 2CF, 3 esc.

Row 7: Chain 2, turn, 3 esc, 2 BPS, 2 esc, 2 BPS, 2 esc, 4 BPS, 2 esc, 2 BPS, 3 esc, 2 BPS, 2 esc, 2 BPS, 2 esc, 4 BPS, 2 esc, 2 BPS, 2 esc, 2 BPS, 3 esc, 2 BPS, 2 esc, 4 BPS, 2 esc, 2 BPS, 3 esc.

Row 8: Chain 2, turn, 3 esc, 2CF, 2 esc, 4CF, 2 esc, 2CF, 3 esc, B4CF, 2 esc, 4 FPS, 2 esc, B4CF, 3 esc, 2CF, 2 esc, 4CF, [2 esc, 2CF] twice, 3 esc.

Row 9: Chain 2, turn, 3 esc, 2 BPS, 2 esc, 2 BPS, 2 esc, 4 BPS, 2 esc, 2 BPS, 3 esc, 4 BPS, [2 esc, 4 BPS] twice, 3 esc, 2 BPS, 2 esc, 4 BPS, 2 esc, 2 BPS, 3 esc.

Row 10: Chain 2, turn, 3 esc, 2CF, 2 esc, 4CF, 2 esc, 2CF, 3 esc, 2 FPS, [add 2 esc stitches between the next 2 stitches, 2 FPS], 2 esc, B4CF, 2 esc, 2 FPS, repeat instructions in [ ] once, 3 esc, 2CF, 2 esc, 4CF, [2 esc, 2CF] twice, 3 esc.

Row 11: Chain 2, turn, 3 esc, 2 BPS, 2 esc, 2 BPS, 2 esc, 4 BPS, 2 esc, 2 BPS, 3 esc, [2 BPS, 2 esc] twice, 4 BPS, 2 esc, repeat instructions in [ ] once, 2 BPS, 3 esc, 2 BPS, 2 esc, 4 BPS, 2 esc, 2 BPS, 3 esc.

Row 12: Chain 2, turn, 3 esc, 2CF, 2 esc, 4CF, 2 esc, 2CF, 3 esc, 2 FPS, 2 esc, B4CB, add 2 esc stitches between the next 2 stitches, B4CB, 2 esc, 2 FPS, 3 esc, 2CF, 2 esc, 4CF, [2 esc, 2CF] twice, 3 esc.

Row 13: Chain 2, turn, 3 esc, 2 BPS, 2 esc, 2 BPS, 2 esc, [4 BPS, 2 esc, 2 BPS, 3 esc, 2 BPS, 2 esc, 4 BPS, 2 esc] twice, 2 BPS, 3 esc.

Row 14: Chain 2, turn, 3 esc, 2CF, 2 esc, 4CF, 2 esc, 2CF, 3 esc, [B4CF, add 2 esc stitches between the next 2 stitches] twice, B4CF, 3 esc, 2CF, 2 esc, 4CF, [2 esc, 2CF] twice, 3 esc.

Rows 15–50: Repeat Rows 3–14 three times.

Row 51: Chain 2, turn, 3 esc, 2 BPS, 2 esc, (2 BPS, 2 esc, 4 BPS, 2 esc, 2 BPS), 3 esc, [4 BPS, 2 esc] three times, esc, repeat instructions in ( ) once, 3 esc.

Row 52: Chain 2, turn, 3 esc, (2CF, 2 esc, 4CF, 2 esc, 2CF), 3 esc, 2 FPS, [add 2 esc stitches between the next 2 stitches, B4CB] twice, add 2 esc stitches between the next 2 stitches, 2 FPS, 3 esc, repeat instructions in ( ) once, 2 esc, 2CF, 3 esc.

Row 53: Chain 2, turn, 3 esc, 2 BPS, 2 esc, 2 BPS, 2 esc, 4 BPS, 2 esc, 2 BPS, 3 esc, 2 BPS, [2 esc, 4 BPS] twice, 2 esc, 2 BPS, 3 esc, 2 BPS, 2 esc, 4 BPS, 2 esc, 2 BPS, 3 esc.

Row 54: Chain 2, turn, 3 esc, 2CF, 2 esc, 4CF, 2 esc, 2CF, 3 esc, 2 FPS, 2 esc, 2 FPS, add 2 esc stitches between the next 2 stitches, B4CF, add 2 esc stitches between the next 2 stitches, 2 FPS, 2 esc, 2 FPS, 3 esc, 2CF, 2 esc, 4CF, [2 esc, 2CF] twice, esc, Dec.

Row 55: Chain 2, turn, [2 esc, 2 BPS] twice, 2 esc, 4 BPS, 2 esc, 2 BPS, 3 esc, 2 BPS, 2 esc, 2 BPS, 2 esc, 4 BPS, [2 esc, 2 BPS] twice, 3 esc, 2 BPS, 2 esc, 4 BPS, 2 esc, 2 BPS, 3 esc.

Row 56: Chain 2, turn, 3 esc, 2CF, 2 esc, 4CF, 2 esc, 2CF, 3 esc, B4CF, 2 esc, 4 FPS, 2 esc, B4CF, 3 esc, 2CF, 2 esc, 4CF, [2 esc, 2CF] twice, Dec.

Row 57: Chain 2, turn, esc, 2 BPS, 2 esc, 2 BPS, 2 esc, 4 BPS, 2 esc, 2 BPS, 3 esc, [4 BPS, 2 esc] twice, 4 BPS, 3 esc, 2 BPS, 2 esc, 4 BPS, 2 esc, 2 BPS, 3 esc.

Row 58: Chain 2, turn, 3 esc, 2CF, 2 esc, 4CF, 2 esc, 2CF, 3 esc, [2 FPS, add 2 esc stitches between the next 2 stitches], 2 FPS, 2 esc, B4CF, 2 esc, repeat instructions in [ ] once, 2 FPS, 3 esc, 2CF, 2 esc, 4CF, 2 esc, 2CF, 2 esc, FPS, Dec in esc and post stitch.

Row 59: Chain 2, turn, esc, BPS, 2 esc, 2 BPS, 2 esc, 4 BPS, 2 esc, 2 BPS, 3 esc, [2 BPS, 2 esc] twice, 4 BPS, 2 esc, repeat instructions in [ ] once, 2 BPS, 3 esc, 2 BPS, 2 esc, 4 BPS, 2 esc, 2 BPS, 3 esc.

Row 60: Chain 2, turn, 3 esc, 2CF, 2 esc, 4CF, 2 esc, 2CF, 3 esc, 2 FPS, 2 esc, B4CB, add 2 esc stitches between the next 2 stitches, B4CB, 2 esc, 2 FPS, 3 esc, 2CF, 2 esc, 4CF, 2 esc, 2CF, 2 esc, Dec in esc and post stitch.

Row 61: Chain 2, turn, 3 esc, 2 BPS, 2 esc, 4 BPS, 2 esc, 2 BPS, 3 esc, 2 BPS, [2 esc, 4 BPS] twice, 2 esc, 2 BPS, 3 esc, 2 BPS, 2 esc, 4 BPS, 2 esc, 2 BPS, 3 esc.

Row 62: Chain 2, turn, 3 esc, 2CF, 2 esc, 4CF, 2 esc, 2CF, 3 esc, [B4CF, add 2 esc stitches between the next 2 stitches] twice, B4CF, 3 esc, 2CF, 2 esc, 4CF, 2 esc, 2CF, esc, Dec.

Row 63: Chain 2, turn, 2 esc, 2 BPS, 2 esc, 4 BPS, 2 esc, 2 BPS, 3 esc, 4 BPS, [2 esc, 4 BPS] twice, 3 esc, 2 BPS, 2 esc, 4 BPS, 2 esc, 2 BPS, 3 esc.

Row 64: Chain 2, turn, 3 esc, 2CF, 2 esc, 4CF, 2 esc, 2CF, 3 esc, 2 FPS, [add 2 esc stitches between the next 2 stitches, B4CB] twice, add 2 esc stitches between the next 2 stitches, 2 FPS, 3 esc, 2CF, 2 esc, 4CF, 2 esc, 2CF, Dec.

Row 65: Chain 2, turn, esc, 2 BPS, 2 esc, 4 BPS, 2 esc, 2 BPS, 3 esc, 2 BPS, [2 esc, 4 BPS] twice, 2 esc, 2 BPS, 3 esc, 2 BPS, 2 esc, 4 BPS, 2 esc, 2 BPS, 3 esc.

Row 66: Chain 2, turn, 3 esc, 2CF, 2 esc, 4CF, 2 esc, 2CF, 3 esc, 2 FPS, 2 esc, 2 FPS, add 2 esc stitches between the next 2 stitches, B4CF, add 2 esc stitches between the next 2 stitches, 2 FPS, 2 esc, 2 FPS, 3 esc, 2CF, 2 esc, 4CF, 2 esc, FPS, Dec in esc and post stitch.

Row 67: Chain 2, turn, esc, BPS, 2 esc, 4 BPS, 2 esc, 2 BPS, 3 esc, 2 BPS, 2 esc, 2 BPS, 2 esc, 4 BPS, 2 esc, 2 BPS, 2 esc, 2 BPS, 3 esc, 2 BPS, 2 esc, 4 BPS, 2 esc, 2 BPS, 3 esc.

Row 68: Chain 2, turn, 3 esc, 2CF, 2 esc, 4CF, 2 esc, 2CF, 3 esc, B4CF, 2 esc, 4 FPS, 2 esc, B4CF, 3 esc, 2CF, 2 esc, 4CF, 2 esc, Dec in esc and post stitch.

Row 69: Chain 2, turn, 3 esc, 4 BPS, 2 esc, 2 BPS, 3 esc, 4 BPS, [2 esc, 4 BPS] twice, 3 esc, 2 BPS, 2 esc, 4 BPS, 2 esc, 2 BPS, 3 esc.

Row 70: Chain 2, turn, 3 esc, 2CF, 2 esc, 4CF, 2 esc, 2CF, 3 esc, [2 FPS, add 2 esc stitches between the next 2 stitches], 2 FPS, 2 esc, B4CF, 2 esc, repeat instructions in [ ] once, 2 FPS, 3 esc, 2CF, 2 esc, 4CF, esc, Dec.

Row 71: Chain 2, turn, 2 esc, 4 BPS, 2 esc, 2 BPS, 3 esc, [2 BPS, 2 esc] twice, 4 BPS, 2 esc, repeat instructions in [ ] once, 2 BPS, 3 esc, 2 BPS, 2 esc, 4 BPS, 2 esc, 2 BPS, 3 esc.

Row 72: Chain 2, turn, 3 esc, 2CF, 2 esc, 4CF, 2 esc, 2CF, 3 esc, 2 FPS, 2 esc, B4CB, add 2 esc stitches between the next 2 stitches, B4CB, 2 esc, 2 FPS, 3 esc, 2CF, 2 esc, 4CF, Dec.

Row 73: Chain 2, turn, esc, 4 BPS, 2 esc, 2 BPS, 3 esc, 2 BPS, [2 esc, 4 BPS] twice, 2 esc, 2 BPS, 3 esc, 2 BPS, 2 esc, 4 BPS, 2 esc, 2 BPS, 3 esc.

Row 74: Chain 2, turn, 3 esc, 2CF, 2 esc, 4CF, 2 esc, 2CF, 3 esc, [B4CF, add 2 esc stitches between the next 2 stitches] twice, B4CF, 3 esc, 2CF, 2 esc, 2CF, FPS, Dec in esc and post stitch.

Row 75: Chain 2, turn, esc, 3 BPS, 2 esc, 2 BPS, 3 esc, 4 BPS, [2 esc, 4 BPS] twice, 3 esc, 2 BPS, 2 esc, 4 BPS, 2 esc, 2 BPS, 3 esc.

Row 76: Chain 2, turn, 3 esc, 2CF, 2 esc, 4CF, 2 esc, 2CF, 3 esc, 2 FPS, [add 2 esc stitches between the next 2 stitches, B4CB] twice, add 2 esc stitches between the next 2 stitches, 2 FPS, 3 esc, 2CF, 2 esc, 2CF, Dec in esc and post stitch.

Row 77: Chain 2, turn, esc, 2 BPS, 2 esc, 2 BPS, 3 esc, 2 BPS, [2 esc, 4 BPS] twice, 2 esc, 2 BPS, 3 esc, 2 BPS, 2 esc, 4 BPS, 2 esc, 2 BPS, 3 esc.

Row 78: Chain 2, turn, 3 esc, 2CF, 2 esc, 4CF, 2 esc, 2CF, 3 esc, 2 FPS, 2 esc, 2 FPS, add 2 esc stitches between the next 2 stitches, B4CF, add 2 esc stitches between the next 2 stitches, 2 FPS, 2 esc, 2 FPS, 3 esc, 2CF, 2 esc, FPS, Dec in esc and post stitch.

Row 79: Chain 2, turn, esc, BPS, 2 esc, 2 BPS, 3 esc, 2 BPS, 2 esc, 2 BPS, 2 esc, 4 BPS, [2 esc, 2 BPS] twice, 3 esc, 2 BPS, 2 esc, 4 BPS, 2 esc, 2 BPS, 3 esc.

Row 80: Chain 2, turn, 3 esc, 2CF, 2 esc, 4CF, 2 esc, 2CF, 3 esc, B4CF, 2 esc, 4 FPS, 2 esc, B4CF, 3 esc, 2CF, 2 esc, Dec in esc and post stitch.

Row 81: Chain 2, turn, esc, BPS, 2 esc, 2 BPS, 3 esc, 4 BPS, [2 esc, 4 BPS] twice, 3 esc, 2 BPS, 2 esc, 4 BPS, 2 esc, 2 BPS, 3 esc.

Row 82: Chain 2, turn, 3 esc, 2CF, 2 esc, 4CF, 2 esc, 2CF, 3 esc, [2 FPS, add 2 esc stitches between the next 2 stitches], 2 FPS, 2 esc, B4CF, 2 esc, repeat instructions in [ ] once, 2 FPS, 3 esc, 2CF, esc, Dec into esc and post stitch.

Row 83: Chain 2, turn, 2 esc, 2 BPS, 3 esc, [2 BPS, 2 esc] twice, 4 BPS, 2 esc, repeat instructions in [ ] once, 2 BPS, 3 esc, 2 BPS, 2 esc, 4 BPS, 2 esc, 2 BPS, 3 esc.

Row 84: Chain 2, turn, 3 esc, 2CF, 2 esc, 4CF, 2 esc, 2CF, 3 esc, 2 FPS, 2 esc, B4CB, add 2 esc stitches between the next 2 stitches, B4CB, 2 esc, 2 FPS, 3 esc, 2CF, Dec.

Row 85: Chain 2, turn, esc, 2 BPS, 3 esc, 2 BPS, [2 esc, 4 BPS] twice, 2 esc, 2 BPS, 3 esc, 2 BPS, 2 esc, 4 BPS, 2 esc, 2 BPS, 3 esc.

Row 86: Chain 2, turn, 3 esc, 2CF, 2 esc, 4CF, 2 esc, 2CF, 3 esc, [B4CF, add 2 esc stitches between the next 2 stitches] twice, B4CF, 3 esc, FPS, Dec in esc and post stitch.

Row 87: Chain 2, turn, esc, BPS, 3 esc, 4 BPS, [2 esc, 4 BPS] twice, 3 esc, 2 BPS, 2 esc, 4 BPS, 2 esc, 2 BPS, 3 esc.

Row 88: Chain 2, turn, 3 esc, 2CF, 2 esc, 4CF, 2 esc, 2CF, 3 esc, 2 FPS, [add 2 esc stitches between the next 2 stitches, B4CB] twice, add 2 esc stitches between the next 2 stitches, 2 FPS, 3 esc, Dec in esc and post stitch.

Row 89: Chain 2, turn, 4 esc, 2 BPS, [2 esc, 4 BPS] twice, 2 esc, 2 BPS, 3 esc, 2 BPS, 2 esc, 4 BPS, 2 esc, 2 BPS, 3 esc.

Row 90: Chain 2, turn, 3 esc, 2CF, 2 esc, 4CF, 2 esc, 2CF, 3 esc, 2 FPS, 2 esc, 2 FPS, add 2 esc stitches between the next 2 stitches, B4CF, add 2 esc stitches between the next 2 stitches, 2 FPS, 2 esc, 2 FPS, 2 esc, Dec.

Row 91: Chain 2, turn, 3 esc, [2 BPS, 2 esc] twice, 4 BPS, [2 esc, 2 BPS] twice, 3 esc, 2 BPS, 2 esc, 4 BPS, 2 esc, 2 BPS, 3 esc.

Row 92: Chain 2, turn, 3 esc, 2CF, 2 esc, 4CF, 2 esc, 2CF, 3 esc, B4CF, 2 esc, 4 FPS, 2 esc, B4CF, esc, Dec.

Row 93: Chain 2, turn, 2 esc, [4 BPS, 2 esc] three times, esc, 2 BPS, 2 esc, 4 BPS, 2 esc, 2 BPS, 3 esc.

Sweater Back Side

Make 1 of the back side of the sweater. The back side consists of two motif patterns, Motif 1 and Motif 2. The row-by-row instructions that follow reference the motif instructions, which begin on page 158. Note: The two motifs have different repeats for the rows. See Charts A and E.

Row 1: Chain 128 (including starting loop), esc in the third chain from hook, and esc across. (126 esc, 1 chain)

Row 2: Chain 2, turn, Motif 1 row 2, Motif 2 row 2, Motif 1 row 2.

Row 3: Chain 2, turn, Motif 1 row 3, Motif 2 row 3, Motif 1 row 3.

Row 4: Chain 2, turn, Motif 1 row 4, Motif 2 row 4, Motif 1 row 4.

Row 5: Chain 2, turn, Motif 1 row 5, Motif 2 row 5, Motif 1 row 5.

Row 6: Chain 2, turn, Motif 1 row 6, Motif 2 row 6, Motif 1 row 6.

Row 7: Chain 2, turn, Motif 1 row 7, Motif 2 row 7, Motif 1 row 7.

Row 8: Chain 2, turn, Motif 1 row 8, Motif 2 row 8, Motif 1 row 8.

Row 9: Chain 2, turn, Motif 1 row 9, Motif 2 row 9, Motif 1 row 9.

Row 10: Chain 2, turn, Motif 1 row 10, Motif 2 row 10, Motif 1 row 10.

Row 11: Chain 2, turn, Motif 1 row 11, Motif 2 row 11, Motif 1 row 11.

Row 12: Chain 2, turn, Motif 1 row 12, Motif 2 row 12, Motif 1 row 12.

Row 13: Chain 2, turn, Motif 1 row 13, Motif 2 row 13, Motif 1 row 13.

Row 14: Chain 2, turn, Motif 1 row 14, Motif 2 row 14, Motif 1 row 14.

Row 15: Chain 2, turn, Motif 1 row 3, Motif 2 row 15, Motif 1 row 3.

Row 16: Chain 2, turn, Motif 1 row 4, Motif 2 row 16, Motif 1 row 4.

Row 17: Chain 2, turn, Motif 1 row 5, Motif 2 row 17, Motif 1 row 5.

Row 18: Chain 2, turn, Motif 1 row 6, Motif 2 row 18, Motif 1 row 6.

Row 19: Chain 2, turn, Motif 1 row 7, Motif 2 row 3, Motif 1 row 7.

Row 20: Chain 2, turn, Motif 1 row 8, Motif 2 row 4, Motif 1 row 8.

Row 21: Chain 2, turn, Motif 1 row 9, Motif 2 row 5, Motif 1 row 9.

Row 22: Chain 2, turn, Motif 1 row 10, Motif 2 row 6, Motif 1 row 10.

Row 23: Chain 2, turn, Motif 1 row 11, Motif 2 row 7, Motif 1 row 11.

Row 24: Chain 2, turn, Motif 1 row 12, Motif 2 row 8, Motif 1 row 12.

Row 25: Chain 2, turn, Motif 1 row 13, Motif 2 row 9, Motif 1 row 13.

Row 26: Chain 2, turn, Motif 1 row 14, Motif 2 row 10, Motif 1 row 14.

Row 27: Chain 2, turn, Motif 1 row 3, Motif 2 row 11, Motif 1 row 3.

Row 28: Chain 2, turn, Motif 1 row 4, Motif 2 row 12, Motif 1 row 4.

Row 29: Chain 2, turn, Motif 1 row 5, Motif 2 row 13, Motif 1 row 5.

Row 30: Chain 2, turn, Motif 1 row 6, Motif 2 row 14, Motif 1 row 6.

Row 31: Chain 2, turn, Motif 1 row 7, Motif 2 row 15, Motif 1 row 7.

Row 32: Chain 2, turn, Motif 1 row 8, Motif 2 row 16, Motif 1 row 8.

Row 33: Chain 2, turn, Motif 1 row 9, Motif 2 row 17, Motif 1 row 9.

Row 34: Chain 2, turn, Motif 1 row 10, Motif 2 row 18, Motif 1 row 10.

Row 35: Chain 2, turn, Motif 1 row 11, Motif 2 row 3, Motif 1 row 11.

Row 36: Chain 2, turn, Motif 1 row 12, Motif 2 row 4, Motif 1 row 12.

Row 37: Chain 2, turn, Motif 1 row 13, Motif 2 row 5, Motif 1 row 13.

Row 38: Chain 2, turn, Motif 1 row 14, Motif 2 row 6, Motif 1 row 14.

Row 39: Chain 2, turn, Motif 1 row 3, Motif 2 row 7, Motif 1 row 3.

Row 40: Chain 2, turn, Motif 1 row 4, Motif 2 row 8, Motif 1 row 4.

Row 41: Chain 2, turn, Motif 1 row 5, Motif 2 row 9, Motif 1 row 5.

Row 42: Chain 2, turn, Motif 1 row 6, Motif 2 row 10, Motif 1 row 6.

Row 43: Chain 2, turn, Motif 1 row 7, Motif 2 row 11, Motif 1 row 7.

Row 44: Chain 2, turn, Motif 1 row 8, Motif 2 row 12, Motif 1 row 8.

Row 45: Chain 2, turn, Motif 1 row 9, Motif 2 row 13, Motif 1 row 9.

Row 46: Chain 2, turn, Motif 1 row 10, Motif 2 row 14, Motif 1 row 10.

Row 47: Chain 2, turn, Motif 1 row 11, Motif 2 row 15, Motif 1 row 11.

Row 48: Chain 2, turn, Motif 1 row 12, Motif 2 row 16, Motif 1 row 12.

Row 49: Chain 2, turn, Motif 1 row 13, Motif 2 row 17, Motif 1 row 13.

Row 50: Chain 2, turn, Motif 1 row 14, Motif 2 row 18, Motif 1 row 14.

Rows 51–68: Repeat Rows 3–20.

Row 69: Chain 2, turn, Dec, esc, [2 BPS, 2 esc, 4 BPS, 2 esc, 2 BPS, 3 esc, 4 BPS, (2 esc, 4 BPS) twice, 3 esc, 2 BPS, 2 esc, 4 BPS, 2 esc, 2 BPS], 3 esc; Motif 2 row 5; 3 esc, repeat instructions in [ ], esc, Dec.

Row 70: Chain 2, turn, 2 esc, [2CF, 2 esc, 4CF, 2 esc, 2CF, 3 esc, (2 FPS, add 2 esc stitches between the next 2 stitches), 2 FPS, 2 esc, B4CF, 2 esc, repeat instructions in ( ), 2 FPS, 3 esc, 2CF, 2 esc, 4CF, 2 esc, 2CF], 3 esc; Motif 2 row 6; 3 esc, repeat instructions in [ ], 2 esc.

Row 71: Chain 2, turn, Dec, [2 BPS, 2 esc, 4 BPS, 2 esc, 2 BPS, 3 esc, 2 BPS, 2 esc, 2 BPS, 2 esc, 4 BPS, (2 esc, 2 BPS) twice, 3 esc, 2 BPS, 2 esc, 4 BPS, 2 esc, 2 BPS], 3 esc; Motif 2 row 7; 3 esc, repeat instructions in [ ], Dec.

Row 72: Chain 2, turn, esc, [2CF, 2 esc, 4CF, 2 esc, 2CF, 3 esc, 2 FPS, 2 esc, B4CB, add 2 esc stitches between the next 2 stitches, B4CB, 2 esc, 2 FPS, 3 esc, 2CF, 2 esc, 4CF, 2 esc, 2CF], 3 esc; Motif 2 row 8; 3 esc, repeat instructions in [ ], esc.

Row 73: Chain 2, turn, esc, [2 BPS, 2 esc, 4 BPS, 2 esc, 2 BPS, 3 esc, 2 BPS, (2 esc, 4 BPS) twice, 2 esc, 2 BPS, 3 esc, 2 BPS, 2 esc, 4 BPS, 2 esc, 2 BPS], 3 esc; Motif 2 row 9; 3 esc, repeat instructions in [ ], esc.

Row 74: Chain 2, turn, esc, [2CF, 2 esc, 4CF, 2 esc, 2CF, 3 esc, (B4CF, add 2 esc stitches between the next 2 stitches) twice, B4CF, 3 esc, 2CF, 2 esc, 4CF, 2 esc, 2CF], 3 esc; Motif 2 row 10; 3 esc, repeat instructions in [ ], esc.

Row 75: Chain 2, turn, esc, [2 BPS, 2 esc, 4 BPS, 2 esc, 2 BPS, 3 esc, 4 BPS, (2 esc, 4 BPS) twice, 3 esc, 2 BPS, 2 esc, 4 BPS, 2 esc, 2 BPS], 3 esc; Motif 2 row 11; 3 esc, repeat instructions in [ ], esc.

Row 76: Chain 2, turn, esc, [2CF, 2 esc, 4CF, 2 esc, 2CF, 3 esc, 2 FPS, (add 2 esc stitches between the next 2 stitches), B4CB, repeat instructions in ( ), B4CB, repeat instructions in ( ), 2 FPS, 3 esc, 2CF, 2 esc, 4CF, 2 esc, 2CF], 3 esc; Motif 2 row 12; 3 esc, repeat instructions in [ ], esc.

Row 77: Chain 2, turn, esc, [2 BPS, 2 esc, 4 BPS, 2 esc, 2 BPS, 3 esc, 2 BPS, (2 esc, 4 BPS) twice, 2 esc, 2 BPS, 3 esc, 2 BPS, 2 esc, 4 BPS, 2 esc, 2 BPS], 3 esc; Motif 2 row 13; 3 esc, repeat instructions in [ ], esc.

Row 78: Chain 2, turn, esc, [2CF, 2 esc, 4CF, 2 esc, 2CF, 3 esc, 2 FPS, 2 esc, 2 FPS, add 2 esc stitches between the next 2 stitches, B4CF, add 2 esc stitches between the next 2 stitches, 2 FPS, 2 esc, 2 FPS, 3 esc, 2CF, 2 esc, 4CF, 2 esc, 2CF], 3 esc; Motif 2 row 14; 3 esc, repeat instructions in [ ], esc.

Row 79: Chain 2, turn, esc, [2 BPS, 2 esc, 4 BPS, 2 esc, 2 BPS, 3 esc, 2 BPS, 2 esc, 2 BPS, 2 esc, 4 BPS, (2 esc, 2 BPS) twice, 3 esc, 2 BPS, 2 esc, 4 BPS, 2 esc, 2 BPS], 3 esc; Motif 2 row 15; 3 esc, repeat instructions in [ ], esc.

Row 80: Chain 2, turn, esc, [2CF, 2 esc, 4CF, 2 esc, 2CF, 3 esc, B4CF, 2 esc, 4 FPS, 2 esc, B4CF, 3 esc, 2CF, 2 esc, 4CF, 2 esc, 2CF], 3 esc; Motif 2 row 16; 3 esc, repeat instructions in [ ], esc.

Row 81: Chain 2, turn, esc, [2 BPS, 2 esc, 4 BPS, 2 esc, 2 BPS, 3 esc, 4 BPS, (2 esc, 4 BPS) twice, 3 esc, 2 BPS, 2 esc, 4 BPS, 2 esc, 2 BPS], 3 esc; Motif 2 row 17; 3 esc, repeat instructions in [ ], esc.

Row 82: Chain 2, turn, esc, [2CF, 2 esc, 4CF, 2 esc, 2CF, 3 esc, (2 FPS, add 2 esc stitches between the next 2 stitches), 2 FPS, 2 esc, B4CF, 2 esc, repeat instructions in ( ) once, 2 FPS, 3 esc, 2CF, 2 esc, 4CF, 2 esc, 2CF], 3 esc; Motif 2 row 18; 3 esc, repeat instructions in [ ], esc.

Row 83: Chain 2, turn, esc, [2 BPS, 2 esc, 4 BPS, 2 esc, 2 BPS, 3 esc, (2 BPS, 2 esc) twice, 4 BPS, 2 esc, repeat instructions in ( ) once, 2 BPS, 3 esc, 2 BPS, 2 esc, 4 BPS, 2 esc, 2 BPS], 3 esc; Motif 2 row 3; 3 esc, repeat instructions in [ ], esc.

Row 84: Chain 2, turn, esc, [2CF, 2 esc, 4CF, 2 esc, 2CF, 3 esc, 2 FPS, 2 esc, B4CB, add 2 esc stitches between the next 2 stitches, B4CB, 2 esc, 2 FPS, 3 esc, 2CF, 2 esc, 4CF, 2 esc, 2CF], 3 esc; Motif 2 row 4; 3 esc, repeat instructions in [ ], esc.

Row 85: Chain 2, turn, esc, [2 BPS, 2 esc, 4 BPS, 2 esc, 2 BPS, 3 esc, 2 BPS, (2 esc, 4 BPS) twice, 2 esc, 2 BPS, 3 esc, 2 BPS, 2 esc, 4 BPS, 2 esc, 2 BPS], 3 esc; Motif 2 row 5; 3 esc, repeat instructions in [ ], esc.

Row 86: Chain 2, turn, esc, [2CF, 2 esc, 4CF, 2 esc, 2CF, 3 esc, (B4CF, add 2 esc stitches between the next 2 stitches) twice, B4CF, 3 esc, 2CF, 2 esc, 4CF, 2 esc, 2CF], 3 esc; Motif 2 row 6; 3 esc, repeat instructions in [ ], esc.

Row 87: Chain 2, turn, esc, [2 BPS, 2 esc, 4 BPS, 2 esc, 2 BPS, 3 esc, 4 BPS, (2 esc, 4 BPS) twice, 3 esc, 2 BPS, 2 esc, 4 BPS, 2 esc, 2 BPS], 3 esc; Motif 2 row 7; 3 esc, repeat instructions in [ ], esc.

Sweater Back Neck Shaping Right Side

This will be the shaping for the neckline on the right side of the sweater back. You will continue the rows from the sweater back but make short rows just on the right side.

Row 88: Chain 2, turn, esc, 2CF, 2 esc, 4CF, 2 esc, 2CF, 3 esc, 2 FPS, [add 2 esc stitches between the next 2 stitches, B4CB] twice, add 2 esc stitches between the next 2 stitches, 2 FPS, esc, Dec.

Sweater Back Neck Shaping Left Side

This will be the shaping for the neckline on the left side of the sweater back. You will cut the yarn from the main body and reattach your yarn on Row 87 thirty-five stitches in from the left side of the sweater back.

Row 88: Chain 2, turn, Dec, esc, 2 FPS, [add 2 esc stitches between the next 2 stitches, B4CB] twice, add 2 esc stitches between the next 2 stitches, 2 FPS, 3 esc, 2CF, 2 esc, 4CF, 2 esc, 2CF, esc.

Row 89: Chain 2, turn, esc, 2 BPS, 2 esc, 4 BPS, 2 esc, 2 BPS, 3 esc, 2 BPS, [2 esc, 4 BPS] twice, 2 esc, 2 BPS, 2 esc.

Row 90: Chain 2, turn, Dec, 2 FPS, 2 esc, 2 FPS, add 2 esc stitches between the next 2 stitches, B4CF, add 2 esc stitches between the next 2 stitches, 2 FPS, 2 esc, 2 FPS, 3 esc, 2CF, 2 esc, 4CF, 2 esc, 2CF, esc.

Row 91: Chain 2, turn, esc, 2 BPS, 2 esc, 4 BPS, 2 esc, 2 BPS, 3 esc, 2 BPS, 2 esc, 2 BPS, 2 esc, 4 BPS, [2 esc, 2 BPS] twice, esc.

Row 92: Chain 2, turn, esc, B4CF, 2 esc, 4 FPS, 2 esc, B4CF, 3 esc, 2CF, 2 esc, 4CF, 2 esc, 2CF, esc.

Row 93: Chain 2, turn, esc, 2 BPS, 2 esc, 4 BPS, 2 esc, 2 BPS, 3 esc, 4 BPS, [2 esc, 4 BPS] twice, esc.

Tie off yarn.

Motif 1 Pattern

Row 2: [3 esc, 2CF, 2 esc, 4CF, 2 esc, 2CF, 3 esc], (4CF, 2 esc) twice, 4CF, repeat instructions in [ ].

Row 3: [3 esc, 2 BPS, 2 esc, 4 BPS, 2 esc, 2 BPS, 3 esc], (4 BPS, 2 esc) twice, 4 BPS, repeat instructions in [ ].

Row 4: [3 esc, 2CF, 2 esc, 4CF, 2 esc, 2CF, 3 esc], 2 FPS, (add 2 esc stitches between the next 2 stitches, B4CB) twice, add 2 esc stitches between the next 2 stitches, 2 FPS, repeat instructions in [ ].

Row 5: [3 esc, 2 BPS, 2 esc, 4 BPS, 2 esc, 2 BPS, 3 esc], 2 BPS, (2 esc, 4 BPS) twice, 2 esc, 2 BPS, repeat instructions in [ ].

Row 89: Chain 2, turn, 2 esc, 2 BPS, [2 esc, 4 BPS] twice, 2 esc, 2 BPS, 3 esc, 2 BPS, 2 esc, 4 BPS, 2 esc, 2 BPS, esc.

Row 90: Chain 2, turn, esc, 2CF, 2 esc, 4CF, 2 esc, 2CF, 3 esc, 2 FPS, 2 esc, 2 FPS, add 2 esc stitches between the next 2 stitches, B4CF, add 2 esc stitches between the next 2 stitches, 2 FPS, 2 esc, 2 FPS, Dec.

Row 91: Chain 2, turn, esc, [2 BPS, 2 esc] twice, 4 BPS, [2 esc, 2 BPS] twice, 3 esc, 2 BPS, 2 esc, 4 BPS, 2 esc, 2 BPS, esc.

Row 92: Chain 2, turn, esc, 2CF, 2 esc, 4CF, 2 esc, 2CF, 3 esc, B4CF, 2 esc, 4 FPS, 2 esc, B4CF, esc.

Row 93: Chain 2, turn, esc, [4 BPS, 2 esc] twice, 4 BPS, 3 esc, 2 BPS, 2 esc, 4 BPS, 2 esc, 2 BPS, esc.

Tie off yarn.

Row 6: [3 esc, 2CF, 2 esc, 4CF, 2 esc, 2CF, 3 esc], 2 FPS, 2 esc, 2 FPS, add 2 esc stitches between the next 2 stitches, B4CF, add 2 esc stitches between the next 2 stitches, 2 FPS, 2 esc, 2 FPS, repeat instructions in [ ].

Row 7: [3 esc, 2 BPS, 2 esc, 4 BPS, 2 esc, 2 BPS, 3 esc], (2 BPS, 2 esc) twice, 4 BPS, (2 esc, 2 BPS) twice, repeat instructions in [ ].

Row 8: [3 esc, 2CF, 2 esc, 4CF, 2 esc, 2CF, 3 esc], B4CF, 2 esc, 4 FPS, 2 esc, B4CF, repeat instructions in [ ].

Row 9: [3 esc, 2 BPS, 2 esc, 4 BPS, 2 esc, 2 BPS, 3 esc], 4 BPS, (2 esc, 4 BPS) twice, repeat instructions in [ ].

Row 10: [3 esc, 2CF, 2 esc, 4CF, 2 esc, 2CF, 3 esc], (2 FPS, add 2 esc stitches between the next 2 stitches), 2 FPS, 2 esc, B4CF, 2 esc, repeat instructions in ( ) once, 2 FPS, repeat instructions in [ ].

Row 11: [3 esc, 2 BPS, 2 esc, 4 BPS, 2 esc, 2 BPS, 3 esc], (2 BPS, 2 esc) twice, 4 BPS, 2 esc, repeat instructions in ( ) once, 2 BPS, repeat instructions in [ ].

Row 12: [3 esc, 2CF, 2 esc, 4CF, 2 esc, 2CF, 3 esc], 2 FPS, 2 esc, B4CB, add 2 esc stitches between the next 2 stitches, B4CB, 2 esc, 2 FPS, repeat instructions in [ ].

Row 13: [3 esc, 2 BPS, 2 esc, 4 BPS, 2 esc, 2 BPS, 3 esc], 2 BPS, (2 esc, 4 BPS) twice, 2 esc, 2 BPS, repeat instructions in [ ].

Row 14: [3 esc, 2CF, 2 esc, 4CF, 2 esc, 2CF, 3 esc], (B4CF, add 2 esc stitches between the next 2 stitches) twice, B4CF, repeat instructions in [ ].

Motif 2 Pattern

Row 2: [4CF, 2 esc] twice, 4CB, 2 esc, 4CB.

Row 3: [4 BPS, 2 esc] three times, 4 BPS.

Row 4: 2 FPS, add 2 esc stitches between the next 2 stitches, B4CF, add 2 esc stitches between the next 2 stitches, B4CF, add 2 esc stitches between the next 2 stitches, B4CB, add 2 esc stitches between the next 2 stitches, 2 FPS.

Row 5: 2 BPS, 2 esc, [4 BPS, 2 esc] three times, 2 BPS.

Row 6: [B4CF, add 2 esc stitches between the next 2 stitches] twice, B4CB, add 2 esc stitches between the next 2 stitches, B4CB.

Row 7: Repeat Row 3.

Row 8: Repeat Row 4.

Row 9: Repeat Row 5.

Row 10: [B4CB, add 2 esc stitches between the next 2 stitches] twice, B4CF, add 2 esc stitches between the next 2 stitches, B4CF.

Row 11: Repeat Row 3.

Row 12: 2 FPS, add 2 esc stitches between the next 2 stitches, B4CB, add 2 esc stitches between the next 2 stitches, B4CB, add 2 esc stitches between the next 2 stitches, B4CF, add 2 esc stitches between the next 2 stitches, 2 FPS.

Row 13: Repeat Row 5.

Row 14: Repeat Row 10.

Row 15: Repeat Row 3.

Row 16: Repeat Row 12.

Row 17: Repeat Row 5.

Row 18: Repeat Row 6.

Sweater Sleeves

Make two sweater sleeves. Note that these sleeves are worked flat and then joined by sewing a seam on the underside of the sleeve.

Row 1: Chain 41 (including starting loop), esc in the third chain from hook, and esc across. (39 esc, 1 chain)

Row 2: Chain 2, turn, [FPS, BPS] 19 times, FPS.

Row 3: Chain 2, turn, BPS, [FPS, BPS] 19 times.

Row 4: Chain 2, turn, esc 38 times, esc twice in the next stitch.

Row 11: Chain 2, turn, esc in each esc stitch, 2CF in first two post stitches, 2 esc, 4CF in 4 post stitches, 2 esc, 2CF in last two post stitches, esc in each esc stitch.

Row 12: Chain 2, turn, esc in each esc stitch, 2 BPS in 2CF stitch, 2 esc, 4 BPS in 4CF stitch, 2 esc, 2 BPS in 2CF stitch, esc in each esc stitch.

Rows 13–60: Repeat Rows 9–12 twelve times.

Row 61: Chain 2, turn, esc in each esc stitch, 2CF in post stitches, 2 esc, 4CF, 2 esc, 2CF in post stitches, esc in each esc stitch.

Row 62: Chain 2, turn, esc in each esc stitch, 2 BPS in 2CF stitch, 2 esc, 4 BPS in 4CF stitch, 2 esc, 2 BPS in 2CF stitch, esc in each esc stitch.

Row 63: Chain 2, turn, esc in each esc stitch, 2CF in first two post stitches, 2 esc, 4CF in 4 post stitches, 2 esc, 2CF in last two post stitches, esc in each esc stitch.

Row 64: Chain 2, turn, esc in each esc stitch, 2 BPS in 2CF, 2 esc, 4 BPS in 4CF, 2 esc, 2 BPS in 2CF, esc in each esc stitch.

Rows 65–92: Repeat Rows 61–64 seven times.

Row 93: Chain 2, turn, Dec, 26 esc, 2CF, 2 esc, 4CF, 2 esc, 2CF, 26 esc, Dec.

Row 94: Chain 2, turn, Dec, 25 esc, 2 BPS, 2 esc, 4 BPS, 2 esc, 2 BPS, 25 esc, Dec.

Row 95: Chain 2, turn, Dec, 24 esc, 2CF, 2 esc, 4CF, 2 esc, 2CF, 24 esc, Dec.

Row 96: Chain 2, turn, Dec, 23 esc, 2 BPS, 2 esc, 4 BPS, 2 esc, 2 BPS, 23 esc, Dec.

Row 97: Chain 2, turn, 2 Dec, 20 esc, 2CF, 2 esc, 4CF, 2 esc, 2CF, 20 esc, 2 Dec.

Row 98: Chain 2, turn, 2 Dec, 18 esc, 2 BPS, 2 esc, 4 BPS, 2 esc, 2 BPS, 18 esc, 2 Dec.

Row 99: Chain 2, turn, 2 Dec, 16 esc, 2CF, 2 esc, 4CF, 2 esc, 2CF, 16 esc, 2 Dec.

Row 100: Chain 2, turn, 2 Dec, 14 esc, 2 BPS, 2 esc, 4 BPS, 2 esc, 2 BPS, 14 esc, 2 Dec.

Row 5: Chain 2, turn, esc twice in the next stitch, 13 esc, 2CF, 2 esc, 4CF, 2 esc, 2CF, 13 esc, esc twice in the next stitch.

Row 6: Chain 2, turn, 15 esc, 2 BPS, 2 esc, 4 BPS, 2 esc, 2 BPS, 15 esc.

Row 7: Chain 2, turn, 15 esc, 2CF, 2 esc, 4CF, 2 esc, 2CF, 15 esc.

Row 8: Chain 2, turn, 15 esc, 2 BPS, 2 esc, 4 BPS, 2 esc, 2 BPS, 15 esc.

Row 9: Chain 2, turn, esc twice in the next stitch, esc in remaining esc stitches, 2CF in post stitches, 2 esc, 4CF, 2 esc, 2CF in post stitches, esc in remaining esc stitches except for one, esc twice in the last stitch.

Row 10: Chain 2, turn, esc in each esc stitch, 2 BPS in 2CF stitch, 2 esc, 4 BPS in 4CF stitch, 2 esc, 2 BPS in 2CF stitch, esc in each esc stitch.

Row 101: Chain 2, turn, 3 Dec, 10 esc, 2CF, 2 esc, 4CF, 2 esc, 2CF, 10 esc, 3 Dec.

Row 102: Chain 2, turn, 3 Dec, 7 esc, 2 BPS, 2 esc, 4 BPS, 2 esc, 2 BPS, 7 esc, 3 Dec.

Row 103: Chain 2, turn, 3 Dec, 4 esc, 2CF, 2 esc, 4CF, 2 esc, 2CF, 4 esc, 3 Dec.

Row 104: Chain 2, turn, 3 Dec, esc, 2 BPS, 2 esc, 4 BPS, 2 esc, 2 BPS, esc, 3 Dec.

Row 105: Chain 2, turn, 2 Dec, 2CF, 2 esc, 4CF, 2 esc, 2CF, 2 Dec.

Row 106: Chain 2, turn, Dec, 2 BPS, 2 esc, 4 BPS, 2 esc, 2 BPS, Dec.

Tie off yarn.

Sweater Assembly Instructions

Place the two sweater fronts on top of the sweater back (front sides of the two sweater fronts facing the front side of the sweater back—i.e., the sweater is inside out) and either sew with a tapestry needle or single crochet join* the two pieces of fabric together on the left and right seam between the sweater fronts and sweater back. Tie off yarn. Repeat on other side of sweater.

Now join the shoulders by attaching the yarn to the top of the shoulders of the sweater front (left or right side) and sweater back, and then sew or crochet join the two pieces of fabric together. Tie off yarn. Repeat on the other shoulder of the sweater. You should now have an inside-out sweater vest; reverse the orientation to right-side-out. If possible, try it on and check the fit.

Join the sweater sleeves to themselves so that they form a cylinder or tube. You can join the sleeves by folding them in half widthwise and then joining the edges from the wrist to the shoulder. Leave the shoulder open for attaching to the sweater vest.

Join the sleeves to the sweater by placing the sweater vest inside out and aligning the inside-out sweater sleeve on the side. If useful, you can pin the sleeve to the sweater vest arm opening to make sure you join the two evenly around the shoulder opening. Join the sweater sleeve to the sweater vest. Perform the sleeve joining on the other sleeve.

Turn the sweater right side out. You should now have a sweater, which is only missing the Waistband and Neckline (button band) edging.

Sweater Edging: Neckline Edging

These instructions add the button band and neckline to the sweater. Attach your yarn at a left or right edge/corner of the sweater at the bottom, and crochet up the front left side, across the neckline of the back side, and down the right front side for the first row of the edging. Then you will turn and crochet back across the previous row of the edging.

Row 1: Chain 2, turn, esc in each stitch.

Rows 2–5: Repeat Row 1 four times.

Tie off yarn.

Sweater Edging: Waistband Edging

These instructions add the ribbed waistband at the bottom of the sweater. Attach your yarn at a left or right edge of the neckline edging of the sweater at the bottom.

Row 1: Chain 3, esc in each stitch.

Row 2: Chain 2, turn, [FPS, BPS], repeat instructions in [ ] around the sweater bottom.

Rows 3–7: Repeat Row 2 five times.

Tie off yarn.

Add decorative buttons in desired locations along the neckline edging.

---

*   A crochet join is an extended single crochet stitch made through the two fabrics at the same time. Simply insert your hook through both fabrics, yarn over, and pull through. Then perform a regular esc stitch.

Crochet Patterns with Color Gradient Yarns

This chapter focuses on yarns that have continuous and extended color gradients. In Chapter 5 we discussed the best use of brightness and hue gradients in crochet projects, such as how to choose gradients that can showcase texture. However, in addition to color considerations with gradients, there are practical concerns for using gradient yarn. With color gradient yarn, you must be careful when you join skeins so that they are at a similar point in the color gradient and therefore the color shift will look continuous in your project. In addition, if you are making a project with one long skein of yarn, you must be careful to fit the size of the project to the length of yarn in the skein. We will address each of these practical issues in the patterns included in this chapter, which include a cable scarf pattern and a throw blanket pattern.

As with all the patterns in this book, my comments on the multicolored yarn used in each pattern are in Chapter 6. These comments focus on the yarn's brightness variation and suitability for textured projects. In addition, Chapter 6 has an image of the swatch (or skein) of the yarn used in both color and black and white. For stitch descriptions, additional pattern instructions, and notes, refer to Chapter 7.

Archil Scarf (Unisex, Intermediate)

Materials

2 skeins of Freia Fine Handpaints Ombre Merino Lace in Flare 19-1 (712 yd./651 m per skein and 2.64 oz./75 g net weight per skein; 100% US Merino wool; #0 lace weight (yarn doubled)

Hook

US size 7 (4.5 mm) crochet hook (7)

Dimensions

3.25 in. (8.3 cm) wide by 104.5 in. (265.4 cm) long

Gauge

Gauge is not critical for this project. Swatch with your chosen yarn and adjust hook size to achieve your desired drape.

Crochet Stitch Video Tutorials

4-Cross Front Cable Stitch (4CF):

 "Four Cross Front Crochet Cable Stitch Tutorial," https://www.youtube.com/watch?v=rzuMC6mB68w&t=1s

4-Cross Back Cable Stitch (4CB):

 "Four Cross Back Crochet Cable Stitch Tutorial," https://www.youtube.com/watch?v=EGBMJaXAcEQ&t=35s

Stitch Diagram

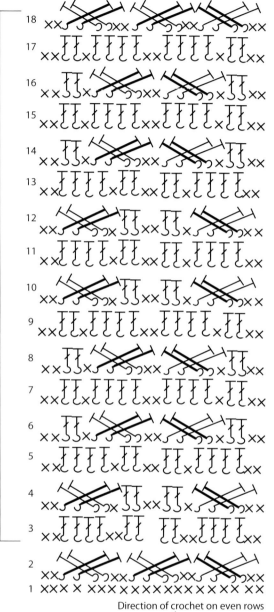

Repeat this section

Direction of crochet on even rows

4CF 4CB

Note: Bold stitches are in front of other stitches
All post stitches in the cables are treble post stitches

⌶ Front Post Double Crochet

⊥ Back Post Double Crochet

✕ Extended Single Crochet

INSTRUCTIONS

Gradient Notes: This scarf is relatively long and narrow. Therefore, I recommend that you make the scarf with as many full repeats as possible with one long gradient skein of yarn. In other words, make the scarf pattern until you run out of yarn. Then frog or rip the scarf back to the last repeat that you finished, cut the yarn there, and tie off the yarn. Don't worry about whether your scarf is shorter than the example scarf; the example scarf made from this pattern is unusually long. This approach will allow you to use as much of the full color gradient as possible with the scarf design.

Tassel Notes: If you would like to add tassels to the scarf (I did not), I recommend cutting the tassels from the beginning of your gradient skein (before you start) and from the end of your gradient skein (leave extra yarn at the end of the skein when you tie off the scarf). If you use this approach, the tassels' color will look close to continuous with the color gradient of the scarf itself.

Row 1: Chain 22 (including starting loop), esc in the third chain from hook, and esc across. (20 esc, 1 chain)

Row 2: Chain 2, turn, 2 esc, 4CF, [2 esc, 4CB] twice, 2 esc.

Row 3: Chain 2, turn, [2 esc, 4 BPS] three times, 2 esc.

Row 4: Chain 2, turn, 2 esc, 4CF, skip a stitch, esc, 2 FPS, add 2 esc stitches between the next 2 stitches, 2 FPS, skip a stitch, esc, 4CB, 2 esc.

Row 5: Chain 2, turn, 2 esc, 4 BPS, esc, 2 BPS, 2 esc, 2 BPS, esc, 4 BPS, 2 esc.

Row 6: Chain 2, turn, 2 esc, 2 FPS, add 1 esc stitch between the next 2 stitches, B4CF, 2 esc, B4CB, add 1 esc stitch between the next 2 stitches, 2 FPS, 2 esc.

Row 7: Chain 2, turn, 2 esc, 2 BPS, esc, 4 BPS, 2 esc, 4 BPS, esc, 2 BPS, 2 esc.

Row 8: Chain 2, turn, 2 esc, 2 FPS, esc, 4CF, 2 esc, 4CB, esc, 2 FPS, 2 esc.

Row 9: Repeat Row 7.

Row 10: Chain 2, turn, 2 esc, B4CF, add 1 esc stitch between the next 2 stitches, 2 FPS, 2 esc, 2 FPS, add 1 esc stitch between the next 2 stitches, B4CB, 2 esc.

Row 11: Repeat Row 5.

Row 12: Chain 2, turn, 2 esc, 4CF, esc, 2 FPS, 2 esc, 2 FPS, esc, 4CB, 2 esc.

Row 13: Repeat Row 5.

Rows 14–17: Repeat Rows 6–9.

Row 18: Chain 2, turn, 2 esc, B4CF, [add 2 esc stitches between the next 2 stitches, B4CB] twice, 2 esc.

Rows 19–370: Repeat Rows 3–18 twenty-two times.

Row 371: Repeat Row 3.

Tie off yarn.

Weave in any loose yarn ends.

Tyrian Purple Blanket (Intermediate)

Materials

4 skeins of Scheepjes Whirl in Lemon Cassis Cream 765 (1093.6 yd./1000 m per skein and 7.8 oz./215 g net weight per skein; 60% cotton and 40% acrylic; #1 super fine weight) (yarn doubled)

Hook

US size H-8 (5.0 mm) crochet hook

Dimensions

36 in. (91.4 cm) wide by 39 in. (99.1 cm) long (including lace edging)

Stitch Diagram

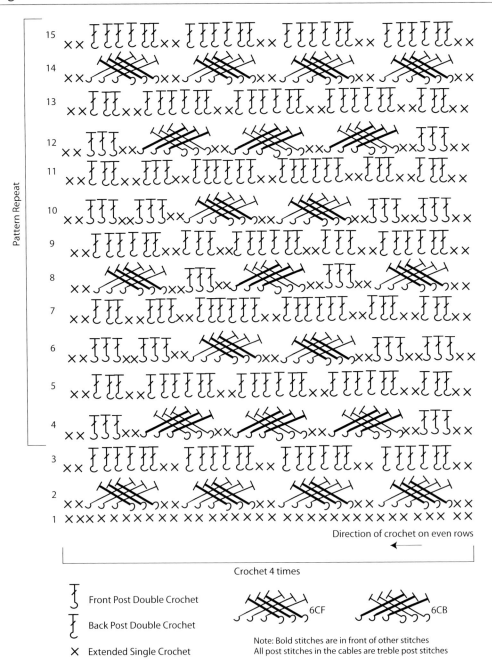

Pattern Repeat

Direction of crochet on even rows

Crochet 4 times

⊥ Front Post Double Crochet

⊥ Back Post Double Crochet

X Extended Single Crochet

6CF

6CB

Note: Bold stitches are in front of other stitches
All post stitches in the cables are treble post stitches

Gauge

7 esc stitches x 7 esc rows = 2 in. x 2 in. (5.1 cm x 5.1 cm)

Crochet Stitch Video Tutorials

 *6-Cross Front Cable Stitch* (6CF): "Six Cross Front Crochet Cable Stitch Tutorial," https://www.youtube.com/watch?v=znjRYYXoRXY

 6-Cross Back Cable Stitch (6CB): "Six Cross Back Crochet Cable Stitch Tutorial," https://www.youtube.com/watch?v=Ldx84gbKVKA&t=1s

Gradient Yarn Notes

To make the color gradient effect, work the blanket instructions until you are halfway through the length of the blanket (if half of the blanket does not finish a whole skein of yarn, put any extra yarn aside). Then tie off your yarn (the first two skeins) and pick up the third and fourth gradient yarn skeins at the same point in the color gradient as you left off with the first two skeins, but now going backward through the color changes you just made. For example, for the yarn used in the sample blanket, the color progression is from magenta to blue to yellow for the first and second skeins. Then the yarn is tied off, and you progress backward in the color progression (using the third and fourth skeins) from yellow to blue to magenta. This means that if you started at the center of the yarn in the first and second skein, the third and fourth skeins will be started from the edge, with any extra yarn removed from the outside. This extra yarn will be used in the lace border. Unravel these parts of the skeins, and then set this extra yarn aside. Finish the blanket center with the third and fourth skeins. When you reach the full number of pattern repeats, tie off your project. You should now have a color gradient that is a mirror image of itself—that is,

magenta to yellow, and then yellow back to magenta (see project image).

For the border around the blanket, you can now use two of the four remaining partial skeins. Start with the lighter of the two ends of the remaining gradient (in this case, the yellow) and crochet until you finish the lace border instructions.

INSTRUCTIONS

Blanket Body

Row 1: Chain 138 (including starting loop), esc in the third chain from hook, and esc across. (136 esc, 1 chain)

Row 2: Chain 2, turn, {[2 esc, 6CF] four times, 2 esc} four times.

Row 3: Chain 2, turn, {[2 esc, 6 BPS] four times, 2 esc} four times.

Row 4: Chain 2, turn, {2 esc, 3 FPS, [add 2 esc between the next 2 stitches, B6CB] three times, add 2 esc between the next 2 stitches, 3 FPS, 2 esc} four times.

Row 5: Chain 2, turn, {2 esc, 3 BPS, [2 esc, 6 BPS] three times, 2 esc, 3 BPS, 2 esc} four times.

Row 6: Chain 2, turn, {[2 esc, 3 FPS] twice, [add 2 esc between the next 2 stitches, B6CF] twice, add 2 esc between the next 2 stitches, (3 FPS, 2 esc) twice} four times.

Row 7: Chain 2, turn, {[2 esc, 3 BPS] three times, 3 BPS, 2 esc, 6 BPS, repeat instructions between [ ] twice, 2 esc} four times.

Row 8: Chain 2, turn, {2 esc, B6CF, 2 esc, 3 FPS, add 2 esc between the next 2 stitches, B6CB, add 2 esc between the next 2 stitches, 3 FPS, 2 esc, B6CF, 2 esc} four times.

Row 9: Chain 2, turn, {2 esc, 6 BPS, 2 esc, 3 BPS, 2 esc, 6 BPS, 2 esc, 3 BPS, 2 esc, 6 BPS, 2 esc} four times.

Row 10: Chain 2, turn, {2 esc, 3 FPS, add 2 esc between the next 2 stitches, 3 FPS, 2 esc, B6CF, add 2 esc between the next 2 stitches, B6CF, 2 esc, 3 FPS, add 2 esc between the next 2 stitches, 3 FPS, 2 esc} four times.

Row 11: Chain 2, turn, {[2 esc, 3 BPS] twice, [2 esc, 6 BPS] twice, [2 esc, 3 BPS] twice, 2 esc} four times.

Row 12: Chain 2, turn, {2 esc, 3 FPS, 2 esc, [B6CB, add 2 esc between the next 2 stitches] twice, B6CB, 2 esc, 3 FPS, 2 esc} four times.

Row 13: Chain 2, turn, {2 esc, 3 BPS, 2 esc, [6 BPS, 2 esc] three times, 3 BPS, 2 esc} four times.

Row 14: Chain 2, turn, {2 esc, [B6CF, add 2 esc between the next 2 stitches] three times, B6CF, 2 esc} four times.

Row 15: Repeat Row 3.

Rows 16–51: Repeat Rows 4–15 three times.

This is the halfway point. Make sure to change your yarn to follow the gradient instructions above.

Rows 52–99: Repeat Rows 4–15 four times.

Tie off yarn.

Weave in any loose yarn ends.

Blanket Border Pattern

This blanket border is a shell stitch border (Rounds 1–5), edged with a clover stitch (Rounds 6 and 7).

Round 1: Attach yarn to the edge of the blanket, chain 2 and then esc evenly around the blanket border. Slip stitch with beginning chain.

Round 2: Chain 2, [shell stitch, skip 4 stitches], repeat instructions in [ ] all the way around the blanket border. Slip stitch with beginning chain.

Round 3: Chain 2, shell stitch in the chain 3 space of each shell stitch of the previous round. Slip stitch with beginning chain.

Round 4: Repeat Round 3.

Round 5: Chain 2, [shell stitch in the chain 3 space of each shell stitch of the previous round, until you reach the 3 shell stitches centered on the next blanket corner; in each of the 3 shell stitches on the blanket corner: make a large shell stitch in the next chain 3 space of a shell stitch], repeat instructions in [ ] three times. Slip stitch with beginning chain.

Round 6: Chain 10, slip stitch with the sixth chain from the hook. Then chain 4. Skip the next shell stitch, and then sc (Note: This sc is between the first and second shell stitch). [Chain 8, slip stitch in the fifth chain from the hook. Chain 4. Skip the next shell stitch and then sc.] Repeat instructions in [ ] around the blanket border. Slip stitch with beginning chain.

Round 7: Chain 3, {[in the next picot loop of the previous round (this is the loop generated when you slip-stitched in the first long chain) make a clover stitch, dc in the next esc], repeat instructions in [ ] until you reach the 3 picot loops (one for each shell stitch in Round 5) centered on the next blanket corner. In each of the 3 stitch repeats on the blanket corner perform the following stitches: chain 2, in the next picot loop of the previous round make a clover stitch, chain 2, dc in the next sc}. Repeat instructions in { } three times. Slip stitch with the beginning chain.

Tie off yarn.

Weave in any loose yarn ends.

12 Crochet Patterns with Stranded Colorwork

In this chapter the methods for utilizing both a solid and a multicolored yarn to make a crocheted item will be explained and explored. Colorwork with multicolored yarn is the most straightforward when only one of the yarns has color variegation, which is the approach we take in these patterns. However, as you gain confidence in color choice and yarn selection, you can combine multiple multicolored yarns to make a symphony of color. For tips and considerations related to crochet textured colorwork, read Chapter 5.

As with all of the patterns in this book, my comments on the multicolored yarn used in each pattern can be found in Chapter 6. These comments focus on the yarn's brightness variation and suitability for textured projects. In addition, Chapter 6 includes an image of the swatch (or skein) of the yarn used in both color and black and white. For stitch descriptions, additional pattern instructions, and notes, refer to Chapter 7.

Orpiment Shawl (Unisex, Experienced)

Materials

- 2 skeins of Spincycle Yarns Dyed in the Wool in Salty Dog (200 yd./182.9 m per skein, and 1.8 oz./50 g net weight per skein; 100% superwash American wool; #2 fine weight)
- 4 skeins of WeCrochet Stroll in Peapod (231 yd./211.2 m per skein and 1.8 oz./50 g net weight per skein; 75% fine superwash Merino wool and 25% nylon; #1 super fine weight)

Hook

US size F-5 (3.75 mm) crochet hook

Dimensions

34 in. (86.4 cm) wide by 43.5 in. (110.5 cm) long

Gauge

11 esc stitches x 11 esc rows = 2 in. x 2 in. (5.1 cm x 5.1 cm) in WeCrochet Stroll

Crochet Stitch Video Tutorials

 4-Cross Front Cable Stitch (4CF): "Four Cross Front Crochet Cable Stitch Tutorial," https://www.youtube.com/watch?v=rzuMC6mB68w&t=1s

 4-Cross Back Cable Stitch (4CB): "Four Cross Back Crochet Cable Stitch Tutorial," https://www.youtube.com/watch?v=EGBMJaXAcEQ&t=35s

Stitch Diagram

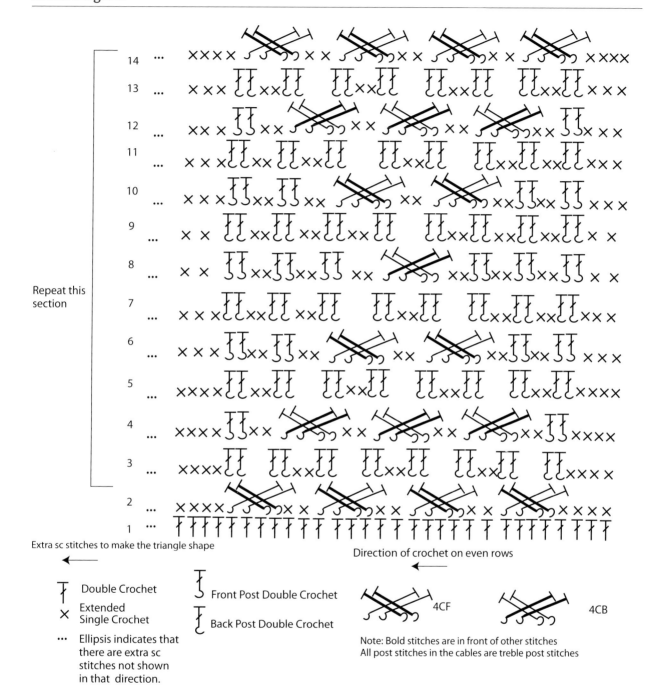

Repeat this section

Extra sc stitches to make the triangle shape

◄

Direction of crochet on even rows

◄

Double Crochet

✗ Extended Single Crochet

… Ellipsis indicates that there are extra sc stitches not shown in that direction.

Front Post Double Crochet

Back Post Double Crochet

4CF

4CB

Note: Bold stitches are in front of other stitches
All post stitches in the cables are treble post stitches

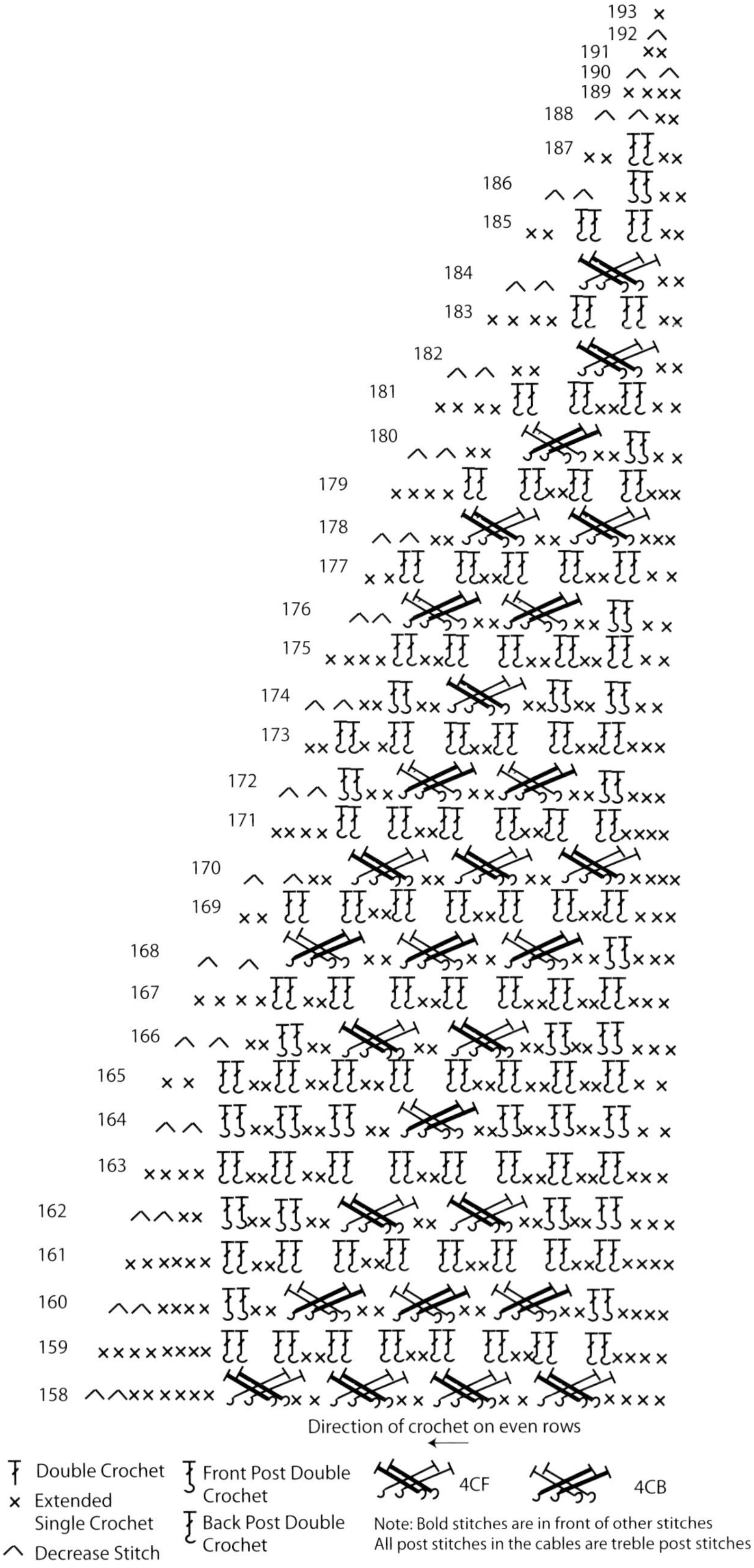

The chart shows rows numbered 158 through 193 (even rows on the left and odd rows indicated) with crochet stitch symbols.

Row numbers visible: 193, 192, 191, 190, 189, 188, 187, 186, 185, 184, 183, 182, 181, 180, 179, 178, 177, 176, 175, 174, 173, 172, 171, 170, 169, 168, 167, 166, 165, 164, 163, 162, 161, 160, 159, 158

← Direction of crochet on even rows

Legend:

⊤	Double Crochet
×	Extended Single Crochet
∧	Decrease Stitch
Front Post Double Crochet	
Back Post Double Crochet	

4CF   4CB

Note: Bold stitches are in front of other stitches
All post stitches in the cables are treble post stitches

INSTRUCTIONS

The blue text in the following instructions indicates all of the stitches used to make the cable pattern on the right edge of the shawl. All of the stitches in blue for Rows 1–158 are diagrammed in the first stitch diagram of this pattern on page 175. The black stitches (following the blue cable stitches) detail the esc stitches that generate the triangle shape of the shawl (represented by ". . ." in the cable pattern diagram). These extra esc stitches decrease in number (or total width) in each row. When you reach Row 166, the extra esc stitches have now decreased to zero, and the decreasing triangle shape impinges on the cable itself. For Rows 158–193 (the decreasing cable portion), the second cable diagram on this page can be used.

The colorwork portion of the shawl is entirely described by the blue text sections (the cable pattern). The multi-colored yarn is used to make the post stitches and cable stitches, and the solid yarn is used to make the esc stitches between the cables. To help distinguish these two stitch types, the stitches that use the multicolored yarn are included in bold type, while the stitches that use the regular yarn are listed in regular type.

Row 1: Chain 195 (including the starting loop), dc in fourth chain from hook, and dc across. (192 dc, 1 chain)

Row 2: Chain 2, turn, 4 esc, [**4CF**, 2 esc] 4 times, 2 esc, 158 esc, Dec twice.

Row 3: Chain 2, turn, 160 esc, 4 esc, [**4 BPS**, 2 esc] 4 times, 2 esc.

Row 4: Chain 2, turn, 4 esc, **2 FPS**, [add 2 esc stitches between the next 2 stitches, **B4CB**] 3 times, add 2 esc stitches between the next 2 stitches, **2 FPS**, 4 esc, 156 esc, Dec twice.

Row 5: Chain 2, turn, 158 esc, 4 esc, **2 BPS**, [2 esc, **4 BPS**] 3 times, 2 esc, **2 BPS**, 4 esc.

Row 6: Chain 2, turn, 3 esc, skip an esc stitch, **2 FPS**, 2 sc, **2 FPS**, [add 2 esc stitches between the next 2 stitches, **B4CF**] twice, add 2 esc stitches between the next 2 stitches, **2 FPS**, 2 esc, **2 FPS**, skip an esc stitch, 3 esc, 154 esc, Dec twice.

Row 7: Chain 2, turn, 156 esc, 3 esc, **2 BPS,** 2 esc, **2 BPS,** [2 esc, **4 BPS**] twice, 2 esc, **2 BPS**, 2 esc, **2 BPS**, 3 esc.

Row 8: Chain 2, turn, 2 esc, skip an esc stitch, [**2 FPS**, 2 esc, **2 FPS,** 2 esc, **2 FPS**], add 2 esc stitches between the next 2 stitches, **B4CB**, add 2 esc stitches between the next 2 stitches, repeat instructions in [ ] once, skip an esc stitch, 2 esc, esc 152 times, Dec twice.

Row 9: Chain 2, turn, 154 esc, 2 esc, [**2 BPS**, 2 esc, **2 BPS**, 2 esc, **2 BPS**], 2 esc, **4 BPS**, 2 esc, repeat instructions in [ ] once, 2 esc.

Row 10: Chain 2, turn, esc, esc twice in the next stitch, **2 FPS**, 2 esc, **2 FPS**, 2 esc, **B4CF**, add 2 esc stitches between the next 2 stitches, **B4CF**, 2 esc, **2 FPS**, 2 esc, **2 FPS**, esc twice in the next stitch, esc, 150 esc, Dec twice.

Row 11: Chain 2, turn, 152 esc, 3 esc, **2 BPS**, 2 esc, **2 BPS**, 2 esc, **4 BPS**, 2 esc, **4 BPS**, 2 esc, **2 BPS**, 2 esc, **2 BPS**, 3 esc.

Row 12: Chain 2, turn, 3 esc, **2 FPS**, 2 esc, [**B4CB**, add 2 esc stitches between the next 2 stitches] twice, **B4CB**, 2 esc, **2 FPS**, 3 esc, esc 148 times, Dec twice.

Row 13: Chain 2, turn, 150 esc, 3 esc, **2 BPS**, 2 esc, [**4 BPS**, 2 esc] three times, **2 BPS**, 3 esc.

Row 14: Chain 2, turn, 2 esc, esc twice in the next stitch, [**B4CF**, add 2 esc stitches between the next 2 stitches] three times, **B4CF**, esc twice in the next stitch, 2 esc, 146 esc, Dec twice.

The next 144 rows (Rows 15–158) will repeat the cable pattern (stitches in blue for each row) twelve times (12 rows x 12 repeats = 144 rows), but gradually decrease the single crochets at the end of each even row (and beginning of each odd row). Every other row decreases the number of stitches by 2 (effectively an average decrease of 1 stitch per row). Therefore, as described in each row below, perform the stitches in blue for the referenced Rows 3–14 and ignore the stitches in black for that referenced row (Rows 3–14).

Row 15: Chain 2, turn, 148 esc, repeat Row 3 stitches in blue.

Row 16: Chain 2, turn, repeat Row 4 stitches in blue, 144 esc, Dec twice.

Row 17: Chain 2, turn, 146 esc, repeat Row 5 stitches in blue.

Row 18: Chain 2, turn, repeat Row 6 stitches in blue, 142 esc, Dec twice.

Row 19: Chain 2, turn, 144 esc, repeat Row 7 stitches in blue.

Row 20: Chain 2, turn, repeat Row 8 stitches in blue, 140 esc, Dec twice.

Row 21: Chain 2, turn, 142 esc, repeat Row 9 stitches in blue.

Row 22: Chain 2, turn, repeat Row 10 stitches in blue, 138 esc, Dec twice.

Row 23: Chain 2, turn, 140 esc, repeat Row 11 stitches in blue.

Row 24: Chain 2, turn, repeat Row 12 stitches in blue, 136 esc, Dec twice.

Row 25: Chain 2, turn, 138 esc, repeat Row 13 stitches in blue.

Row 26: Chain 2, turn, repeat Row 14 stitches in blue, 134 esc, Dec twice.

Row 27: Chain 2, turn, 136 esc, repeat Row 3 stitches in blue.

Row 28: Chain 2, turn, repeat Row 4 stitches in blue, 132 esc, Dec twice.

Row 29: Chain 2, turn, 134 esc, repeat Row 5 stitches in blue.

Row 30: Chain 2, turn, repeat Row 6 stitches in blue, 130 esc, Dec twice.

Row 31: Chain 2, turn, 132 esc, repeat Row 7 stitches in blue.

Row 32: Chain 2, turn, repeat Row 8 stitches in blue, 128 esc, Dec twice.

Row 33: Chain 2, turn, 130 esc, repeat Row 9 stitches in blue.

Row 34: Chain 2, turn, repeat Row 10 stitches in blue, 126 esc, Dec twice.

Row 35: Chain 2, turn, 128 esc, repeat Row 11 stitches in blue.

Row 36: Chain 2, turn, repeat Row 12 stitches in blue, 124 esc, Dec twice.

Row 37: Chain 2, turn, 126 esc, repeat Row 13 stitches in blue.

Row 38: Chain 2, turn, repeat Row 14 stitches in blue, 122 esc, Dec twice.

Row 39: Chain 2, turn, 124 esc, repeat Row 3 stitches in blue.

Row 40: Chain 2, turn, repeat Row 4 stitches in blue, 120 esc, Dec twice.

Row 41: Chain 2, turn, 122 esc, repeat Row 5 stitches in blue.

Row 42: Chain 2, turn, repeat Row 6 stitches in blue, 118 esc, Dec twice.

Row 43: Chain 2, turn, 120 esc, repeat Row 7 stitches in blue.

Row 44: Chain 2, turn, repeat Row 8 stitches in blue, 116 esc, Dec twice.

Row 45: Chain 2, turn, 118 esc, repeat Row 9 stitches in blue.

Row 46: Chain 2, turn, repeat Row 10 stitches in blue, 114 esc, Dec twice.

Row 47: Chain 2, turn, 116 esc, repeat Row 11 stitches in blue.

Row 48: Chain 2, turn, repeat Row 12 stitches in blue, 112 esc, Dec twice.

Row 49: Chain 2, turn, 114 esc, repeat Row 13 stitches in blue.

Row 50: Chain 2, turn, repeat Row 14 stitches in blue, 110 esc, Dec twice.

Row 51: Chain 2, turn, 112 esc, repeat Row 3 stitches in blue.

Row 52: Chain 2, turn, repeat Row 4 stitches in blue, 108 esc, Dec twice.

Row 53: Chain 2, turn, 110 esc, repeat Row 5 stitches in blue.

Row 54: Chain 2, turn, repeat Row 6 stitches in blue, 106 esc, Dec twice.

Row 55: Chain 2, turn, 108 esc, repeat Row 7 stitches in blue.

Row 56: Chain 2, turn, repeat Row 8 stitches in blue, 104 esc, Dec twice.

Row 57: Chain 2, turn, 106 esc, repeat Row 9 stitches in blue.

Row 58: Chain 2, turn, repeat Row 10 stitches in blue, 102 esc, Dec twice.

Row 59: Chain 2, turn, 104 esc, repeat Row 11 stitches in blue.

Row 60: Chain 2, turn, repeat Row 12 stitches in blue, 100 esc, Dec twice.

Row 61: Chain 2, turn, 102 esc, repeat Row 13 stitches in blue.

Row 62: Chain 2, turn, repeat Row 14 stitches in blue, 98 esc, Dec twice.

Row 63: Chain 2, turn, 100 esc, repeat Row 3 stitches in blue.

Row 64: Chain 2, turn, repeat Row 4 stitches in blue, 96 esc, Dec twice.

Row 65: Chain 2, turn, 98 esc, repeat Row 5 stitches in blue.

Row 66: Chain 2, turn, repeat Row 6 stitches in blue, and then 94 esc, Dec twice.

Row 67: Chain 2, turn, 96 esc, repeat Row 7 stitches in blue.

Row 68: Chain 2, turn, repeat Row 8 stitches in blue, 92 esc, Dec twice.

Row 69: Chain 2, turn, 94 esc, repeat Row 9 stitches in blue.

Row 70: Chain 2, turn, repeat Row 10 stitches in blue, 90 esc, Dec twice.

Row 71: Chain 2, turn, 92 esc, repeat Row 11 stitches in blue.

Row 72: Chain 2, turn, repeat Row 12 stitches in blue, 88 esc, Dec twice.

Row 73: Chain 2, turn, 90 esc, repeat Row 13 stitches in blue.

Row 74: Chain 2, turn, repeat Row 14 stitches in blue, 86 esc, Dec twice.

Row 75: Chain 2, turn, 88 esc, repeat Row 3 stitches in blue.

Row 76: Chain 2, turn, repeat Row 4 stitches in blue, and then 84 esc, Dec twice.

Row 77: Chain 2, turn, 86 esc, repeat Row 5 stitches in blue.

Row 78: Chain 2, turn, repeat Row 6 stitches in blue, 82 esc, Dec twice.

Row 79: Chain 2, turn, 84 esc, repeat Row 7 stitches in blue.

Row 80: Chain 2, turn, repeat Row 8 stitches in blue, 80 esc, Dec twice.

Row 81: Chain 2, turn, 82 esc, repeat Row 9 stitches in blue.

Row 82: Chain 2, turn, repeat Row 10 stitches in blue, 78 esc, Dec twice.

Row 83: Chain 2, turn, 80 esc, repeat Row 11 stitches in blue.

Row 84: Chain 2, turn, repeat Row 12 stitches in blue, 76 esc, Dec twice.

Row 85: Chain 2, turn, 78 esc, repeat Row 13 stitches in blue.

Row 86: Chain 2, turn, repeat Row 14 stitches in blue, 74 esc, Dec twice.

Row 87: Chain 2, turn, 76 esc, repeat Row 3 stitches in blue.

Row 88: Chain 2, turn, repeat Row 4 stitches in blue, 72 esc, Dec twice.

Row 89: Chain 2, turn, 74 esc, repeat Row 5 stitches in blue.

Row 90: Chain 2, turn, repeat Row 6 stitches in blue, 70 esc, Dec twice.

Row 91: Chain 2, turn, 72 esc, repeat Row 7 stitches in blue.

Row 92: Chain 2, turn, repeat Row 8 stitches in blue, 68 esc, Dec twice.

Row 93: Chain 2, turn, 70 esc, repeat Row 9 stitches in blue.

Row 94: Chain 2, turn, repeat Row 10 stitches in blue, 66 esc, Dec twice.

Row 95: Chain 2, turn, 68 esc, repeat Row 11 stitches in blue.

Row 96: Chain 2, turn, repeat Row 12 stitches in blue, 64 esc, Dec twice.

Row 97: Chain 2, turn, 66 esc, repeat Row 13 stitches in blue.

Row 98: Chain 2, turn, repeat Row 14 stitches in blue, 62 esc, Dec twice.

Row 99: Chain 2, turn, 64 esc, repeat Row 3 stitches in blue.

Row 100: Chain 2, turn, repeat Row 4 stitches in blue, 60 esc, Dec twice.

Row 101: Chain 2, turn, 62 esc, repeat Row 5 stitches in blue.

Row 102: Chain 2, turn, repeat Row 6 stitches in blue, and then 58 esc, Dec twice.

Row 103: Chain 2, turn, 60 esc, repeat Row 7 stitches in blue.

Row 104: Chain 2, turn, repeat Row 8 stitches in blue, 56 esc, Dec twice.

Row 105: Chain 2, turn, 58 esc, repeat Row 9 stitches in blue.

Row 106: Chain 2, turn, repeat Row 10 stitches in blue, 54 esc, Dec twice.

Row 107: Chain 2, turn, 56 esc, repeat Row 11 stitches in blue.

Row 108: Chain 2, turn, repeat Row 12 stitches in blue, 52 esc, Dec twice.

Row 109: Chain 2, turn, 54 esc, repeat Row 13 stitches in blue.

Row 110: Chain 2, turn, repeat Row 14 stitches in blue, 50 esc, Dec twice.

Row 111: Chain 2, turn, 52 esc, repeat Row 3 stitches in blue.

Row 112: Chain 2, turn, repeat Row 4 stitches in blue, 48 esc, Dec twice.

Row 113: Chain 2, turn, 50 esc, repeat Row 5 stitches in blue.

Row 114: Chain 2, turn, repeat Row 6 stitches in blue, 46 esc, Dec twice.

Row 115: Chain 2, turn, 48 esc, repeat Row 7 stitches in blue.

Row 116: Chain 2, turn, repeat Row 8 stitches in blue, 44 esc, Dec twice.

Row 117: Chain 2, turn, 46 esc, repeat Row 9 stitches in blue.

Row 118: Chain 2, turn, repeat Row 10 stitches in blue, 42 esc, Dec twice.

Row 119: Chain 2, turn, 44 esc, repeat Row 11 stitches in blue.

Row 120: Chain 2, turn, repeat Row 12 stitches in blue, 40 esc, Dec twice.

Row 121: Chain 2, turn, 42 esc, repeat Row 13 stitches in blue.

Row 122: Chain 2, turn, repeat Row 14 stitches in blue, 38 esc, Dec twice.

Row 123: Chain 2, turn, 40 esc, repeat Row 3 stitches in blue.

Row 124: Chain 2, turn, repeat Row 4 stitches in blue, 36 esc, Dec twice.

Row 125: Chain 2, turn, 38 esc, repeat Row 5 stitches in blue.

Row 126: Chain 2, turn, repeat Row 6 stitches in blue, 34 esc, Dec twice.

Row 127: Chain 2, turn, 36 esc, repeat Row 7 stitches in blue.

Row 128: Chain 2, turn, repeat Row 8 stitches in blue, 32 esc, Dec twice.

Row 129: Chain 2, turn, 34 esc, repeat Row 9 stitches in blue.

Row 130: Chain 2, turn, repeat Row 10 stitches in blue, 30 esc, Dec twice.

Row 131: Chain 2, turn, 32 esc, repeat Row 11 stitches in blue.

Row 132: Chain 2, turn, repeat Row 12 stitches in blue, 28 esc, Dec twice.

Row 133: Chain 2, turn, 30 esc, repeat Row 13 stitches in blue.

Row 134: Chain 2, turn, repeat Row 14 stitches in blue, 26 esc, Dec twice.

Row 135: Chain 2, turn, 28 esc, repeat Row 3 stitches in blue.

Row 136: Chain 2, turn, repeat Row 4 stitches in blue, 24 esc, Dec twice.

Row 137: Chain 2, turn, 26 esc, repeat Row 5 stitches in blue.

Row 138: Chain 2, turn, repeat Row 6 stitches in blue, 22 esc, Dec twice.

Row 139: Chain 2, turn, 24 esc, repeat Row 7 stitches in blue.

Row 140: Chain 2, turn, repeat Row 8 stitches in blue, 20 esc, Dec twice.

Row 141: Chain 2, turn, 22 esc, repeat Row 9 stitches in blue.

Row 142: Chain 2, turn, repeat Row 10 stitches in blue, 18 esc, Dec twice.

Row 143: Chain 2, turn, 20 esc, repeat Row 11 stitches in blue.

Row 144: Chain 2, turn, repeat Row 12 stitches in blue, 16 esc, Dec twice.

Row 145: Chain 2, turn, 18 esc, repeat Row 13 stitches in blue.

Row 146: Chain 2, turn, repeat Row 14 stitches in blue, 14 esc, Dec twice.

Row 147: Chain 2, turn, 16 esc, repeat Row 3 stitches in blue.

Row 148: Chain 2, turn, repeat Row 4 stitches in blue, 12 esc, Dec twice.

Row 149: Chain 2, turn, 14 esc, repeat Row 5 stitches in blue.

Row 150: Chain 2, turn, repeat Row 6 stitches in blue, 10 esc, Dec twice.

Row 151: Chain 2, turn, 12 esc, repeat Row 7 stitches in blue.

Row 152: Chain 2, turn, repeat Row 8 stitches in blue, 8 esc, Dec twice.

Row 153: Chain 2, turn, 10 esc, repeat Row 9 stitches in blue.

Row 154: Chain 2, turn, repeat Row 10 stitches in blue, 6 esc, Dec twice.

Row 155: Chain 2, turn, 8 esc, repeat Row 11 stitches in blue.

Row 156: Chain 2, turn, repeat Row 12 stitches in blue, 4 esc, Dec twice.

Row 157: Chain 2, turn, 6 esc, repeat Row 13 stitches in blue.

Rows 158–193 are shown in the second diagram of this pattern on page 176.

Note: On Row 166 you will start to decrease the cable width. To do this, you will be making esc and Dec stitches into post stitches as instructed. The diagram may be helpful for this portion of the shawl.

Row 158: Chain 2, turn, repeat Row 14 stitches in blue, 2 esc, Dec twice.

Row 159: Chain 2, turn, 4 esc, repeat Row 3 stitches in blue.

Row 160: Chain 2, turn, repeat Row 4 stitches in blue, Dec twice.

Row 161: Chain 2, turn, 2 esc, repeat Row 5 stitches in blue.

The stitches worked in the multicolored yarn are bold and in black from now on.

Row 162: Chain 2, turn, 3 esc stitches, skip an esc stitch, **2 FPS**, 2 esc, **2 FPS**, [add 2 esc stitches between the next 2 stitches, **B4CF**] twice, add 2 esc stitches between the next 2 stitches, **2 FPS**, 2 esc, **2 FPS**, 2 esc, Dec twice.

Row 163: Chain 2, turn, esc, repeat Row 7 stitches in blue.

Row 164: Chain 2, turn, 2 esc, skip an esc stitch, [**2 FPS**, 2 esc, **2 FPS**, 2 esc, **2 FPS**], add 2 esc stitches between the next 2 stitches, **B4CB**, add 2 esc stitches between the next 2 stitches, repeat instructions in [ ] once, and then Dec twice.

Row 165: Chain 2, turn, repeat Row 9 stitches in blue.

Row 166: Chain 2, turn, esc, esc twice in the next stitch, **2 FPS**, 2 esc, **2 FPS**, 2 esc, **B4CF**, add 2 esc stitches between the next 2 stitches, **B4CF,** 2 esc, **2 FPS**, 2 esc, make a Dec stitch in the next 2 post stitches, Dec in 2 esc stitches.

Row 167: Chain 2, turn, 4 esc, **2 BPS**, 2 esc, **4 BPS**, 2 esc, **4 BPS**, 2 esc, **2 BPS**, 2 esc, **2 BPS**, 3 esc.

Row 168: Chain 2, turn, 3 esc, **2 FPS**, 2 esc, [**B4CB**, add 2 esc stitches between the next 2 stitches] twice, **B4CB**, Dec twice.

Row 169: Chain 2, turn, 2 esc, [**4 BPS**, 2 esc] three times, **2 BPS**, 3 esc.

Row 170: Chain 2, turn, 2 esc, esc twice in the next stitch, [**B4CF**, add 2 esc stitches between the next 2 stitches] three times, make a Dec stitch in the next two post stitches, Dec in two sc stitches.

Row 171: Chain 2, turn, 4 esc, [**4 BPS**, 2 esc] three times, 2 esc.

Row 172: Chain 2, turn, 3 esc, skip a stitch, **2 FPS**, [add 2 esc stitches between the next 2 stitches,

B4CB] twice, add 2 esc stitches between the next 2 stitches, **2 FPS**, Dec twice.

Row 173: Chain 2, turn, 2 esc, **2 BPS**, [2 esc, **4 BPS**] twice, 2 esc, **2 BPS**, 3 esc.

Row 174: Chain 2, turn, 2 esc, skip an esc stitch, **2 FPS**, 2 esc, **2 FPS**, add 2 esc stitches between the next 2 stitches, **B4CF**, add 2 esc stitches between the next 2 stitches, **2 FPS**, 2 esc, make a Dec stitch in the next 2 post stitches, Dec in 2 esc stitches.

Row 175: Chain 2, turn, 4 esc, **2 BPS,** 2 esc, **4 BPS,** 2 esc, **2 BPS,** 2 esc, **2 BPS,** 2 esc.

Row 176: Chain 2, turn, 2 esc, **2 FPS**, 2 esc, **B4CB**, add 2 esc stitches between the next 2 stitches, **B4CB**, Dec twice.

Row 177: Chain 2, turn, 2 esc, **4 BPS**, 2 esc, **4 BPS**, 2 esc, **2 BPS**, 2 esc.

Row 178: Chain 2, turn, esc, esc twice in the next stitch, [**B4CF**, add 2 esc stitches between the next 2 stitches] twice, make a Dec stitch in the next 2 post stitches, Dec in 2 esc stitches.

Row 179: Chain 2, turn, 4 esc, **4 BPS**, 2 esc, **4 BPS**, 3 esc.

Row 180: Chain 2, turn, 2 esc, skip an esc stitch, **2 FPS**, add 2 esc stitches between the next 2 stitches,

B4CB, make an esc stitch in each of the next 2 post stitches, Dec twice.

Row 181: Chain 2, turn, 4 esc, **4 BPS**, 2 esc, **2 BPS**, 2 esc.

Row 182: Chain 2, turn, 2 esc, **B4CF**, make an esc stitch in each of the next 2 post stitches, Dec twice.

Row 183: Chain 2, turn, 4 esc, **4 BPS**, 2 esc.

Row 184: Chain 2, turn, 2 esc, **4CF**, Dec twice.

Row 185: Chain 2, turn, 2 esc, **4 BPS**, 2 esc.

Row 186: Chain 2, turn, 2 esc, **2 FPS**, make a dec stitch in the next 2 post stitches, Dec in 2 esc stitches.

Row 187: Chain 2, turn, 2 esc, **2 BPS**, 2 esc.

Row 188: Chain 2, turn, 2 esc, make a Dec stitch in the next 2 post stitches, Dec in 2 esc stitches.

Row 189: Chain 2, turn, 4 esc.

Row 190: Chain 2, turn, Dec twice.

Row 191: Chain 2, turn, 2 esc.

Row 192: Chain 2, turn, Dec once.

Row 193: Chain 2, turn, esc.

Tie off yarn.

Weave in any loose yarn ends.

Verdigris Scarf (Unisex, Experienced)

Materials

- 1 skein of Spincycle Yarns Dyed in the Wool in Salty Dog (200 yd./182.9 m per skein, and 1.8 oz./50 g net weight per skein; 100% super-wash American wool; #2 fine weight)
- 1 skein of Blue Sky Fibers Woolstok Light in Spring Ice No. 2320 (218 yd./200 m per skein, and 1.8 oz./50 g net weight per skein; 100% fine Highland wool; super fine weight #1)

Hook

US size E-4 (3.5 mm) crochet hook

Dimensions

4 in. (10.2 cm) wide by 39 in. (99.1 cm) long (excluding tassels)

Gauge

10.5 esc stitches x 10 esc rows = 2 in. x 2 in. (5.1 cm x 5.1 cm) in Blue Sky Fibers Woolstok Light

Crochet Stitch Video Tutorials

4-Cross Front Cable Stitch (4CF): "Four Cross Front Crochet Cable Stitch Tutorial," https://www.youtube.com/watch?v=rzuMC6mB68w&t=1s

4-Cross Back Cable Stitch (4CB): "Four Cross Back Crochet Cable Stitch Tutorial," https://www.youtube.com/watch?v=EGBMJaXAcEQ&t=35s

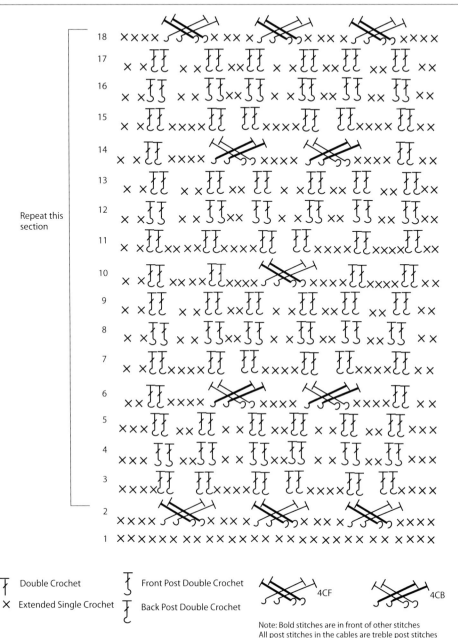

Repeat this section

Double Crochet

X Extended Single Crochet

Front Post Double Crochet

Back Post Double Crochet

4CF

4CB

Note: Bold stitches are in front of other stitches
All post stitches in the cables are treble post stitches

INSTRUCTIONS

Colorwork Instructions: The multicolored yarn is used to make all of the post stitches and cable stitches, and the solid yarn is used to make the esc stitches between the cables. To help distinguish between these two stitch types, the stitches that use the multicolored yarn are included in bold, while the stitches that use the solid yarn are listed in regular type.

Row 1: Chain 30 (including starting loop), esc in third chain from hook, and esc across. (28 esc, 1 chain)

Row 2: Chain 2, turn, [4 esc, **4CF**] 3 times, 4 esc.

Row 3: Chain 2, turn, [4 esc, **4 BPS**] 3 times, 4 esc.

Row 4: Chain 2, turn, 3 esc, skip an esc, [**2 FPS**, add 2 esc between the next 2 stitches, **2 FPS**, skip an esc, 2 esc, skip an esc] twice, **2 FPS**, add 2 esc between the next 2 stitches, **2 FPS**, skip an esc, 3 esc.

Row 5: Chain 2, turn, 3 esc, [**2 BPS**, 2 esc, **2 BPS**, 2 esc] twice, **2 BPS**, 2 esc, **2 BPS**, 3 esc.

Row 6: Chain 2, turn, 2 esc, skip an esc, **2 FPS**, [{esc twice in the next stitch} twice, **B4CB**] twice, repeat instructions in { } twice, **2 FPS**, skip an esc, 2 esc.

Row 7: Chain 2, turn, 2 esc, **2 BPS**, [4 esc, **4 BPS**] twice, 4 esc, **2 BPS**, 2 esc.

Row 8: Chain 2, turn, 2 esc, [**2 FPS**, skip an esc, 2 esc, skip an esc, **2 FPS**, add 2 esc between the next 2 stitches] twice, **2 FPS**, skip an esc, 2 esc, skip an esc, **2 FPS**, 2 esc.

Row 9: Chain 2, turn, 2 esc, [**2 BPS**, 2 esc] six times.

Row 10: Chain 2, turn, 2 esc, **2 FPS**, [{esc twice in the next stitch} twice, **2 FPS**], repeat instructions in { } twice, **B4CF,** repeat instructions in [ ] twice, 2 esc.

Row 11: Chain 2, turn, 2 esc, **2 BPS**, [4 esc, **2 BPS**], 4 esc, **4 BPS,** repeat instructions in [ ] twice, 2 esc.

Row 12: Chain 2, turn, 2 esc, [**2 FPS**, skip an esc, 2 esc, skip an esc] twice, **2 FPS**, add 2 esc stitches between the next 2 stitches, repeat instructions in [ ] twice, **2 FPS**, 2 esc.

Row 13: Chain 2, turn, 2 esc, [**2 BPS**, 2 esc] 6 times.

Row 14: Chain 2, turn, 2 esc, **2 FPS**, [{esc twice in the next stitch} twice, **B4CB**] twice, repeat instructions in { } twice, **2 FPS**, 2 esc.

Row 15: Chain 2, turn, 2 esc, **2 BPS**, [4 esc, **4 BPS**] twice, 4 esc, **2 BPS**, 2 esc.

Row 16: Repeat Row 8.

Row 17: Repeat Row 9.

Row 18: [{Esc twice in the next stitch} twice, **B4CF**] three times, repeat instructions in { } twice.

Rows 19–178: Repeat Rows 3–18 ten times.

Tie off yarn.

Weave in any loose yarn ends.

Tassel Instructions

1. Cut yarn segments (10 segments per tassel) about 9 in. (22. 9 cm) in length.

2. Align the 10 segments (1 tassel) and fold them in half.

3. Take the loop at the half mark of the tassel and insert it into the scarf edge (from the front of the shawl to the back).

4. Take the ends of the yarn segments and pull them through the loop (pull tight).

5. Make and place 9 tassels on each end of the scarf, equally spaced.

6. Trim tassel ends to make them even.

ABBREVIATIONS

Note: For instructions on how to work stitches, see "Stitch Descriptions" on page 71.

2CB	2-cross back cable stitch		**BPS**	double crochet back post stitch
2CF	2-cross front cable stitch		**dc**	double crochet
4CB	4-cross back cable stitch		**dc2tog**	double crochet 2 together
4CF	4-cross front cable stitch		**Dec**	extended single crochet decrease
6CB	6-cross back cable stitch		**DecDBPS**	decrease back post double crochet
6CF	6-cross front cable stitch		**DecDFPS**	decrease front post double crochet
8CB	8-cross back cable stitch		**esc**	extended single crochet
8CF	8-cross front cable stitch		**FPS**	double crochet front post stitch
B2CB	bridging 2-cross back cable stitch		**Inc**	extended single crochet increase
B2CF	bridging 2-cross front cable stitch		**Reverse sc**	extended reverse single crochet
B4CB	bridging 4-cross back cable stitch		**sc**	single crochet
B4CF	bridging 4-cross front cable stitch		**TBS**	twist back stitch
B6CB	bridging 6-cross back cable stitch		**TFPS**	triple crochet front post stitch
B6CF	bridging 6-cross front cable stitch		**TFS**	twist front stitch
BDecDFPS	bridging decrease front post double crochet			

GLOSSARY

Analogous Color Plan: A color combination that utilizes a set of neighboring colors on the color wheel (Figures 1.7 and 1.8 on pages 10 and 11).

Color afterimage: The opponent color that appears after the prolonged viewing of a given color. For example, after viewing a red computer monitor, a white monitor will be perceived to have a green tint because red and green are an opponent color pair (see Color opponency).

Color opponency: The theory that colors are perceived by humans in opponent pairs (red-green and blue-yellow) based on the push-pull processing of color by ganglion cells in the retina of the eye.

Color wheel: A simplified version of the three-dimensional color space (defined by hue, lightness, and saturation) into a two-dimensional disk, which includes the properties of hue (varying along the edge of the wheel) and lightness (varying from the center of the wheel outward) (Figure 1.6 on page 9).

Complementary Color Plan: A color combination that utilizes two or more colors on opposite sides of the color wheel (Figures 1.7 and 1.9 on pages 10 and 12).

Complementary colors: Two or more colors on opposite sides of the color wheel.

Cones: Light-sensing cells in the eye that are used to perceive color. Humans typically have three cone types, which sense different wavelengths of light. The brain interprets the differences among the activation levels of the three cones to generate the perception of color.

Electromagnetic spectrum: The range of wavelengths of electromagnetic radiation. In particular, the division of different types of electromagnetic radiation into categories based on an approximate range of wavelengths or energies, such as microwaves, radio waves, and visible light (Figure 1.1 on page 3).

Felting: The substantial shrinking and stiffening of fabrics made from animal hair, wool, or fur following exposure to water, physical agitation, and heat.

Gauge: The number of stitches and rows per inch achieved with a given yarn and stitch pattern. It is used to generate consistency in crocheted fabric size across yarn types and crocheter tension.

Grayscale: Images made from gradations or shades of gray, ranging from white to black. Images with the absence of color.

Highlights: Bright regions on a fabric or a surface where the light hits the cable stitch or bump and reflects more light.

Hue: A color's hue determines whether the color is perceived as blue, red, or yellow, among others; in other words, it defines the perceived variation of colors within the rainbow (Figure 1.4 on page 8).

Isoluminant colors: Two or more colors with the same level of lightness (or brightness, colloquially).

Lateral brightness adaptation: The influence of the brightness of neighboring colors on each other (Figure 1.11 on page 15).

Lateral chromatic adaptation: The influence of the saturation and hue of neighboring colors on each other (Figure 1.11 on page 15).

Lightness: A measure of how "white" a color appears. It ranges from black through gray to white. Lightness is also frequently called brightness colloquially and relates to a different balance among the types of cones activated in the eye (Figure 1.5 on page 9).

Loft (of yarn): The amount of fuzziness or halo of a given type of yarn.

Monochromatic Color Plan: A color combination that utilizes a set of colors with one shared hue but varied saturation and lightness.

Ply (of yarn): The number of small threads that are twisted together to make up a yarn. Yarn ply can be single ply (no smaller threads, just one large thread twisted), two ply (two threads twisted), three ply (three threads twisted), or more.

Retina: The layer of photosensitive cells at the back of the eye that senses light and processes visual information before communicating it to the brain.

Saturation: The pureness of a color. It ranges from the pure color to complete gray for a given level of hue and lightness (Figure 1.5 on page 9).

Shadows: Darker regions on a fabric or a surface adjacent to a protrusion caused by the blocking of oblique light by that bump.

Stranded colorwork: A technique for using multiple colors while crocheting an item, in which each yarn is used in sequence and is carried along the back of the fabric when not in use.

Swatch: A small rectangle of crocheted fabric that is used to test the yarn gauge and appearance when worked by a particular crocheter.

Tension: The firmness with which a crocheter holds the yarn while crocheting. Stitches made with high tension are tighter and smaller, whereas stitches made with low tension are larger and looser.

Triadic Color Plan: A color combination that utilizes a set of three colors that are equally spaced around the color wheel (Figures 1.7 and 1.10 on pages 10 and 13).

Trichromatic color theory (three-color theory): The theory that colors perceived by humans can be represented with three colors (red, green, and blue) because human color vision is generated from three types of light-sensing cone cells.

Wavelength: A property of electromagnetic waves (such as microwaves, radio waves, and visible light) that can be used to calculate the wave's energy. Electromagnetic waves are an oscillation between a magnetic field and an electric field, and the wavelength is the physical distance that the wave must travel for one full oscillation of the magnetic field and electric field to occur (Figure 1.1 on page 3).

Yarn dye lots: Yarn dyeing is frequently performed in batches, and the resulting color of the yarn can vary among the batches. Therefore, each batch is given a dye lot designation to allow consumers to easily purchase yarn skeins or cakes of consistent color for fiber projects.

ACKNOWLEDGMENTS

I would like to acknowledge the editorial feedback, guidance, and scientific advice of my husband and colleague, Armand R. Tanguay Jr., in writing this book. He was a constant support and cheerleader and even did the housework to give me time to crochet, write, and edit. He also gave frequent and instantaneous feedback on all of the crochet designs, color choices, and motifs with a thoughtful aesthetic sense and constant patience.

I very much appreciate my family, including my grandparents, parents, sister, aunts, uncles, and cousins, as well as my close friends, Camille McAvoy and Charlotte Yang, for their encouragement, enthusiasm, and support through the long process of writing this book.

I would also like to thank Candi Derr at Stackpole Books for her thoughtful feedback on my book drafts and for encouraging me to add introductory material to the book on colors and cables.

I appreciate the yarn support that I received from WeCrochet for select patterns that are included in the book. I would also like to thank Andrea Mowry from Drea Renee Knits, Herrschners, Jennifer Steingass from Knit.Love.Wool, and Kirsten Ballering from Haak Maar Raak Crochet for providing permission to use their knitting or crochet design photos to showcase different color plans in Chapter 1. I also appreciate Spincycle Yarns and Freia Fibers for providing permission to use images that they provided of their yarn skeins and cakes.

ABOUT THE AUTHOR

*N*oelle R. B. Stiles is an assistant professor in the Department of Neurology at the Robert Wood Johnson Medical School at Rutgers University, with joint appointments in the Department of Ophthalmology and Visual Science at the New Jersey Medical School as well as in the Department of Biomedical Engineering in the School of Engineering at Rutgers. She is a core member of the Center for Advanced Human Brain Imaging Research within the Brain Health Institute at Rutgers. She was a vision research scientist at the University of Southern California in the Department of Ophthalmology for over five years and earned a doctorate in neuroscience from the Computation and Neural Systems Program at the California Institute of Technology.

Her research investigates how the brain changes and adapts when vision is lost and is subsequently restored. She currently works with retinal prosthesis patients who have vision restored by means of a biomedical implant and performs psychophysical evaluations and neuroimaging investigations with these individuals. She also studies how the senses interact and has innovated new multisensory illusions such as the Audiovisual Rabbit Illusion (https://www.youtube.com/watch?v=yCpsQ8LZOco), which has received over half a million views on YouTube.

Dr. Stiles has always been artistically as well as scientifically inclined (perhaps inherited from her artist paternal grandmother and math-teacher maternal grandmother). She has been crocheting for two decades and designing award-winning crochet items for over eight years. She was the winner in the Baby Category for the 2017 Herrschners Grand National Afghan Contest. Under her designer label, Rebecca's Stylings (https://www.rebeccasstylings.com/), she has designed patterns for Red Heart Yarns and has published over 150 crochet patterns on Love Crafts, WeCrochet, Ravelry, and Etsy. The focus of her fiber art is complex Aran-style cabling made with standard crochet stitches.

This texture-rich fabric created in bright modern colors is the perfect canvas for her intricate, yet intuitive, designs.

INDEX OF TERMS

VISUAL INDEX

Indigo Hat (Women,
Intermediate)   104

Terre Verte Scarf
(Unisex, Intermediate) 108

Ultramarine Champagne
Tote (Intermediate)   113

Absinthe Scarf
(Unisex, Intermediate) 119

Absinthe Hat
(Unisex, Experienced)   123

Crochet Patterns with Multicolored Yarns: Clothing   128

Vermilion Shawl (Unisex,
Intermediate)   129

Cerulean Shawl (Unisex,
Intermediate)   133

Sepia Poncho (Women,
Intermediate)   137

Amaranth Cardigan
(Women, Experienced) 143

Crochet Patterns with Color Gradient Yarns   162

Archil Scarf
(Unisex, Intermediate) 163

Tyrian Purple Blanket
(Intermediate)   167

Crochet Patterns with Stranded Colorwork   172

Orpiment Shawl
(Unisex, Experienced) 173

Verdigris Scarf
(Unisex, Experienced) 184